NINE MEN

NINE MEN

A Political History
of the Supreme Court
from 1790 to 1955

by FRED RODELL

RANDOM HOUSE · NEW YORK

Seventh Printing

FOR Janet and Mike
with thanks and love

Contents

FOREWORD

ONE Powerful, Irresponsible, and Human 3

TWO From the Gleam in the Founding Fathers' Eyes to the Birth of Supreme Court Power 33

THREE Government by John Marshall, the Great Chief Justice 73

FOUR Not States Against Nation but South Against North as the Court Leads on to War 111

FIVE The Court Rides Back to Power on the Nation's Surge to the West 141

SIX Associate Justice Holmes, Dissenting 179

SEVEN The Court Collides with the New Deal and Wins the Battle by Defaulting the War 213

EIGHT A Court Attuned to a Liberal Key Develops Its Own Discordance 255

NINE Yesterday's Court, the Court Today, and a Court That Could Be Tomorrow 301

INDEX 333

Foreword

THIS BOOK is the oh-hell-I-might-as-well-try-it-myself
result of many years of wishing someone else would write
it. Reviewing a couple of contemporary works about the
Supreme Court, not quite two decades ago, I said: "Some-
where between these two books a really first-rate job has
yet to be done on the Supreme Court. It would not spare
personalities, yet it would not be content to give its readers
the cheap thrill of vicariously peeping through keyholes at
undressed Justices. It would not skimp the past history of
the Court, but would use that history to point up an incisive
inspection of the Court's place in our scheme of government today." This is not to imply by any means that mine
is a "first-rate job"; but it is at least an A-for-effort
attempt to do what I have so long hoped some other, abler
soul might do—and to do it so that any halfway literate
non-lawyer can understand it. My chief editor of words
and phrases has been my fourteen-year-old son, Mike; my
chief editor of ideas has been my wife, Janet, who knows as
little about law as I do about her field, child psychology.

If people cannot understand this book, it will be because Janet and Mike are too bright for her skirts and his breeches.

It may be that lawyers will not understand it, because it is not written down to them. I have done my best not to use the easy slang (once you have learned it) of long-worded legal language, which too often lets off-the-real-point thinking become a habit. More than that, I have kept completely away from matters that would interest only lawyers —from Supreme Court cases that deal with anything other than the part the Court plays in the way this nation is run; Erie *v.* Tompkins, "a great legal landmark," (what it said was that federal judges, when handling private legal squabbles, should use a different set of rules from those they had used before) is not even mentioned—except here. My interest and, I think, most people's interest in the Court is in what it—or rather the men who man it—have done on the (dirty word) political scene for 165 years.

This book has no footnotes, no here's-where-to-look-it-up lists of cases or sources. It is meant for reading, not for easy reference by lazy scholars. Of course, the quotations and facts have been checked and are accurate—in so far as a fallible human, meaning me, can make them accurate— though on matters of opinion, as opposed to fact, I hope I make it clear that the views I express are mine. Moreover, it would be impossible, literally, for me to list where all the stuff came from that stuck in my head throughout more than a quarter-century of reading and hearing—with intent fascination, but with nary a filing-cabinet except the universal filing-cabinet of the mind—about the Court and its past and present Justices. I dare say the reading has included all or parts of over a thousand books and over ten thousand articles, not counting the daily newspapers and the Court's own official reports. And bits of the whole that is here between covers have been filched, with their faces washed and lifted, from the fifty-odd pieces I have written myself, about the Court and the Justices, in the rather recent past.

Beyond that, I am prejudiced, as all men are prejudiced, by my own ideas and ideals. But I like to think that my slant toward people, especially those I know or have known (and Supreme Court Justices are people), is based on those ideas and ideals, not on petty, personal things. If Justice Holmes is one of the major heroes of this book, it is not because I once spent in his home an intellectually exciting afternoon; if Justice McReynolds appears as one of the book's near-villains, it is not because my visit with him was far less pleasant; the reasons come closer to running the other way round. I once took law-school courses from both Justice Douglas and Justice Frankfurter, when they were mere professors of law—and Professor Frankfurter gave me the higher grade and made the more of me, then and for some years after. If Justice Douglas is today my friend, and is also rated in this book considerably above Justice Frankfurter, *both* facts are by my choice and *both* stem from my estimate of them as Justices, as government-serving men.

The ideas and ideals—or prejudices—by which I judge men in public life (or in private life) are mainly two. As even he who reads on the run will easily discover, I am one of that great and unlike group that is fuzzily labeled "liberal"—so I tend, of course, to admire liberals or

lookers-after-the-other-fellow more than I admire conservatives; yet awareness of my own leaning has led me,
throughout this book, to try to give the devils their more
than due. My other ideal or prejudice is more important. I
confess an almost fanatical devotion to that kind of personal
integrity that combines intellectual honesty with courage.
"Better a plain-speaking conservative than a weak and
weaseling liberal" might well be my motto in appraising
men. The man who says what he means, and means and
acts what he says, can almost always win me—which goes,
of course, for Supreme Court Justices.

All this is by way of what the lawyers (and how did
they creep in?) call "full disclosure." No one who goes
beyond these words can now say he wasn't warned. Happy
reading.

F. R.

Bethany, Connecticut
March, 1955

NINE MEN

NINE MEN

CHAPTER 1

Powerful, Irresponsible, and Human

AT THE TOP LEVELS of the three branches of the civilian government of the United States sit the Congress, the President plus his Cabinet, and the Supreme Court. Of these three—in this unmilitary, unclerical nation—only one wears a uniform. Only one carries on its most important business in utter secret behind locked doors—and indeed never reports, even after death, what really went on there. Only one, its members holding office for life if they choose, is completely irresponsible to anyone or anything but themselves and their own consciences. Only one depends for much of its immense influence on its prestige as a

semi-sacred institution and preserves that prestige with the
trappings and show of superficial dignity rather than
earning it, year after working year, by the dignity and
wisdom of what it is and does. Under our otherwise democratic form of government, only one top ruling group uses
ceremony and secrecy, robes and ritual, as instruments of
its *official* policy, as wellsprings of its power.

The nine men who are the Supreme Court of the United
States are at once the most powerful and the most irresponsible of all the men in the world who govern other
men. Not even the bosses of the Kremlin, each held back by
fear of losing his head should he ever offend his fellows,
wield such loose and long-ranging and acountable-to-no-
one power as do the nine or five-out-of-nine Justices who
can give orders to any other governing official in the
United States—from the members of a village school board
who would force their young charges to salute the flag, to a
President who would take over the steel industry to keep
production going—and can make those orders stick. Ours
may be, for puffing purposes, a "government of checks and
balances," but there is no check at all on what the Supreme
Court does—save only three that are as pretty in theory as
they are pointless in practice. (These are the Senate's
power to reject a newly named Justice, used only once this
century, and in the past usually unwisely; the power to
impeach a Justice, only once tried and never carried
through; the power of the people to reverse a Supreme
Court decision by amending the Constitution, as they have
done just three times in our whole history.) The nine
Justices sit secure and stand supreme over Congress,
President, governors, state legislatures, commissions,

administrators, lesser judges, mayors, city councils, and dog-catchers—with none to say them nay.

Lest these words sound like arrant overstatement, here are what three of the most thoughtful men who ever held high national office said about the Supreme Court's flat and final power of government. Thomas Jefferson, who was President when the Court first fully used this power, exploded, prophetically but futilely: "Our Constitution . . . intending to establish three departments, coordinate and independent, that they might check and balance one another, . . . has given, according to this opinion, to one of them alone the right to prescribe rules for the government of the others, and to that one, too, which is unelected by and independent of the nation. . . . The Constitution, on this hypothesis, is a mere thing of wax in the hands of the judiciary which they may twist and shape into any form they please." Jefferson was talking of the Court's then brand-newly wielded power to override Congress and the President. More than a century later, Justice Holmes, revealingly in dissent, berated his brethren for freely using their judicial power to upset *state* laws: "As the decisions now stand I see hardly any limit but the sky to the invalidating of those rights [*'the constitutional rights of the states'*] if they happen to strike a majority of this Court as for any reason undesirable. I cannot believe that the [Fourteenth] Amendment was intended to give us carte blanche to embody our economic or moral beliefs in its prohibitions." And a few years after, Justice Stone, he too in dissent, exclaimed: "The only check upon our own exercise of power is our own sense of self-restraint."

In Stone's same angry protest against the Court's six-to-three veto of the first Agricultural Adjustment Act—a protest that helped spark Franklin Roosevelt's "Court-packing" plan and later led FDR to reward its author with the Chief Justiceship—he also said: "Courts are not the only agency of government that must be assumed to have capacity to govern." This statement, while true on its face, is essentially and subtly—though of course not deliberately —misleading. No "agency of government" governs; no "court" governs; only the men who run the agency of government or the court or the Supreme Court do the governing. The power is theirs because the decisions are theirs; decisions are not made by abstractions like agencies or courts. Justice Stone, who knew what he meant, might a little better have said: "Five or six of the nine men who make up this Court are not the only men in our government who must be assumed to have the capacity to govern." And he might have added: "Nor are they necessarily the wisest in their judgments; I work with them and have reason to know."

For the old saw, beloved of history textbooks and political speeches, that "ours is a government of laws, not of men," is an insult and an undemocratic canard. Laws are words, nothing more. Laws do not write or enforce or interpret themselves. Even constitutions are no more than words except as men give them flesh and muscle and meaning in action; then the flesh and muscle are molded and the meaning in action is directed by men. The words of the Soviet constitution are in many ways more democratic than those of ours—as are the words of the constitutions of several Latin-American countries now run by dictators. And the cold truth about "laws, not men" was never better put than by one of the Founding Fathers, John Mercer of Maryland, who said what all of them were wise enough to know as they hammered out the U.S. Constitution back in 1787: "It is a great mistake to suppose that the paper we are to propose will govern the United States. It is the men whom it will bring into the government and interest in maintaining it."

Among those men, and most powerful of all of them for the past century and a half, are the Justices of the U.S. Supreme Court. They may say—and often do—that it is not *they* who make the decisions, lay down the rules, give orders to every other governing official in the land; they may say they do nothing but "interpret" the laws, including the Constitution; they may talk at times as though they neither had nor need human minds, as though they might almost as well be a nine-headed calculating machine, intricately adjusted to the words of the Constitution and of lesser laws, and ready to give automatic answers to any attorneys who drop their briefs in the proper slot and push the button. But even non-lawyers have come to find a trifle naïve and unconvincing the old fantasy that our government, especially its judicial branch, is mechanically controlled by laws, not by men. If it were, how explain split Supreme Court decisions (5–4, 6–3, 7–2, even 8–1); how explain dissenting opinions that too often make more sense than the majority "opinions of the Court"; how explain the "overruling" of past decisions—a term which means that the same question, decided one way before, is now decided exactly the opposite way? There was more truth than lawyerly discretion in the comment of Charles Evans Hughes, before he became Chief Justice of the United

States: "We are under a Constitution, but the Constitution is what the judges say it is."

The judges who say what the Constitution is have ranged throughout our history from the wise to the stupid, from the broad and brilliant to the narrow-minded and uninformed. No more than election to Congress or the Presidency ensures the ability of the man who is elected, does appointment to the Supreme Court ensure an able judge. For every Marshall, for every Holmes—who comes along sadly seldom, as does a Jefferson or a Lincoln—there will be scores of merely competent or middling or quite inept Justices, who can often outweigh by numbers alone, if not by depth of insight or clarity of vision, their more capable colleagues. It is a telling and disturbing fact that no Supreme Court Justice in the past half-century, save only Hughes, has achieved a generally acknowledged greatness except in dissent.

When a lame-duck Senator is named to the Court to pay off a party's political debt to him, or a querulous Attorney-General is kicked upstairs to the Court, or a lawyer-politician attains the Court because the President, by happenstance, knows and likes him personally, he does not become, by the process of donning a black gown and a solemn mien, a different man. He retains the same mind, the same personality, the same political perspectives and prejudices—plus the same ability or inability to govern wisely. But he has now been entrusted with tremendous governmental power, untrammeled by anyone except his own colleagues, who may be as unable—or as able—as he. Warren G. Harding is not widely regarded as one of our first-rate presidents, but most people assume that his influence on national policy ended when death cut short his term of office. What is too easily forgotten is that the four mediocre or worse-than-mediocre Justices whom he appointed dominated the Court and, through it, the country for years after his death. It has been said that the good a President does is oft interred with his bones but his choice of Supreme Court Justices lives after him. It has also been said that "the Supreme Court follows the election returns" —although Mr. Dooley might have added "of ten or twelve years before." The truth implicit in both these remarks is that the nine Justices are not judicial automatons but highly human and hence inevitably political men.

Being men, the Justices sometimes seem to change their more lightly or expediently held political opinions after they have achieved the security of the Court. McReynolds and Jackson, both of them rampagingly liberal Attorneys-General under crusading Presidents, became eloquent spokesmen of conservatism as Justices; Calvin Coolidge caught a Tartar when he named his old friend, Harlan Stone, a former corporation lawyer and hence a presumably safe and solid Republican choice; Theodore Roosevelt was outraged when Justice Holmes, in a touted trust-busting case, voted against the administration on what was one of T.R.'s pet projects, shortly after T.R. appointed Holmes; and Franklin Roosevelt would doubtless be outraged today at many of the votes and views of two of his New Deal appointees—Frankfurter and Reed. Yet none of these men—nor any other—changed his true colors by the act of ascending the bench, although a few may have been sailing under false colors before. The Presidents who chose them merely misjudged them—as men often misjudge other men. And ever since the time when John Adams put John Marshall in a position, as Chief Justice, to carry on Federalist policies long after the Federalists had been voted out of power, the history of the Court has been replete with the picking of Justices who stuck precisely, permanently, and often stubbornly to the policies and politics that their appointing Presidents expected them to stick to.

If there is anything sinister or wrong about the system whereby every President naturally tries to appoint Justices whose slant toward the big problems of government follows and fits with the appointing President's slant, the wrongness does not lie in the fact that Justices are still men—and that the men are still themselves. The wrongness lies rather in the fact that these men—remaining themselves, attaining the power of Justices, and retaining that power for sometimes more than thirty years—inevitably act as a check, a lag, on the forward momentum of government and on the democratic directing of national policy by other men who are perpetually responsible to the voters (as the Justices are not responsible) for what they don't and what they do. Especially in times of crisis and change, a reluctant and backward-looking Supreme Court, dominated by a man or group of men who owe their power to a repudiated President or party, can create at least friction, at most chaos, in the running of a nation.

Just as John Marshall's Federalist Court slowed down the operations of Andrew Jackson's popular administration thirty-odd years after reactionary John Adams named Marshall Chief Justice, so Roger Taney's pro-Southern Court, in its fateful Dred Scott decision, bucked the shifted popular will and helped bring on the Civil War, twenty years after Andrew Jackson appointed Taney. That the voters, in 1892, elected a Democratic President and a Democratic-Populist Congress, dedicated to the passage of an income tax, did not stop five hangover Supreme Court Justices from throwing out that income tax after it was enacted. And in the 1930's, a high bench top-heavy with the Four Horsemen of the Old Deal brought the Court, as an institution, to one of its lowest ebbs and greatest crises when it flouted the nation's voters by vetoing much of Franklin Roosevelt's New Deal. In each of these instances, as so often in our history, a majority of the Justices were behind the political times.

In a sense, it is inevitable that the Court, if it be anything, should be a brake on the rest of our machinery of government. By the very nature of the way it works, the Court, for all the power its members hold, is only a negative—never an affirmative—force. It cannot create, it cannot initiate, it cannot put into action any government policy of any kind (except in the governmental sideline dealing with the mechanics of how the Court itself, and lesser courts, carry on their job). All the Justices can do is to say Yes or No to a policy or a program or a part of a policy or program that has been started by someone else in some other branch of government. All they can do is to approve or disapprove—after they are asked to do so—a law passed by a legislature, an order given by an executive, a ruling made by a commission, an effort made by a law-enforcing official to fine somebody or put somebody in jail.

In the course of saying Yes or No—though the Justices

never say it that briefly—or in the course of explaining, in
legal language and commonly for the exclusive edification
of lawyers, just why they are saying Yes or No, they may
suggest, wittingly or unwittingly, a shift or an extension
or perhaps a detour in the policies or programs of men in
the affirmative branches of government. A decision throwing out a newly written law may hint to the lawmakers
how to get the same thing done in a different way which
the Justices will then approve. A decision that OK's the
disputed act of some official—be it under some federal law
on patents or monopolies or labor relations, or under, say,
a state regulation of automobiles, or under a city ordinance
about public meetings—may contain signposts telling the
official he can go still farther along the same road if he
chooses. Or a decision that forbids an official to act as he
is now acting may outline to the official, in the very detail-
ing of what he may not do, precisely what he may do.

Yet in every such instance—and there are scores of
them—the Justices can do nothing but impotently point
toward future action after Yessing or Noing past action by
men in a position to act. And this very lack of capacity to
go forward, this easy if inevitable isolation from all the
choice-making, chance-taking responsibility that goes with
governing actively and affirmatively, makes even more un-
democratically dangerous the Justices' almost cavalier
power to keep the nation and its government standing still.

If the Court is irresponsible—as it is—in the sense of
being beyond all discipline, all direction, all effective cen-
sure, by the voters or by any other governing group, and
if it is also irresponsible—as it is—in the sense of sitting
in final judgment without ever facing the far tougher task

of making first judgments (imagine a President who had nothing to do but veto or not veto), the Court is irresponsible in yet a third sense. For the Justices, by their own sole choice, can even duck, whenever they please, the secondary responsibility of merely giving a Yes or a No. They can shuck off any issue, no matter how important, which somebody asks them to settle finally with the final power they hold, by simply refusing to hear or to decide the issue— by saying, in effect: "This isn't our business; we can't be bothered."

One of the ways the Justices retreat from making decisions is to label a problem "political" rather than "legal" and announce that therefore it is not up to them to solve it. This is the word game the Court used, for instance, to get out of deciding whether Illinois, under the Constitution, had to change its voting districts to fit its shifts in population; one set of Illinois politicians wanted the change and one set did not, but both sets put their claims before the Court; the Justices listened and bowed themselves out —"political," not "legal." In the light of the hundreds of political issues the Justices have not even hesitated, much less balked, at wading into whenever *they* wished, over the past 150 years—issues ranging from segregation of Negroes in the South to strikes in wartime and loyalty programs and state-against-federal claims to tidelands oil— the political-not-legal excuse would be farcical if it were not so essentially shocking in its underlining of judicial irresponsibility.

Another system the Justices use to turn away from uncomfortable questions is to find and inflate some petty point of technical legal procedure—a minor flaw in the way the case was argued or the briefs written, a lawyer's slip—and hide behind that as a device for postponing or evading a meaningful decision on the real issue. Many a major government problem, many a queer and question-able criminal conviction, has been left hanging unresolved, literally for years, while the lawyers ran the gauntlet of the lower courts for the second, sometimes the third, time —because the Justices had ordered them to start all over and mind their methods and their legal manners. And after the gauntlets and the years, the Court may dismiss the case as "moot" or too-late-for-an-effective-decision (a pro-tested ruling may meanwhile have been varied or someone in the case may have died)—and small wonder. This pur-poseful putting off making up their minds about a thorny problem, on a legalistic procedural excuse, is one of the Justices' favorite self-protections.

Yet the political-not-legal evasion and the procedural-error evasion, where the Justices listen and run away, are as nothing compared to the Court's chief refuge of ir-responsibility. For, as few non-lawyers are at all aware, the Court is its own exclusive judge of which problems, whose disputes—and how many or how few—it will deign to decide. With a couple of rare exceptions, required by the Constitution, the Justices for the past thirty years have enjoyed—and the verb is accurate—the power to refuse to hear any case that anybody, railroaded convict or President of the United States, tries to bring before them. Reason-ably and responsibly used, this power would protect the Justices from wasting their time on trivial or patently futile and desperate appeals, and would let them devote their minds and energies to important matters only. But this power, since it is absolute, is a free ticket to open abuse, an invitation to laziness, incompetence, even cowardice, and it has been precisely so abused in the recent past.

Chief Justice Vinson's take-it-easy Court heard about half as many cases a year as did Chief Justice Hughes' hustling Court a mere decade before. Nor was this for lack of critical cases, of urgent issues begging for a hearing, and turned down. The question whether a city-helped housing project may discriminate against a Negro war veteran (which split the top court of New York state, four to three); the question whether a radio station is "obstructing justice" when it broadcasts a defendant's alleged out-of-court confession during a murder trial (which pits one civil liberty against another—the guarantee of a fair trial against the guarantee of free speech and press); the question whether a fugitive from a Georgia chain gang must be sent back from his hard-won asylum in another state to what the Constitution calls "cruel and unusual punishment"; the question whether movies, like newspapers and books, are protected from narrow local censorship by freedom of the press: all these questions and dozens like them, within the short space of two Court terms, were deemed by Vinson and company not worthy of decision—or perhaps too hot to handle. Nor could any power on earth then force the unjudging Justices to handle them.

Along with this we-won't-even-take-the-case facet of Supreme Court irresponsibility, there goes an attitude so autocratic as to be looked at askance even by many people who otherwise approve of the Court's autocracy. When the

Justices hear and decide a case, though they do their actual deciding in forever secret conference, they at least write opinions which explain—or try to explain or purport to explain—why they are saying Yes or No. But when they simply refuse to take a case, no reason is ever given for that refusal. True, the Justices have let it be known that, by their own self-made rule, if four of them vote—in secret, of course—to hear a case, that case will be heard. And increasingly, in recent years, a couple of the more industrious and courageous Justices, Douglas and Black, have gone to the unusual extreme of recording their protests, time after time, not against a decision by their brethren (which would be a regular dissent) but against the refusal of their brethren to so much as hear and handle many an important issue. Yet even these often disgusted, often angry protestants, bound by the rules of the lodge, never tell—if indeed they always know—why at least six of their fellows have voted themselves out of doing a job that the protestants think ought to be done. Here, in the Court's unwillingness to explain its own seemingly indiscriminate, and perhaps inexplicable, refusals to act, is the ultimate of undemocratic power abused to a point akin to arrogance.

This arrogance is further compounded by a strange fiction, a judicial fairy tale which many Justices mouth and maybe believe, about what their turning down of a case or problem means. The fiction is that the Court, in *not* taking and *not* deciding a case, which it has the power to take and decide, is actually deciding absolutely nothing. As Justice Frankfurter, the most persistent of recent Justices in flaunting this fiction, put it not long ago: "All that a denial of a petition for a writ of certiorari means [*that being lawyers' language for the commonest way of refusing to hear a case*] is that fewer than four members of the Court thought it should be granted." But ignored by this pseudo-explanation, which (Frankfurter again speaking) "the Court has stated again and again," is the plain fact that no case, no problem, vanishes into the blue with the Court's refusal to hear it.

Technically, what happens is that the judgment of some lower court stands just as inexorably, just as finally, as if the Supreme Court had heard the case and affirmed—or said Yes to—the lower court's decision. Practically, what happens is that the Negro war veteran does not get an apartment in the Stuyvesant Town housing project in New York City; that certain movies, offensive to city censors, can *not* be shown in Atlanta, Georgia; that the Baltimore murder suspect whose supposed confession, bought or cajoled from him without legal safeguards and broadcast for all the jurors—or their friends and families—to hear, may be hanged. When the Justices downed their thumbs against listening to Alger Hiss's appeal from his conviction for perjury, none other than Richard Nixon, a lawyer who was then a U.S. Senator and is now Vice-President of the United States, remarked: "Now that the Supreme Court has finally *written the decision* [*italics added*] in the case of Alger Hiss, I should like to take this opportunity to give due credit . . ." But according to the Justices themselves and their insistent fairy story, they had done nothing, much less "write the decision," in the case of Alger Hiss. They had only denied a petition for a writ of certiorari—and: "All that a denial of a petition for a writ of certiorari means is that fewer than four members of the Court thought it should be granted."

If a law—say on uniform rules for divorce throughout the forty-eight states—should be proposed in Congress (as it has been) and the proposed law should never be brought to vote, perhaps by the device of letting it be buried in committee, it is hard to imagine that any voter, any newspaper, any pressure group that had backed such a law, would accept the bland explanation that Congress had made no decision whatever about it. If such a law should be passed by Congress, and then the President, by simply doing nothing—by failing to sign or to veto it for ten days—should let it go into effect, it is inconceivable that anyone, pro or con, would swallow a White House statement that the President had made no decision. But if such a law should go into effect, after passage by Congress and no veto by the President, and a case should be taken to court by someone who claimed the law was unconstitutional, and the case should go through the lower courts until the Supreme Court was asked to decide it, and the Justices should "deny certiorari" or refuse to hear the case —then the third branch of our tripartite federal government would officially announce, and expect both lawyers and non-lawyers to believe, that it had made no decision at all as to whether the new national divorce law was valid or invalid, good or bad.

Of course this is patent poppycock—and the reason why it is poppycock, even when intoned by a spokesman for the solemn and black-robed nine, is that wherever the power to govern, to make decisions on policy, indubitably exists, it is used every bit as effectively by a deliberate refusal to use it as by its firm and forthright use. Practically speaking, Calvin Coolidge governed just as surely by the near non-exercise of his Presidential power, by *letting* things be done that he wanted done, as did Franklin Roosevelt by the active exercise of the same power, by *getting* things done that he wanted done. Practically speaking, a Supreme Court that lets issues be decided by turning its collective head away from them decides them just as surely as does a Court that meets them head-on. Failure to use the power to govern is one way of governing.

Throughout the whole history of the Court as a governing power and not just as a final forum for lawyers arguing points of private law about contracts and torts and procedure and property and the rest of the stuff that lawyers argue about—that is, ever since John Marshall boldly annexed for the Court a top political spot in the running of the nation—political theorists, from thesis-writing seekers for Ph.D.'s to college professors to the Justices themselves, have worried the problem of an active Court as against a passive Court, of a set of Justices that grabs the reins as against one that lets things roll, or slide. In the current jargon, one set is praised or damned as "judicial activists" and the other set praised or damned as apostles of "judicial self-denial." But the so-called split between the two is a silly circular self-deception on the part of those who worry and debate it. So long as the passivists, the judicial-self-denial boys, the alleged advocates of non-interference in legislative or executive decisions, refuse to go so far as to say that the Court has no *power* to interfere, refuse to urge abdication by the Justices of the role that Marshall won for them, the Court will continue to interfere, and continue to govern, merely by the imminent omnipresence of that power.

Those Justices, after the Civil War, who struck down *state* efforts to regulate business because they wanted a national economy to thrive were no more activists, in so acting, than were Franklin Roosevelt's New Deal Justices when they passively failed to strike down *federal* efforts to regulate business—because they too wanted a national economy to thrive. Those Justices who bow today to whatever lawmakers or law-enforcers may do to cut down our ancient constitutional liberties are no more passivists than are other Justices who would *act* to return to the people's Bill of Rights—despite its legislative or executive disregard. No matter whether a majority of the Justices answer Yes or No, or by shunning a case answer nothing, to a government problem brought before them, their action or inaction settles that case, decides that problem. A genuine judicial passivist, on or off the Court, would urge that the Constitution be amended to take from the Justices all power to make political decisions. No Justice, self-denying or not, has ever so urged (although Holmes once said that he scarcely thought the nation would fall apart if the Court were deprived of its right to veto the rest of the *federal* government). Men, for all their sometime talk of pious self-denial, rarely want to really relinquish power.

Yet to say that the power of the nine Justices—as cannot be said too strongly—is essentially an autocratic and irresponsible power which is quite as potent when not used as when used, *because it is there*, is not necessarily to condemn that power; or at least is not to condemn it altogether. Our government is far from being a genuine democracy, New England town-meeting fashion, or even a democracy only diluted in so far as final decisions are made not by the people but by their elected representatives in their stead. For in such a democracy a constitution saying that certain things may not be done by government, or must only be done in certain ways, as does our Constitution, would be a senseless superfluity, a mere piece of paper—as indeed, though for different and scarcely democratic reasons, is the constitution of the U.S.S.R. In such a democracy the people, by majority vote of themselves or their elected representatives, could make or change any laws or rules they pleased, constitution or no. And one of the oldest dilemmas of all political thinkers who approve of constitutions, but also favor democracy, is the question *who* is then to decide whether the act of a law-maker or law-enforcer goes against a written constitution. Whatever men are entrusted with that ultimate decision, especially if they are not elected to that position of trust, their power cannot but be an autocratic power—for it lets them reverse the choice of a contemporary majority and so defeat the democratic will.

The defeat of the democratic will of a contemporary majority by some sort of autocratic decision—the holding back of the many by a few—is called for, under our Constitution, in one especial and many-faceted field of government. That field of government—or, more accurately, of non-government—is the protection of the civil liberties of all the people from infringement *by* their government. It is the protection, in particular, of unpopular people and groups of people, of suspected criminals and suspected Communists, of religious and racial and noisy political minorities, from the excesses of mob rule and the little-less-than-lynching that are all too often aimed at them, nationally, statewise, or locally, under the guise of law.

The Constitution guarantees, against any muzzling by Congress, the rights of free speech and a free press, those basic means of free political expression. That guarantee is flatly stated and altogether unqualified: "Congress shall make no law . . . abridging the freedom of speech, or of the press"; if Congress then passes such a law, in defiance of the Constitution—as it did within the first ten years of the nation's life and has done sporadically ever since—what but an autocratic power can defend, not so much the Jacobins of 1799 or the Communists of 1949 as the very Constitution itself, against the lawmakers' disregard of its words? The Constitution guarantees, against unequal treatment by any state, the right of every citizen to be given the same legal privileges and protection that are given to every other citizen. If a democratically chosen state government then passes and puts in force a law that treats citizens of African or Mexican or Japanese ancestry less well than it treats "white" citizens—as many states have done—what but an autocratic power can order that the Constitution be obeyed? The Constitution guarantees to everyone accused of crime the right of fair treatment and a fair trial—and does it in considerable detail. If, as probably happens daily somewhere in the U.S., a confession is wrung from a suspect by third-degree methods, or his home is searched without a search-warrant, or his so-called trial, as in an espionage or kidnapping case, with public opinion inflamed for revenge and a prejudiced judge and jury, more nearly resembles a formalized lynching—what but an autocratic power can reverse, in the name of the Constitution, the popularly approved acts of overzealous law-enforcing officials? In short, if there is any place in a near-democracy for the proper use of ultimate political power by an autocratic group like the nine Justices, that place is in protecting the few against the legalized tyrannies, major or minor, of the many. It is in giving man-backed meaning and force to the civil liberties that our parchment Constitution can "guarantee" only with wishful words.

Yet the one field of government in which the Supreme Court's majority, throughout the whole history of the Court, have been most bumblingly bashful, most reluctant to assert the autocratic power they hold, is precisely in the realm of civil liberties. Justices who do not hesitate to strike down duly enacted economic laws—laws regulating business or taxing wealth—will meekly "defer to the legislative will" when laws come before them which restrict the personal freedom of individuals in ways more important than the making or keeping of money. Justices may, without blinking, distort the constitutional stop-sign against any state's depriving anyone of "life, liberty, or property without due process of law" in order to veto the will of a majority that sweatshops for women be abolished, or that bakers not cheat housewives with short-weight loaves of bread, or that life insurance rates be kept reasonable; but the same Justices will turn away from using the same admonition against taking "life, liberty, or property without due process of law" to achieve the original meaning of the phrase—which was, quite simply, that nobody should be executed (deprived of life), jailed (deprived of liberty), or fined (deprived of property) without proper legal procedure including a fair trial. And over the years, the Justices have not hesitated to overturn federal laws that—to list a few examples out of scores—limited the extension of slavery into the western territories, imposed a graduated income tax, put an end to almost all child labor, brought help to the nation's farmers hard hit by depression, and regulated the chaotic coal industry—while letting the federal government do as it pleased, and the Constitution be damned, to browbeat unpopular political minorities all the way from the infamous Alien and Sedition Acts at the end of the eighteenth century to the strikingly similar Smith and McCarran Acts today.

Indeed, the bald record of the Court's use of its autocratic power to overturn federal, not state or local, laws is perhaps the most telling single fact about the kind of part it has played in U.S. political history. On the state and local level, the Justices have acted often to uphold civil liberties against their official restriction—though not nearly so often as they might well have acted, and not nearly so often as they have acted to slap down laws that were stepping on someone's financial interests, not on someone's personal freedoms. That Chief Justice Vinson and his confreres, despite some of the most formidable and far-reaching anti-libertarian decisions in the Court's whole life, won a reputation as a civil-liberties Court, largely by upholding against state and local abuses the rights of a comparatively few Negroes and of a tiny religious sect called Jehovah's Witnesses, merely illustrates how very little has come to be expected of the Justices as champions of civil liberties. But the Court's over-all freedom-defending record *below* the national level of government towers majestic and impressive next to its score as the people's constitutional watchdog against abuses by, or with the approval of, the Congress of the United States.

Since Marshall made of the Court a sort of super-legislature, back in 1803, thousands upon thousands of people and companies have sought the Court's help in protesting, under the Constitution; against some law passed by Congress and (if not re-passed over his veto) signed by the President. Most of these thousands of pleas have been turned away by the Justices—most, although far from all of them, properly. Of the hundreds left that the Court has heard, perhaps half, at a calculated guess, dealt exclusively with money matters and half with one or another facet of civil liberties (granted no black-and-white line divides the two: a slavery question, pre-Civil War, touched one man's wealth and another man's freedom; a low-wage employer, banned by the Wagner Act from anti-union appeals to his workers, could reasonably claim infringement of his freedom of speech). In the hundreds of cases the Court has heard where a federal law was attacked as unconstitutional for either a money reason or a civil-liberties reason, the Justices have held less than eighty times that that law—or a part of it or the way it was working in action—did violate the Constitution. But of those seventy-eight decisions overruling the Congress, and usually the President too, practically all the untrivial ones threw out a law or part of a law that hurt some person or company in the pocketbook or the bank account alone. Only three of those seventy-eight decisions in 150 years could conceivably be classed as significant, if still small-scale, protections of personal, not financial, freedoms. Only three notable times in the Court's entire history have a majority of the Justices, in defense of civil liberties, declared an Act or part of an Act of Congress unconstitutional.

Here, then, are nine non-elected and often haphazardly chosen men wielding the top political power in an otherwise democratic national government, and using that autocratic and triply irresponsible power in a strange and onesided manner. For they use it nearly exclusively to stymie the majority will where the two elected branches of government have acted to control or affect the business life of the nation in ways that five or more of the nine happen to disapprove. They use it almost never toward the kind of end that would thoroughly justify the place of an autocratic group in a constitutional democracy—that is, as a final defender *against* the majority will of unpopular minorities, under the Constitution. Indeed, the only minority in whose behalf the Justices have regularly and effectively used their power, to block the majority will as expressed in federal laws, is the minority of the well-to-do.

How come? How have the Justices managed to maintain their political supremacy so long despite the misuse—and the frequent and maybe frightened non-use—of their power? Why did most of the nation, not just the lawyers of bench and bar, rise in indignant protest when Franklin Roosevelt proposed to add six new Justices—to make a Supreme Court of fifteen men, and also to help outvote, he hoped, the majority of the Nine Old Men who were then judicially murdering the New Deal, which most of the

nation applauded? Why the popular championing of a
government institution whose members were making
unpopular decisions—in order to defeat the countermove
of a popular President, which move not one lawyer in all
the nation could, or did, brand as unconstitutional? Part
of the answer, and a large part, lies in the ceremony and
the ritual of the Court, the robes and the secrecy and the
solemn pronouncements in lumbering legal language, the
whole panoply of a surface-deep dignity that is deliberately
donned to impress its audience and that has invested the
Court, in the popular mind, with a symbolic sacredness, an
aura of being above such petty and temporal things as the
making of political decisions and the wielding of political
power. Most U.S. citizens regard the Court with much the
same automatic respect and reverence that British citizens
feel for their royalty—and for much the same reasons.

But beyond the hypnotic effects of the show that the
Court puts on to look and sound and seem so awe-
inspiring, no matter how weak or unwise may be the
things it does or fails to do, there are two interrelated
reasons, both of them basically myths, that mainly account
for the Court's continuing political power. The first myth
is that the Court is a sort of single force, an integrated
institution, a collective mind that operates as a *unit* of
government instead of as nine distinct and disparate
human beings. This myth is nurtured by the odd notion
that the Justices do not *make* law when they make decisions
but merely get together to discover what the law is, and
was all along. It feeds on the Court's official ukases which
always announce "the opinion of the Court"—although
"the opinion of the Court" has more than once been the

opinion of the Justice who wrote it and his alone, with the other Justices who voted the same way writing separate or "concurring" opinions to explain their reasons why. (One Justice recently rebuked a lawyer who referred, in argument, to "your former opinion, Mr. Justice," by snapping: "You don't mean *my* opinion; you mean the opinion of the *Court*.") The myth has also been fostered by almost all legal scholars who write about the Court; the more naïve discuss "the Court's" work, "its" philosophy, "its" shifting points of view, as though "it" were a strange creature with eighteen legs and one brain; the more sophisticated deplore, particularly of late, the Court's failure to act as they think "it" ought to act—that is, as a single-purposed, predictable, and perforce mono-minded institution, for all its being made up of nine men. Yet neither scholars nor ordinary citizens expect the Senate or the House or, for that matter, any town council to behave other than as a collection of individuals who react to, think about, vote on different government problems in their own individual ways. So too, despite the myth, do Supreme Court Justices.

The second and related myth, even more deeply imbedded in our folklore of government, has it that the men who become Justices become simultaneously—or ought to become if they don't—politically sterile; that they put on, or should put on, with their robes a complete impartiality or indifference toward the nation's social and economic problems; that they switch, or should switch, their minds to neutral in dealing with every issue outside the verbal needlework of the law. A lawyer who has spent his professional life in the service of corporate clients, to whose interests he has been sincerely sympathetic, is supposed, by the myth, to forget it all, to turn it off like a faucet on appointment to the Court. A legislator who has spent his political life in behalf of liberal measures, in which he has deeply believed, is supposed to take the veil, politically, on becoming a Justice; so goes the myth.

This myth, which extends to the whole judiciary, not just the Supreme Court, is further illustrated by the condemnation of any judge who indulges in any remotely political activity—except the deciding of cases. When Justice Douglas, a few years back, made a series of public speeches urging that the Constitution's Bill of Rights be zealously followed and jealously guarded, especially in explosive times like these—a sentiment scarcely out of keeping with the duties or office of a high judge sworn to uphold the Constitution—he was bitterly criticized by much of the press and most of the bar for stooping to political partisanship and so sullying his judicial robes and judicial integrity. Although not yet deprived of their right, as citizens, to cast their votes every November, Supreme Court Justices—off the bench as well as on it—are deemed by the myth to be, properly, apolitical persons, unaffected by what goes on in the nation outside their marble temple, aloof and remote from the workaday world.

Like the other myth which helps uphold the power of the Justices, no matter how they use, abuse, or fail to use that power, this myth is of course arrant nonsense. The idea that a human being, by a conscious act of will, can rid his mind of the preferences and prejudices and political slants or values that his whole past life has accumulated in him, and so manage to think in the rarefied atmosphere of simon-pure objectivity, is simply a psychological absurdity. Granted, a wise Justice like Holmes, out of tolerance for the views of others, may try to temper those of his private biases of which he himself is aware. But only a dull-witted Justice would suppose, and only an intellectually dishonest one pretend—and the Court has been manned by far too many of both—that he could ever purge his thinking processes, for the purpose of making decisions, of all his personal predilections even of the conscious kind, much less the unconscious and unrecognized. Myths or no myths, solemn show or no solemn show, the Supreme Court is nothing other than nine sometimes wise, sometimes unwise, but always human, men.

And so it is superficial, however technically true, to say, for example, that "the Supreme Court," in 1935, declared unconstitutional the New Deal's railroad retirement act (under which all railroads would have had to chip in to a compulsory insurance fund to pay annuities to retired railroad workers over the age of 65). It is somewhat more accurate, more meaningful, and more revealing to say that five Supreme Court Justices—one of whom made the legal reputation that led to his Justiceship as a lawyer for the Great Northern, the Northern Pacific, and the Chicago, Burlington, and Quincy railroads (Butler); one of whom was kicked upstairs to the Court because of his cantankerousness as Attorney-General, including his reluctance to prosecute the New York, New Haven, and Hartford Railroad on anti-trust charges (McReynolds); one of whom had made a small fortune and a large legal name for himself by representing, in government and out, the Union Pacific Railroad (Van Devanter); one of whom had been a close Senate friend of a certain Senator Harding who later, as President, named him to the Court, after the voters of Utah had refused to re-elect him because of his reactionary Senate record in behalf of corporations, including railroads (Sutherland); and one of whom, as a former Philadelphia lawyer, had counted among his several large corporate clients the Pennsylvania Railroad plus its affiliates (Roberts)—that these five Justices outvoted their four considerably abler colleagues (Hughes, Brandeis, Cardozo, and Stone—who dissented) and thus negated the will of Congress, the will of the Administration, and presumably the will of the people of the country, as well as, quite coincidentally of course, saving money for the railroads. Not all of the Supreme Court's constitutional decisions are as easy to explain as this one, or as crystal-clear in meaning and in motive. But none of those decisions can be explained or analyzed or understood on any other than a sheerly superficial, legalistic level, except in terms of the Justices, the *men*, who made them.

Hence any attempt to explore and evaluate the Court's role in our national history—past, present, and future—must stem from and come constantly back to the men who really play that role in the Court's name. It must cut through all the falderol of ceremony and sanctimony; it must not be taken in by the quaint notion that words, whether of constitution or statute, can govern, without men to use the words as the men see fit to use them; it must kept straight that the so-called reasons the Justices give for what they do, in their long and legal-languaged opinions, are as often self-justifying excuses, wittingly or unwittingly made, as they are genuine sources of decision.

Any such attempt must recognize too, in a realistic way, that the overwhelming political power held by the Justices is triply an irresponsible power—in that they are accountable to no one but themselves; in that they never take, nor can they take, responsibility for affirmative government action; and in that they can either use or refuse to use their power as they please, without ever so much as telling why. And last—and first—any such attempt must consider the proper part, if any, to be played by a small and autocratic group of men who make authoritarian decisions within the framework of a constitutional democracy.

Only so can the Court as a political institution be seen in its true colors and in perspective. Only so can a light be shined on what the Justices, over the years—good and bad Justices, wise and less than wise, farsighted and astigmatic —have done for the nation and done to the nation. Only so can a long look at the Supreme Court of the United States make sense.

CHAPTER 2

From the Gleam in the
Founding Fathers' Eyes to the
Birth of Supreme Court Power

IN NO OTHER NATION on earth does a group of judges
hold the sweeping political power—the privilege in
practice, not just in theory, of saying the last governmental
word—that is held by the nine U.S. Supreme Court Justices. Whence came this unique judicial supremacy over all
other branches and levels of government? What is its
source; did it spring, like Minerva, fullblown from the
foreheads of the Founding Fathers, or did it, like Topsy,
just grow? The answer is neither so black-or-white simple
nor yet so difficult, nor even so important, as the scholarly

squabbles of historians and political scientists would sometimes make it seem. In brief summary, the Supreme Court's political power was conceived, if furtively, during the drafting of the Constitution; it was carefully nourished prenatally by the Federalist Party during the early years of the nation's life while that Party controlled the entire federal government; it was skillfully and timely midwived by Chief Justice John Marshall soon after the Federalists had lost the Congress and the Presidency; and, with only a few short lapses, it has gradually grown in strength and stature ever since.

The origins of Supreme Court power are of little real import today save to academicians and antiquarians simply because that power indubitably exists. No delving into its roots, no research into its legitimacy in history or in logic, can refute or reverse its stark presence as a political force. Only in a rather negative way—in exploding misconceptions about what the Court "should" be today, based on misconceptions about what it was at its birth, in dispelling illusions about the Court being any other than an essentially political body, and being so intended, from its very creation—only so may a look at the earliest sources and uses of its power carry some current bite. If the Founding Fathers, or many of them, meant the Court to wield a sort of superlegislative shillelagh to protect the rights of property against laws that would chip away those rights, perhaps the conservative Four Horsemen who were the judicial bane of the New Deal were scarcely abusing their *historic* function, as so many New Dealers claimed. If so high-minded a President as George Washington could staff the first Court exclusively with fellow Federalists, passing over such anti-Federalist brilliants as patriot Patrick Henry, maybe Franklin Roosevelt can be forgiven —or better understood—for naming only Democrats to the Court; and if one of Washington's appointees, the legally quite undistinguished James Iredell, was so honored largely to pay off a political debt, perhaps Harry Truman should not be too severely censured for making Tom Clark a Justice.

Those who see the past through the rosy glow of fable with which time tends to fog the facts too readily misapprehend the present. For the last quarter-century, the Court as a whole and each of its separate Justices have been bitterly criticized—now from the left, now from the right, now from the left—and the bulk of that criticism has flayed the intrusion of downright partisan politics, now conservative, now liberal, into the judicial process, while urging the Court to go back to being above partisanship, disinterested, politically numb, "as it was and was meant to be in the beginning." It never was. From its very inception—in its nascent and then surgent governmental strength, in the choosing of its personnel, in its practices and policies and declarations and decisions—the Court has been an instrument, as the Justices have been both agents and exercisers, of sheer political power.

Most palaver about the governmental power of the Justices, be it scholarly or more mundane, by lawyers or by laymen, centers solely on one aspect of that power, the right of judicial review, which is what the lawyers and scholars call the Justices' now accepted authority to veto any law—national, state, or local—or anything done under any such law, by saying that it is forbidden by the

U.S. Constitution. This right of judicial review is indeed the most potent and pregnant facet of Supreme Court power; and its most dramatic and controversial manifestation is in the vetoing by the Justices of things done by the other two supposedly equal branches of the national government, the Congress and the President. It is this ultimate supremacy of the judiciary within the federal government itself—plus the uses to which it has been put and the motives behind those uses—that is so widely misunderstood today as being, originally and properly, remote from the realm of ordinary political affairs. Because it is thus misunderstood, a look at its sources and its history may help bring its present into sharper perspective.

But before going briefly back to the Founding Fathers for a preview of judicial review, it should be clear that the Justices hold and have always held yet another political weapon, as generally underrated as it has been commonly overlooked in judicial review's long shadow. That weapon is their unquestioned right—and more than that, their duty—to "interpret" the laws passed by Congress, to tell what the words of a law mean whenever that meaning is in dispute. And lest this sound like a trivial source or a piddling type of power, be it remembered—in Mr. Dooley's phrase—that a statute which reads like a stone wall to a layman can become in the hands of a lawyer a triumphal arch—and that the Justices are lawyers.

The Justices, with Taft as their Chief, wielded pure political power when they "interpreted" the Clayton Act's famous Section 20—which was called, when passed, "labor's Magna Charta" because its words seemed so clearly to restrict court injunctions against unions—as *not* restricting court injunctions against unions and not so intended. And so, on the other side, did the New Deal Justices wield political power twenty years later when they "interpreted" the anti-trust laws as almost never applying to labor unions at all. As in countless other cases of mere "interpretation," each of these decisions, one conservative, one liberal, carried a political punch far greater than many a Court ruling declaring a law unconstitutional. And much of the Justices' influence over the nation has always come from reading federal tax laws, labor laws, patent laws, business-regulating laws one way or another way, for business or against business, for or against the other two branches of the federal government.

The chief difference between this kind of Supreme Court power and the judicial-review variety is that here the Justices' decision, however potent, is not necessarily final. Congress, if sufficiently displeased by judicial "interpretation" of any of its laws, can if it wishes amend or rewrite that law more plainly and more specifically to get done what it wants done. In fact, Congress once revised the wording of part of the federal estate tax statute the very day after the Court had handed down a political "interpretation" of the old wording so patently incorrect as to be absurd. But when the Justices brand an act of Congress unconstitutional, there is nothing further Congress can do —save perhaps try to achieve the same end in a different and devious way or else hope for a radical shift in the Court's membership. Here is judicial supremacy at its supremest; and it does indeed stem from the work of the Founding Fathers.

But not from their words—or at least, not from the

words of the U.S. Constitution which they drafted in the
famous Convention of 1787. Nowhere in that document,
nor anywhere in any of its amendments, is there so much
as a mention of the right of judicial review. Article III
sets up a Supreme Court, lists the kinds of cases it is to
handle, *not* including those where a law is said to violate
the Constitution, and leaves the rest to "such regulations
as the Congress shall make." Endless and pointless controversy has raged ever since about whether the founders
meant the right of judicial review to be implied from between the lines of the written Constitution.

Those who say No point to the meticulous care with
which the machinery of a federal government was detailed
in the document and scoff at the notion that anything so
important, if intended, should have been omitted. Those
who say Yes claim that the right of judicial review was so
widely accepted and practiced at the time that it did not
need to be specified and was simply taken for granted by
the founders. Actually, neither argument holds water.
The founders might well have wanted judicial review and
still not dared to say so in black and white for fear that the
open grant of such power to the courts might keep the
people, who trusted their legislatures more than they
trusted judges, from ratifying the Constitution. As for the
claim that judicial review was the regular order of the day,
quite the contrary was the case, with the British Parliament
dominant over the British judiciary, just as it still remains,
and with early American legislatures overturning court
decisions far more frequently than the one or two instances
where an early American court boldly balked at applying a
duly enacted law. Only in the striking down by King

George's Privy Council of laws passed by colonial legislatures had there been anything resembling widespread judicial review—and that had been one of the causes of the Revolution.

The fact is that some of the men who drafted the Constitution clearly favored judicial review, some clearly opposed it, and some had no strong opinion either way. Those who favored it, though well aware it would be a governmental innovation, were the most forthright conservative and property-minded members of the Convention like Alexander Hamilton, James Wilson (later a Supreme Court Justice), and Oliver Ellsworth (later a Supreme Court Chief Justice). They feared that an unchecked Congress might run riot in passing, even over the President's veto, the sort of "leveling laws," as they called them, that helped the poor at the expense of the wealthy, just as many state legislatures had done; and they feared too the domination of the new federal judiciary by the legislature, as had also happened in the states. The founders who opposed judicial review, perhaps with pre-Revolutionary repression of self-government more vividly in their minds, feared rule by the people's representatives less and rule by an oligarchy, whether of His Majesty's agents or of home-grown judges, more; as Benjamin Franklin plainly stated this side of the case, it would be "improper to put it in the power of any man to negative a law passed by the legislature because it would give him the control of the legislature."

Actually, the right of judicial review never became an issue at the Constitutional Convention because even those who hoped the judges would use it did not propose that it be designated in the document. References to it were incidental to discussion of a "council of revision"—to be made up of the President and two Supreme Court Justices, with a partial power to veto acts of Congress—which *was* proposed and was voted down. Reports of the Convention record only eleven members of the fifty-five as taking a stand either way on judicial review, and of these, six were for and five against—scarcely a score to warrant a confident conclusion about "what the Founding Fathers intended." And even though other members expressed themselves outside the Convention at other times, no count has ever put those who spoke in favor of judicial review higher than twenty-five, or three less than a majority, and no count has ever put those who spoke against it nearly that high.

But if wrangles over "the intent of the founders" with respect to judicial review are then futile, as they are, and this largely because the founders never made it an issue they had to face officially at the Convention, judicial review nevertheless became a very live and important issue when they presented the finished Constitution to the people of the then-sovereign states for ratification. As all but devotees of the Parson Weems approach to American history are aware, the question of ratifying or not ratifying the new Constitution—of creating or not creating a real United States—set off one of the bitterest, no-holds-barred political battles in all our history. By and large, the Constitution-backers were the men of wealth and substance, the creditors or well-propertied class, the commercial traders of the North and the slave-holding plantation owners of the South. Suspicious or hostile were the small farmers and mechanics, the debtor class, the men who, from the fishermen on the coast to the frontiersmen clearing the Western wilderness, did their day's work with their hands. And one of the most suspect, if still implicit, wrinkles of the proposed new Constitution was the threat, perceived by many, that a national judiciary topped by a Supreme Court might try to overturn laws passed by the people's legislatures, including Congress.

In countering these suspicions, the more active and articulate of the Federalists—as the pro-Constitution party came to be called—did not deny the possibility of judicial review. Instead, they cleverly claimed that such review would be used mainly to protect the whole of the people, not the propertied class, against unfair laws like "bills of attainder" (by which individuals are picked out and punished by a legislature without court trial). As historian J. Allen Smith once described this shrewd campaign, overstating it only slightly: "The advocates of judicial supremacy were careful to support it not as a conservative safeguard but as a means—assumed to be necessary—of protecting popular rights and enforcing the constitutional checks on public officials. Every effort was made to create the impression that the Supreme Court of the United States was designed to protect the people. . . . There is probably no other instance in the whole history of constitutional development where public opinion has been so misled as to the fundamental nature of a political arrangement. . . . The real purpose was to centralize political authority largely in the Supreme Court of the United States, and through the power of final interpretation, to make the Constitution an adequate bulwark of conservatism."

Though the Constitution did not in so many words set up the right of judicial review, though the overt intent of the founders was inconclusively hazy, though the high hopes in this respect of the pro-ratification spokesmen were stated with strategic indirection, it took little time to translate those Federalist hopes into substantial action, once the Constitution was adopted and the brand-new U.S. government had taken over. That government was, of course, a Federalist government, with George Washington, who had chairmanned the constitutional convention, as its President, and with a Congress, chosen in quick elections by a small fraction of America's adult males, overweighted with ardent Federalists. And one of the very first things done by this very first of U.S. Congresses, early in 1789, was to write a system of national courts, plus a set of rules for those courts to follow, into a law much more pointed and meaningful and far-reaching than the Constitution specified or required.

The Judiciary Act of 1789, which remains even today the foundation of the whole federal court system, was one of the most remarkable statutes ever enacted by any legislative body in the world. That it set up a Supreme Court—then composed of only six Justices—and two kinds of lower federal courts was not so remarkable. Nor was the staffing of these courts with marshals, U.S. attorneys, and all the personal paraphernalia needed to try cases and enforce decisions. What was remarkable was the listing of the kinds of cases—in addition to those named in the Constitution itself—which the Supreme Court was to hear on appeal. For in the course of that listing, a national legislature, by its own voluntary act, deliberately made itself subordinate to and reversible by a national judiciary.

Even here, the Supreme Court's right of judicial review was not written out plain and bold for all to read. But Section 25 of the Judiciary Act would have made no sense at all unless understood as bestowing on the Justices the right of judicial review. What Section 25 did was to give the Supreme Court the flat power to affirm or reverse, on appeal, any decision by the highest court of a state holding that a *state* law was valid, constitutional, good, or that a *federal* law was bad. At the extreme of technical strictness, this would only allow the Supreme Court to overrule *Congress* after a state court had done so first—though the Justices' full supremacy over *state* legislatures is bluntly stated. But to suppose that so nation-minded a political assemblage as the first Congress meant to concede, as does Section 25, to the courts of the states a power to veto Congress, subject to Supreme Court approval, and *not* give that same power to the Supreme Court, acting initially or in review of lower federal courts, would be the depth of absurdity. No member of Congress, when the Section was debated (and judicial supremacy over Congress, not the states, was flayed by a militant minority) so supposed.

Why this strange renunciation of power by men in a position to keep that top power in their own hands—a renunciation which, incidentally, has never been reversed or retracted by any Congress since (though the right to renounce power by passing a law embodies the right to reclaim it by repealing that law)? Why this gift to the judges, as on a platter, of a king-of-the-castle role among the three supposedly equal branches of federal government?

Because the Federalists were political realists. Because the Federalist Congress and the Federalist President knew that *they* were not renouncing *their* power in any but an abstract and theoretical way. To future Congresses and future Presidents, the renunciation might—as it did— become meaningful. But no Federalist-appointed judiciary was going to balk the Congress that created it nor the President that named its members; the notion of a truly independent and apolitical batch of judges, despite the high-flown falderol that had helped sell the Constitution to the people, would have brought snickers from all but the least sophisticated Federalists.

More than that, these men were aware that the Congressmen among them held office for only two years and then had to be re-elected—or rejected—by the people; that the Senators among them held office, at most, for six years and then had to be re-chosen—or not—by state legislatures elected by the people; that the President held office for four years and then had to be given—or denied— a second term by electors picked by the people. They had not forgotten, these Federalists, by how close a squeak their Constitution had run the gauntlet of ratification in the face of potent popular opposition (two of the thirteen "original" states had still not joined the union when the Judiciary Act was drafted); and they also foresaw that many of the measures and policies of the new government would not be calculated to add to its, or their, widespread popular support. In short, they and their Federalist Party could not count on staying in office, and in control, for more than four years, much less forever.

But federal judges, including Supreme Court Justices,

were to be appointed, not elected—and moreover, appointed for life. What could a Federalist Congress lose by blessing with ultimate national power the men who were sure to wield that power longest? The Judiciary Act of 1789, with its Section 25, was no renunciation of any sort of power that the practical men of the first Congress cared about. It was rather a foresighted extension of Federalist domination into a future when the Party might lose—as it did—the executive and the legislature, and only the judges would be left to hold the fort of Federalist policies.

Implicit in all of this, of course, and essential to an understanding of otherwise inexplicable Section 25, was the assumption that President Washington would choose his judges and Justices in much the same manner that he picked his Cabinet, and for much the same reason—to assure that the new government, its judicial branch not excepted, would be exclusively in the hands of its friends, of the political leaders who wrote the Constitution and fought to get it ratified, of the Federalists. The assumption was warranted; President Washington did not fail them.

No President since Washington has had the chance to pack the entire federal judiciary with men of his own political persuasion and no President since Washington ever did a more thorough job with whatever chance he had to fill federal judgeships with party bedfellows. Indeed, Washington seemed to rate the courts as of greater political importance than the Cabinet; to his Cabinet he at least named Thomas Jefferson, who had looked askance at the Constitution from the beginning and was soon to become the anti-Federalists' leader; but every judgeship, high and low and without exception, went to a full-blown Federalist faithful. Rarely has any statesman of comparable stature demonstrated more pointedly his awareness that the men, not the laws, control and direct even the judicial branch of government.

To the first Supreme Court Washington appointed three Northerners and three Southerners, thus initiating the rather ridiculous practice of roughly equal geographical representation on a *national* tribunal which has, ever since, kept many first-rate men off the Court and helped put less able Justices on. All six were, of course, ardent Federalists, wealth-conscious and conservative in the extreme, and although three or perhaps four of them could be said to have merited their Justiceships on the basis of ability and legal reputation, the others could not hold a lawyer's candle to many well-known but less politically appealing luminaries, of whom Patrick Henry was only one. (Some years later, when age and illness had softened the "give me liberty or give me death" patriot to comparative conservatism, Washington did offer him a vacant Justiceship, which Henry declined.)

As first Chief Justice of the United States, Washington chose land-rich John Jay of New York, experienced as a judge and diplomat and main draftsman of his state's first constitution. His slant toward matters governmental is hinted by his opposition to the Declaration of Independence, though he afterward supported the Revolution, and is shouted by his credo that "those who own the country ought to govern it." Able, aloof, aristocratic, a high-minded right-winger, Jay somewhat resembled in political and personal temperament a subsequent Chief Justice from the same state, Charles Evans Hughes.

That Washington picked Jay over his two top rivals for the post, James Wilson and John Rutledge, was either fortuitous or inspired—for it would scarcely have added to the fledgling Supreme Court's popular prestige to have its Chief Justice go insane, as Rutledge later did, or spend his last days jumping from one state to another to avoid being arrested for debt, as did Wilson. But both Wilson, who had literally applied for the Chiefship, and Rutledge, whose friends had campaigned for him, were named Associate Justices. Both were learned and practiced in the law, both were wealthy and belligerently tough-minded about the protection of wealth by government, both had helped draft and put across the Constitution, and each was largely responsible for a provision in it that looked to the financial welfare of himself and his friends—Rutledge, from South Carolina, for the legalizing of the slave trade for twenty more years, and Wilson for the tricky little phrase forbidding any state to pass a law "impairing the obligation of contracts." (Such a law would almost always favor debtors at the expense of creditors; Wilson was not to become a debtor himself until years later.) In short, both men were naturals for the kind of Court the Federalists contemplated and wanted.

Yet neither man contributed, in net, to the Court as a government institution; Washington was only the first of many Presidents to pre-misjudge men named as Justices. Rutledge for two years never attended a session of the Court (he did have the farthest to travel and the Court had almost no business at the start); he then resigned to take what seemed to him the more important post of chief justice of South Carolina. Appointed U.S. Chief Justice at his own oblique request when Jay resigned in 1795, he presided over the Court for one term until the Senate refused to confirm him—the only nominee for Chief Justice ever so dishonored—simply because he had recently made a political speech that sounded anti-Federalist; at which point Rutledge went crazy.

Wilson, by contrast, carried more than his share of the Court's work for the nine years from his appointment until his death, and faithfully followed on the bench the Federalists' political line. But Wilson's penchant for land speculation and other get-rich-quick—or rather, get-richer-quick—schemes of a questionable character brought him into increasing disrepute even before the failure of one of his biggest plunges set the sheriffs after him with arrest warrants. He might have been named Chief Justice, after the Senate rejected Rutledge, had not his recent major participation in the smelly Yazoo land frauds—which involved the open bribing of the Georgia legislature—outweighed on the minus side, in terms of the Court's influence and integrity, the plus of his substantial judicial record. As John Jay's personal rectitude made him a Court asset, so the comparative personal fraility of the deeper-thinking, harder-working Wilson (Justices are human beings) made him an ultimate liability.

Compared to Jay, Rutledge, and Wilson, their three colleagues on the first Supreme Court were mental lightweights—although William Cushing, who had served the creditor class well as chief justice of Massachusetts, was rather highly regarded in concentric legal circles, partly because of his judicial ancestry, partly because of the surface dignity which he affected, as in insisting on wearing a full wig after all other American judges had discarded it. Cushing's chief claim to fame is that, by refusing to retire from the Court even after senility had rendered him quite incompetent, he managed to extend his undistinguished career there to twenty years, or more than twice as long as any of the other original Justices.

The remaining two members of the first Court were appointed as so many too many second- or third-rate Justices have been appointed since. Gentleman John Blair, who was later to get rich by gambling heavily in government securities, had played an inconsequential part in the Constitutional Convention and had also, as a minor judge in Virginia, early proclaimed the right of judicial review, but neither of these facts accounts for his appointment; he was George Washington's close personal friend. Young James Iredell had been a mediocre minor judge in North Carolina but he was named to the Court because, as militant head of the North Carolina Federalists, he had just succeeded in getting that reluctant state to join the Union—a sheer political reward. The only thing of note in either man's career as a Justice came when Iredell was presiding in a lower federal court, as the Justices then did regularly, and the Federalist Party was on its way out of power; dealing with a farmer named Fries who had resisted a federal tax collector, Iredell actually urged and upheld Fries' indictment and conviction for treason against the United States. (After re-conviction in a second trial and sentence by equally vindictive, equally Federalist Justice Chase that he be hanged, Fries got a Presidential pardon.)

Here, then, was the first Supreme Court of the United

States, made up of six men all of whose appointments were, in whole or in part, politically inspired and motivated —and in the most partisan sense of the word "politically." A distinguished and decent, but neither profound nor brilliant, Chief Justice whose conception of the importance of his post, and of an independent judiciary, was soon to be indicated by his twice running for governor of New York without resigning from the Court, and then resigning when he was elected; two extremely able Associate Justices, one of whom did not deign to waste an iota of his ability on the Court's work until, after resigning, he later served a brief term as Chief Justice, and one of whom served the Court arduously but also came to disgrace it with his personal financial peccadilloes; an Associate Justice of considerable narrowly legalistic competence who, when age and illness put an end to this competence, became and remained for years a drag on the Court and a hindrance to its work; and two Associate Justices who had no business being on the Court at all, and could scarcely have achieved such eminence save for the happenstance of Presidential friendship or gratitude. If so great a President as Washington could choose no more wisely than this—and his subsequent appointments were of much the same stripe— it may be that later Presidents should rather be praised for their sometime selection of good Justices than damned for their designation of so-so or bad ones.

The first official meeting of the now high-and-mighty Supreme Court of the United States, held in the Wall Street section of New York City early in 1790, must have been a singularly unimpressive affair. Only three Justices bothered to attend, the Southern trio apparently not rating the trip worth the trouble. The half-Court stayed in session for a few days, admitting lawyers to practice before it, obviously in the future, and then adjourned. Indeed, the Court did not hear a single case during the first two years of its existence, the only case brought before it in that period being summarily dismissed on a legal technicality. Thus it might be said that the very first precedent established by the Court—a precedent still in robust health today —was the tossing out of cases for "procedural error," the delaying of substantial decisions and the penalizing of litigants for their attorneys' technical mistakes.

Seen in the light of the Court's initial inactivity, Rutledge's resignation to head the supreme court of South Carolina—a resignation also sparked by pique at not having been named Chief Justice—does not seem too surprising. Nor does it seem surprising that Washington had to offer the vacant post to three men, including Rutledge's nephew, before he got an acceptance from an insignificant Maryland judge named Johnson—who in turn resigned two years later, to be replaced by William Paterson of New Jersey, a wealthy former Founding Father who knew far less of law than he did of business and politics, the latter being, of course, of the Federalist brand.

Yet to say that the *Court* did almost nothing for the first few years of its life does not mean that the Justices themselves were idle. For under the Judiciary Act they had to ride circuit—and riding meant just that in the eighteenth century—in order to sit in the lower federal courts, called Circuit Courts, which regularly met in each section of the nation. Each Circuit Court, at the start,

required the presence of two Justices, but the number was
soon reduced to one to lighten their literally physical burden—and the requirement was eventually eliminated
save for rare occasions when, even today, Supreme Court
members sit with their judicial inferiors in a few types of
cases. Except as unrealism would distinguish an abstract
institution from the human beings who man it, most of
the Supreme Court's work and its most important work,
for the first decade of its existence, was performed by the
Justices, not as a six-man team at the top of the judicial
heap but in pairs or singly as they ran the show in a lower
technical echelon of the federal judiciary.

It was here in the Circuit Courts that Justices of the
Supreme Court first dared to brand an Act of Congress
unconstitutional—eleven years before John Marshall, in
his most famous decision, proclaimed the same judicial
supremacy for the Supreme Court itself. The law that four
of the original Justices, in two separate cases, called bad
in 1792, a scant two years after the federal judiciary first
began to operate, was peculiarly wide open to the *effective*
flaunting of the right of judicial review, even over Congress. Had these early Justices been so bold as to order
anyone in the legislative or executive branches of the
government not to obey a Congressional mandate, their
decisions might well have been flouted or ignored. But the
law in question ordered federal judges, including the Justices themselves, to act as commissioners in awarding
pensions to disabled veterans of the Revolution. So when
the Justices held this unconstitutional in giving to the
judiciary a job that was not properly a judicial job (and
so offending the famous "separation of powers" between

the three branches of government), they had only to say, in effect, *We* refuse to take it on—and how and by whom could they be forced to do it? Actually, most of the Justices offered to do the work voluntarily, but in a private capacity, not as members of the Supreme Court—a distinction to delight the devious legal mind. This absurdity was brought full circle when a case came up later, questioning the validity of the pension awards made by the Justices acting voluntarily, whereupon the same Justices, sitting now as the Supreme Court, held that they had had no authority to do what they had done. Thus the disabled veterans were left holding an empty bag; the nonsense was doubly promulgated that a man is not the same man when he is a judge as when he is not a judge; and judicial supremacy over Congress was tentatively but officially written into the law reports for the first time.

It was in the Circuit Courts too that the Justices began to assert their dominance of state legislatures and their right to veto state laws under the U.S. Constitution. In 1792, the same year when they first balked at taking orders from Congress, two Justices held that a Rhode Island statute, relieving a hard-pressed debtor, violated the little "obligation of contracts" clause that had been thoughtfully inserted into the Constitution by Justice, then-Founding-Father, James Wilson. Then a Georgia statute went the same way for the same reason, then a South Carolina statute, then a Pennsylvania one. The Justices, on circuit, had started in earnest to slap down the "leveling laws" that the founders had, with property-minded near-unanimity, deplored and that the Federalists had counted on *their* judges to take care of.

Meanwhile, a few cases had finally trickled into the Supreme Court itself, most of them suits by people who claimed that different states owed them money and who knew they could never collect in the state courts. This was an especially touchy matter because, although some of the words of the Constitution could be read as contemplating suits of this sort, the Federalists, during the fight over ratification, had given solemn assurance that no such slur on state sovereignty as letting a state be sued by a citizen in a federal court had been intended or would ever be tolerated; the point had seemed so important at the time that, without this assurance, the Constitution would probably not have been ratified.

Nevertheless, old assurances or no, the Federalist Supreme Court set out to uphold these claims against the states—and, in so doing, got itself embroiled in its first big political brawl. One of these claims was against the then truculently democratic and proud state of Georgia, and Georgia refused to so much as dignify the suit by appearing in court to defend against it. Content to hear only one side of the case, the Court held against Georgia, with Chief Justice Jay, who had personally participated in the pledges that nothing like this would ever happen, leading the pack, and only Iredell registering the first Supreme Court dissent. The immediate result throughout the country was a shock of resentment and indignation at so blatant a breaking of faith; in Georgia, one house of the legislature passed a bill—which never became law—that any federal marshal who tried to carry out the Supreme Court's decision would be hanged "without benefit of clergy," and actually the decision was never enforced. The ultimate result was the quick adoption of the Eleventh Amendment to the Constitution, specifically banning suits of this kind in all federal courts. The Justices had lost their first open battle with the people—but the Court was young, and it was not often to lose again.

Nor did it lose its next political set-to, though this was no tempestuous and publicized issue but only a mild little family disagreement between the Court and the Washington Administration. Its repercussions, nonetheless, have echoed down the intervening years with a significance far greater than the semi-sentimental stuff involved in suits against the states. Out of the French Revolution, of the war it spawned between France and England, and of the old defensive alliance between the U.S. and France, arose a cluster of knotty problems in international law, as applied especially to the capture of American ships, to the service of U.S. citizens on warring foreign vessels, and to the setting up of so-called "prize-courts" to handle conflicting claims about the captured "prizes." President Washington, bent on keeping this country out of war, sent to the Supreme Court a series of legal questions about the technical aspects of neutrality, foreign treaties, and like matters—asking the Justices for their professional advice just as a President today would consult his Attorney-General. The Justices politely replied that it was none of their business to hand out legal opinions of this sort, even to a President, even to help keep the U.S. out of war; their only responsibility was deciding cases properly brought before them.

Soon after this mannerly putting-in-his-place of a U.S. President (plus telling him what they thought *their* place to be) the Justices did get a case that covered most of the major questions Washington had asked, and decided those questions just as Washington would have liked them decided. (In brief, U.S. national sovereignty was upheld and foreign nations, at war or not, were warned to respect it.) But the long-term significance of all this lay not so much in the Court's first venture into international law, nor even in the judicial upholding of Administration policy in foreign relations. The long-term significance lay rather in the Justices' firm refusal to sully or jeopardize what they conceived to be their judicial independence by ruling on concededly legal problems—though of vast and vital national import, though bound to be brought before them eventually—in any other than the conventional, dilatory way of waiting for an actual case to arise and reach them. For all the Justices might have cared, their refusal could have helped put the nation at war before the case arose; at least, *they* would not have overstepped the bounds of judicial propriety.

This apparently self-abnegating attitude of we-won't-touch-it-unless-it-comes-to-us-in-the-correct-and-ortho-dox-manner, religiously adhered to by the Supreme Court ever since, has been lavishly lauded by almost all lawyers and most political scientists as a hallmark of the federal judiciary's proud freedom from contamination by the other branches of government, as a living testament to the separation of powers. It is, of course, nothing of the sort. Supreme Court Justices can be just as influenced by, or just as servile to, a Congress or a President when they make their politically consequential decisions in actual cases, a year or five years later, as if they had given the legislature or the executive preliminary legal advice. George Washington got the decision he wanted even though he had to wait for it—and so have Presidents, and Congresses, since.

Moreover, though this insistence on real litigation, on the militant lining-up for the Court of the arguments on both sides in an actual lawsuit, has some excuse as applied to little private legal squabbles (for all its being, at bottom, a hangover from medieval trial by battle), it has virtually no excuse at all as applied to the big problems of government that the Court handles. Rarely, at best, does the eloquence or cogency of an attorney switch a Justice's mind as to whether a minimum-wage law is constitutional, or whether insurance companies or the baseball business are covered by the anti-trust acts. If full-fledged fighting litigation were needed to get the right decision, the Justices would have to throw out of Court, as they do not, the many "friendly suits," dressed up to resemble the genuine article, that are staged to get important problems decided less slowly. And if live political issues with legal overtones required real cases in order to be properly solved —or to preserve judicial independence—then the systems of justice of the several states which *do* authorize *their* supreme courts to give "advisory opinions" to other government branches, without benefit of lawsuits, should long since have broken down. Massachusetts, for one, had been indulging in this practice back in the eighteenth century, even before its former chief justice, Cushing, joined with his Supreme Court brethren in self-righteously refusing an advisory opinion to President Washington.

What the Supreme Court's 160-year-old tradition—of

never giving advice and never laying down the law except
in a formal "case or controversy"—really adds up to is
not nearly so admirable as the safeguarding of an independent federal judiciary or the assurance that every issue
will be decided on its well-argued merits. What it adds
up to is mainly a trio of practical and quite unadmirable
consequences. The first is the entrenching of delay, sometimes interminable delay, in the federal judicial process,
regardless of the impact or the immediacy of the political
problem that cries for a solution. If Congress had been
forewarned that the Missouri Compromise would be tossed
aside by the Court as unconstitutional thirty-odd years
later, other means might have been found to deal with
the extension or non-extension of slavery to the Western
territories; the inflammatory Dred Scott decision would
never have been handed down, fantastically late, from on
high; and the Civil War might conceivably have been
averted. The National Industrial Recovery Act, bulwark
of the original New Deal, was vigorously—and presumably illegally—enforced throughout half of Franklin Roosevelt's first Administration before a unanimous Supreme
Court got around to proclaiming that the NRA, blue eagle
and all, had been unconstitutional, improper, void, from
the beginning. Countless people and companies have paid
all sorts of federal taxes for years before being informed
by the Justices, after a formal protest against this or that
tax came to the Court's attention in the accepted, leisurely manner, that the taxes were invalid and need never
have been paid at all (and in most instances—insult on
injury—that it was too late to recover them). None of
these injustices or worse would likely have occurred or

could normally occur, as they still do, today if the Court would deign to be consulted initially, and officially, instead of still following the too-proud-to-advise lead of George Washington's early Justices.

The second and more subtle consequence of the Court's unwillingness to give out governmental advice except by deciding cases is that it thus retains its dominant position, its precious power to say the last word in political affairs. If the Justices had counseled Washington as to what they deemed his proper conduct according to international law, he might have discarded their counsel or accepted it only in part, for the decision would still have been his to make. If any set of Justices should ever consent to advise any President or Congress about a contemplated law or a planned course of government action, even from a strictly legal angle—which is all that could be asked or expected—the failure of the executive or the legislature to take this advice would mean the partial subordination of the judiciary to them, instead of vice versa. Only so long as the Justices insist on speaking last, after the other two branches have decided and acted, can they surely and automatically retain their supremacy.

And herein lies the third unadmirable consequence of the Court's old hands-off-until-we-get-a-case habit. By always speaking last, by always waiting for a case to come before them in which they need only say Yes or No to something already done, the Justices guarantee and underscore their freedom from all responsibility for the *affirmative* operations of government. It is not the independence of the federal judiciary but rather one facet of its irresponsibility that is made secure by its rigid refusal to speak or act except in the course of deciding litigated cases. Here was perhaps the most telling contribution to future federal jurisprudence—and to the nation's political picture, seen in long-term perspective—of the young Supreme Court under the Chief Justiceship of John Jay.

Jay remained Chief Justice for only five years and spent one of those years on a diplomatic mission to Great Britain —a service to the President which scarcely stressed the alleged independence of the judiciary and which subjected Jay to considerable criticism, much like that leveled at Justice Robert Jackson a century and a half later, when he took a year off from the Court to help prosecute the Nazis at Nuremberg after World War II. But Jay was little criticized for running twice for governor of New York without resigning his judicial post—an act which would bring a storm of protest, and probable impeachment, to-day, when Justices are supposed to keep clean of all politics. Barely missing election the first time, Jay made it on his second try and quit the Court.

John Rutledge had written Washington, just before Jay resigned, that he had shared his friends' feeling, five years before, that "my pretensions to the office of Chief Justice were at least equal to Mr. Jay's in point of law-knowledge, with the additional weight of much longer experience and much greater practice." Washington took the hint, and the man who had never honored the Court with his presence during his two earlier years as an Associate Justice presided over it for one short term until the Senate refused to confirm him—not because the Senators disagreed with Rutledge's less than modest self-estimate but simply because he had recently pulled a political boner that hurt and irked the Federalist Party. The job was then offered, too late, to no-longer-fiery Patrick Henry and next to the oldest sitting Justice, Cushing—both of whom rejected it; it was rather conspicuously not offered to able Justice Wilson, who was already embarrassing his brethren and the Administration with his financial follies. Finally, the begging Chiefship fell to proper and well-propertied Oliver Ellsworth of Connecticut, a shrewdly successful lawyer-politician-banker who had cut an influential figure at the Constitutional Convention and had once suggested, out of his aristocratic Anglophilia, that the U.S. President be called "His Highness."

Meanwhile, mild Justice Blair had resigned and Washington had replaced him with his exact temperamental opposite—a huge, rude, choleric Marylander named Samuel Chase, a man of indubitable and explosive intellectual capacity who almost immediately took over the leadership of the Court from his seniors and his Chief, and went on to become the most unabashedly active political partisan in the Court's whole history. Chase had once been a fire-eating rebel, a rioting member of the "Sons of Liberty," a signer of the Declaration of Independence, and—paradoxically, in the light of what was to come—a violent advocate of freedom of the press. But his subsequent conversion into a dedicated Federalist—as when a Communist today turns Catholic—had been complete and unqualified; and his unjudicial crusading, on and off the bench, for the cause he now espoused was to make him the only Supreme Court Justice ever impeached, although he was not convicted.

The Court which Ellsworth formally headed and Chase

dominated for the five final years of the eighteenth century could easily be rated the worst in U.S. history, but could also contend for honors as the most honest; its members pulled no verbal punches and made no polite bones about being active agents of the fast-fading Federalist Party. Cushing and Paterson remained Justices throughout this period. Wilson died in the middle of it and was replaced, President John Adams now doing the appointing, by the ex-President's nephew, Bushrod Washington—sloppy, snuff-sniffing, slight of build and slight of mentality—whose chief qualification was obviously his name and who was to stick on the Court for thirty-one years, dully mouthing old Federalist doctrine to the very end. Later, Iredell died and his seat went to another North Carolinian, Alfred Moore, who at least had the grace to retire after four years of judicial ineptitude. Shifting personnel did not vary the Court's caliber, except slightly for the worse, and Justice Chase continued throughout to run the show.

That the show Chase ran was a garish sideshow to the final Federalist Administration, fighting tooth and nail to save the Party from defeat and extinction, was not, by realistic standards, the reason why the Chase-Ellsworth Court was a fourth-rate Court. Fourth-rateness lay not in political forthrightness—for a Court less openly, more cleverly dedicated to the same ends would have been worse—but in the Justices' flagrant perversion of the plainest words of the Constitution, to try to thwart the popular will. Where an autocratic super-legislature might justify its place in a democracy by defending the civil liberties of a *minority* under the Constitution, the Chase-Ellsworth crew managed to be doubly undemocratic in trampling on the civil liberties of a *majority* whose political views they despised and sought to kill. And once more the bulk of the Justices' work—now political party work— was done not with the imprimatur of the Supreme Court itself but instead by its separate members, sitting in lower federal courts and laying down punitive, Federalist Party law.

The transatlantic reverberations of the French Revolution plus the eloquent home-grown pamphleteering of Thomas Paine in behalf of the "Rights of Man" had for some years been deepening the political-financial-emotional breach between the "rich and well-born" Federalists and their less favored but increasingly more numerous domestic opponents, at the time when Associate Justice Chase took effective command of the Supreme Court. As the Federalists had grown more and more pro-British, once independence was assured, so the anti-Federalists had grown pro-French—to the point where they now called themselves Republicans, a title then tinged with overtones of the French revolutionaries. What the Federalists called them was "Jacobins," after the ruthless French extremists —and they used the word with the same combination of hatred, contempt, and horror that "Communists" evokes in twentieth-century America, and with the same implication of treason. But by contrast to the dwindling number and political puniness of U.S. Communists today, the Jacobin-Republicans elected their leader, Thomas Jefferson, to the Vice-Presidency in 1796 and continued to grow in influence and power. In a last desperate effort to stifle the Republican Party by muzzling it, the frightened Federalists, against the advice of their wiser adherents, enacted the infamous Alien and Sedition Laws—and so gave Chase and his fellow Justices a chance to show their mettle as guardians of the rights guaranteed by the Constitution.

Though the Alien Act was never enforced, the Sedition Act was soon filling the federal courts with defendants. Under its terms, among other things, it was made a crime, punishable by fine and imprisonment, to "write, print, utter or publish any false, scandalous and malicious writing . . . against the government of the United States, or either house of the Congress . . . or the President of the United States, with intent . . . to bring them . . . into contempt or disrepute. . . ." To a Federalist judge —and all federal judges were Federalists—almost any mild criticism of his Party's leaders was, *per se*, "false, scandalous and malicious"—so not only Republican political speakers but bystanders at Federalist meetings who booed or made spontaneous Republican cracks were hauled into court and convicted of sedition. And, as might be expected, the most vicious enforcement of the Act was visited on editors of Republican papers—though their criminal remarks were often less intemperate than the castigations of Franklin Roosevelt by this century's quite different Republicans, in print, or of the Eightieth Congress by this century's Trumanite Democrats.

In the forefront of this vindictive campaign against anti-Federalist editors were the Justices of the Supreme Court —presiding almost gleefully over Sedition Act trials, charging juries with angry righteousness to bring in convictions, sentencing respectable men who had published

Republican sentiments (a U.S. Congressman, Matthew Lyons, or a well-known philosopher, Dr. Cooper) to long terms in jail. It did not bother the Justices that Jefferson, aided and backed by James Madison, "the father of the Constitution," got the legislatures of Kentucky and Virginia to pass resolutions condemning the Sedition Act as unconstitutional and urging other states to join in defying it. Nor, far more significantly, did it bother the Justices that the First Amendment to the Constitution forbids Congress to pass any law "abridging the freedom of speech, or of the press." To them, the uncertain future of the Federalist Party was more important than the upholding of the Constitution.

In Northern, Middle, and Southern states, in Vermont and Massachusetts and Pennsylvania and Virginia, the Justices sent editors to jail. Moreover, without so much as Congressional sanction, non-editing friends and confederates sometimes went to prison with, or in place of, the offending editors—by an early use of the doctrine of guilt by association. A group who started to raise money with a lottery to pay the fine of an impoverished editor, and so get him out of jail a little sooner, found that they too were therefore guilty of sedition; and so was the editor of a neighboring paper for merely printing a paid advertisement of the lottery. To prison, elsewhere, went one editor's brother who had nothing to do with the "seditious" published remarks, except that he ran the printing-press; since the editor was dying and unable to stand trial, the brother was convicted in his stead. But the low-water mark of this American Inquisition was undoubtedly the double conviction of farmer Fries—first

under Iredell, then under Chase, who ordered him hanged
—on the ground that resistance to a federal tax collector
amounted not just to sedition but to treason. President
Adams, in pardoning Fries, showed that he at least respected the Constitution's rigid definition of treason more
than did two Supreme Court Justices—although no more
than they did he respect its guarantee of free speech and
a free press.

Before the Sedition Act was repealed, its prisoners
pardoned, and almost all the fines imposed under it re-
funded—as happened shortly after Jefferson rode to the
Presidency, thanks in part to popular revolt against this
Federalist indecency—how did the Supreme Court manage, even in legal language, to square the Act with its
patent prohibition by the plain words of the First Amendment? By what reasoning did the Court call the Act constitutional? The answer is that it never had to try; no case
asserting that the Act was unconstitutional ever reached
the high Court itself—and small wonder, since not even
from behind bars was any of the Act's victims fool enough
to suppose that the Justices, *en masse*, would react differently than they had been reacting, and with enthusiastic
vigor, on their own. Such efforts as were made to argue
the unconstitutionality of the Act during the actual lower-
court trials of its hapless defendants were either ignored
or shouted down from the bench as quite irrelevant to the
issue at hand. Not by the Supreme Court but by its separate members, not by head-on meeting of the legal problem but by taking for granted of the political answer, was
the Sedition Act upheld. Here was a judiciary performing,

without shame and without pretense, a partisan political role.

Nor can it be convincingly contended that perhaps the Justices were a little leery still of matching their judgment against Congress's judgment, of using to the ultimate the right of judicial review. For, despite the active part they played in the lower federal courts during the dark years at the close of the eighteenth century—a part that smacked more of prosecutor than of judge—the Justices found time to hear and decide a few cases as the Supreme Court of the United States. And one of the cases they took on demanded a decision whether a new federal tax on carriages was or was not constitutional. With only three Justices sitting—and these the most politically minded and motivated of the six—and with Chase writing the chief opinion for himself and Paterson and Iredell, the tax was upheld; which fact was not nearly so important as that the Supreme Court, for the first time as a Supreme Court, undertook without so much as blinking to pass on the validity of an Act of Congress. Since the Act was held valid, the practical result was precisely the same as though the Court had never heard the case, and the decision, however historic in theory and in retrospect, created no stir at the time.

But even a Federalist Court, which was now well on its way toward declaring itself the supreme and final interpreter of the U.S. Constitution, did not dare go so far as to assert a similar protective domination over the constitutions of the states. In another of the few cases heard by the Chase-Ellsworth Court, the Justices bowed themselves out of deciding whether a *state* law offended that *state's* constitution—though in the course of doing so Chase and Iredell took separate pains to point out in windy and wide-of-the-point opinions that the U.S. Constitution was their ward, even if the state constitutions were not. That the meaning of state constitutions belongs to state courts to determine is still the Supreme Court's rule today; it might not have been had not the Justices of 1798—who were scarcely shrinking violets in claiming government power for themselves—realized in full that a contrary ruling in those explosive times could well have sparked a real revolt of the state-proud national populace against the federal judiciary, and perhaps the whole of the federal Administration.

The revolt, when it came, was peaceful but it did not include the judiciary in its sweep, simply because judges could not be voted out of office—as were Congressmen, Senators, and a President in the elections of 1800 that brought Thomas Jefferson to the brand-new White House. Despite their personal lifetime tenure, the Justices did their best to avert this Federalist catastrophe. Iredell, Cushing, Paterson, and of course Chase had for some years been making straight political speeches from the bench, and these had been faithfully circulated by the Federalist press. In the last Supreme Court term before the election, Chase never sat at all because he was out stumping the state of Maryland for Adams's re-election. Since Cushing was sick throughout that term and Chief Justice Ellsworth was away doing his Federalist bit on a diplomatic mission to prevent a war with France—not that the ineffectual Chief's absence made much of a dent in the Court—only three Justices were left to carry on the Court's official business.

The only decision of any note they handed down was based on their finding that the U.S. was then engaged in a sort of cold war—"limited, partial war" they called it—with France, a finding that did not exactly jibe with what their Chief was at that moment trying to accomplish abroad, but that warmed some stubbornly Francophobian Federalist hearts. None of these activities, not even Chase's callously unjudicial campaigning, could stem the Republican tide.

Routed at the polls, the lame-duck Federalists still had time to set booby-traps for their incoming Republican enemies, and the obvious place to set them was around the one branch of government destined to stay Federalist. In the Judiciary Act of 1801, the outgoing Party made its big bid for retention of power, through the courts. This Act provided, by way of the first Court-packing, or perhaps Court-unpacking, plan, that at the death of the first sitting Justice (Cushing was inaccurately expected to die soon) the number of Justices on the Supreme Court should be reduced to five—which would patently deprive Jefferson of his first Court appointment. In a more maliciously clever move, the Act also relieved Supreme Court Justices of their circuit-riding duties and set up sixteen new federal circuit courts, complete with new judges who would, of course, be appointed by President Adams and confirmed by the Federalist Senate before the Republicans took over.

The cleverness of this last provision was two-edged. Except for the timing, which advertised its partisan motivation, this step would have been a wise and widely applauded revision of the federal judiciary. For more than a decade the Justices had been griping, quite justifiably, about their circuit duties (Iredell once dubbed himself "a travelling post boy"); these duties were the reason or excuse for several Court declinations or resignations, including Rutledge's, and also for the comparatively little work done by the Justices as a Supreme Court; had the move been made ten, or two, years earlier it would have won even Republican support. Now, it was damned by Republicans as everything from "a bill for providing sinecure places and pensions for thorough-going Federalist partisans" to the establishment of "an army of Judges . . . [who] . . . may deprive us of our liberties . . . for we cannot remove them."

And herein lay the second edge of the 1801 Judiciary Act's sword. The Federalists well knew that the Republicans could and probably would (as they did) repeal the Act as soon as the government changed hands. But how about the flat mandate of the Constitution that federal judges were to hold office "during good behavior"— meaning for life, short of impeachment? The Republicans might abolish the circuit courts, but what could they do about lifetime-appointed circuit judges who, if jettisoned, could appeal to the still-Federalist Supreme Court, under the Constitution, to keep their jobs? What eventually happened was that none of these judges had sense, courage, or perhaps money enough to make such an appeal—a fact which detracts nothing from the ingenuity of the Federalists' last-ditch scheme to enlarge their hold on the federal judiciary by simply enlarging the judiciary that they held.

Yet the midnight move that *did* work, and that was destined to save for the Federalists the upper hand—not just for a few years but for thirty-four years, not just over

the judiciary but over the government of the entire nation
—went strangely unheralded when it was made; the newspapers of the day barely reported it. Ellsworth, sick and
tired, had resigned his Chief Justiceship just before Jefferson's election; John Jay had refused reappointment to his
old position. President Adams, brushing aside the strong
claims of Paterson for the post, named to the Chiefship a
well-respected and powerful forty-five-year-old Virginia
politician who had had almost no formal education, legal
or otherwise (he was actually born and reared in a log
cabin), and no judicial experience whatsoever, and whose
government slant was revealed in a casual comment on
Jefferson's election to the Presidency: "The Republicans
are divided into speculative theorists and absolute ter-
rorists. With the latter, I am disposed to class Mr.
Jefferson."

This new Chief Justice took over the Supreme Court
just one month before the Republicans took over, for
twenty-four solid years, the rest of the federal government. He outlasted them by a decade. His name was John
Marshall.

CHAPTER 3

Government by
John Marshall,
the Great Chief Justice

BY EVERY SENSIBLE STANDARD, John Marshall deserves superbly his sobriquet of "the great Chief Justice." He deserves it, that is, by every standard save only the mincing and squeamish view of a "proper" judicial attitude that prevails in these milk-toast times. For, almost all that the man believed and lived and brought to life would be sheer anathema to those who honor his name in happy ignorance as they damn any current Justice who dares to do his current job with the same contempt for legalism, the same concern for the end product, the same

conception of the Court as a stark political instrument,
that marked the work of Marshall. Marshall was great
because he saw the law as a servant, not as a master, of
the functions and goals of government—and because he
used the Court as a means to achieve the goals he was
after, however he had to bend or twist the law to achieve
them. Scorning past legal precedents to fabricate his own,
turning tiny technical points into ringing and far-reaching
political principles, making a mockery of the nice-Nelly
notion of "judicial self-restraint" that contemporary scholars hold in such high esteem, he ran his Court with a
realistic gusto as refreshing in retrospect as it would be
deemed improper, even indecent, today. If ever a figure
in U.S. history embodied in his career clear proof that
ours is a government of men, not of laws, that figure is
John Marshall, the great Chief Justice.

To say that a man was great is not to say that he was
always wise, for greatness does not perforce imply wisdom. There are many who still question the wisdom of
much that Franklin Roosevelt did; there are few who
would deny him a place among the great Presidents. The
point is that Roosevelt used the powers of his high office
to the full and, in doing so, greatly affected—for good or
ill—the course of the nation. So did John Marshall. Looking at Marshall's greatness from another angle, there are
many who would rate Holmes above him as the wisest
Justice who ever sat on the Court. But Holmes was wise
almost exclusively in dissent, where present ineffectiveness
coupled with indignation often makes comparatively easy
the eloquent expression of wisdom; by contrast, Marshall
spoke almost exclusively with the authority of the Court

behind him, so that his words were not merely something he *said* but official statements of what he and his Court—whether wisely or unwisely—effectively did.

What Marshall did, and well-nigh single-handed—for the force and warmth of his personality swung even his political adversaries on the Court to his side—was to mold the government of a new nation to his own ideas of how that nation ought to be run. More than any other man, more than Washington or Jefferson or Lincoln, he put flesh on the skeletal structure, the bare bones of the Founding Fathers' Constitution—and put it there to stay. Most of what he did to steer for his own times and chart for the future the main course of the country's development, economically, socially, politically, is with us yet, 150 years later, courtesy of the precedents he set and the respect in which they are still held, and in this fact lies the real mark and monument of Marshall's greatness.

Marshall thought the nation ought to be run by a strong central government to which the states played strictly second fiddle. So the bulk of his most momentous decisions either enlarged the powers of the federal government—over finance, commerce, business affairs—by what is commonly called a "broad construction" of those words of the Constitution that list what the federal government may do, or else restricted and cut down, by a narrow interpretation of other constitutional language, the similar and sometimes conflicting powers of the states. From banking to bankruptcy, from higher education to inland waterways, Marshall slapped down state attempts to control or regulate or supervise, and upheld, at least by inference, the hand of the central government. Yet strangely—and this has gone little noted—Marshall's passionate attachment to national supremacy sometimes faded slightly when it came to supporting federal Administration acts or policies which failed to win his personal approval.

For Marshall not only thought the nation should be run by a strong central government; he also thought the nation and its government should be run by and for his kind, his political and economic class—meaning, of course, the creditor-capitalists, the Federalists, the financial conservatives. And so, although most of his significant decisions can be read—and usually are—as sparked primarily by a disinterested preference for federal, as against state, control of national affairs, not one of those significant decisions fails to fit the pattern of protecting and fostering the long-range or short-run security of private property. From the wholesale endowing of corporations with the property rights of individuals to the repeated upholding of land claims or money claims clearly based, originally, on bribery or flagrant fraud, Marshall served not only honest investors but less scrupulous speculators well. Practically all his anti-state and pro-federal-government rulings were as welcome to the well-to-do as they were deplored and denounced by the relatively poor, the "common men" of the time.

Thus an entertaining poser arises as to what John Marshall's political views and his legal leanings would have been had he lived and served on the Court in the middle of the twentieth century instead of at the beginning of the nineteenth. For in Marshall's day the states were still the chief citadels of a "liberal" or "leveling" political philosophy, controlled by and responsive to the mass of the people, whereas the central government, even under Jefferson and his followers, was more respectful of property rights. In recent times the situation has been the precise reverse, so that solid citizens are now states'-righters and liberals put greater faith in the federal government, even under conservative auspices. Where, then, would Marshall stand, faced with a New Deal, a Fair Deal, or even a New Look, and unable to champion simultaneously a strong central authority and the interests of the creditor class? Would he love national power more or leveling laws less? The probable answer must stem from the ineluctable fact that Marshall, like the Founding Fathers, was an eminently practical man, far more concerned with down-to-earth political realities than with the abstractions of government theory, more bent on achieving results than expounding principles. So, paradoxical as it may sound, there is little doubt that John Marshall, for all the tremendous part he played in giving the federal government strength and supremacy back in the early nineteenth century, would be a states' rights advocate today. Except —and quite an exception—in one regard:

Just as Marshall, for practical reasons, wanted the federal government dominant over the states and worked successfully to make it so, he also wanted one branch of that government dominant over the other two branches— and for identical practical reasons. Nor would Marshall, if he were living now, have any cause to regret what is generally rated his greatest, and was surely his most complete and spectacular, political achievement. In establishing unshakably the supremacy of the judiciary over both the legislature and the executive—and this in the face of a

series of Congresses and Presidents who were either ex-
plosively or seethingly hostile—Marshall built a bastion
for the rights of property, no matter how careless of those
rights the rest of the federal government might come to
be, that has stood secure and firm through all the intervening years and that a contemporary Marshall would still
approve, with pardonable pride. For it was under Marshall
that the Supreme Court, officially and as a whole Court,
first proclaimed and exercised the right of judicial review
in its ultimate and most radical sense—by holding a part
of an Act of Congress unconstitutional. And from that
most famous of all the famous Marshall decisions, in the
case of Marbury *v.* Madison—a decision that drew the
battle lines between the new Chief Justice and his bitter
antagonist, President Jefferson—until, toward the close
of his career, Marshall made the ruling that brought forth
President Andrew Jackson's perhaps apocryphal but essentially accurate snort: "Well, John Marshall has made
his decision; now let him enforce it" (and the decision was
reluctantly obeyed nonetheless), Marshall forced on his
foes and flaunted to the nation the doctrine of judicial
supremacy.

It was an extraordinary hierarchy of pyramided political
power that Marshall built, with himself at its apex. The
pyramid encompassed the entire governmental structure
of the nation, and at every level Marshall had to drive or
win his way to the top against massed majority opposition. Beginning at the bottom, there was the basic issue
whether, under a system of "dual sovereignty," the
centralized federal government or the proudly separate
states should prevail; the climate of opinion backed by the

weight of popular pressure was strongly with the states at the time; Marshall won supremacy for the union. At the next level up, the question was which branch of the federal government would hold sway over the other two; Marshall for over thirty years contended and coped with Presidents and Congresses who wanted the last word for themselves; he won conclusive supremacy for the judiciary. (Within the judiciary the Supreme Court was already, and naturally, dominant; it was easy for Marshall to rivet this supremacy over lower federal courts—and over top state courts as well.) As the final step, Marshall had to assert and maintain his own personal authority over his colleagues on the Supreme Court itself; as his Court was early infiltrated, and later numerically overweighted, by Justices whose political slant ran counter to his own, it was no simple task to line them up behind him; but until, shortly before his death, he was barely defeated on a big decision—and wrote one of the nine dissents he ever had to express in this thirty-four years on the high bench—Marshall never faltered and never importantly failed in keeping himself supreme over his fellow Justices.

Thus the great Chief Justice, by dominating the Supreme Court which dominated the judiciary which dominated the federal government which dominated the states —and with each of these steps substantially his own indomitable doing—himself effectively dominated the nation for a third of a century, and left it a lasting legacy in the conduct of its government. His accomplishment is all the more fabulous considered in the light of the personal and institutional statuses from which Marshall raised first himself, then the Court, to glory.

The likely key to Marshall's unyielding economic conservatism, and perhaps to his dynamic drive as well, is the fact that, in the common phrase, he was a self-made man who came up the hard way. Like so many who fight their way to the top against original odds, he had scant sympathy for those less able or less fortunate or less determined whom he left behind and beneath; successful, respected, well-to-do by dint of his own efforts, he identified himself completely with the class to which he had climbed. His was a primitive, frontier childhood; his was the meagerest of formal educations, later supplemented by a couple of months of law lectures at William and Mary; his was the suffering through the awful winter at Valley Forge as a soldier in the Revolution. By persistence and native brilliance, he rose in both law and politics, hewing straighter and straighter, the farther he rose, to the Federalist line. As a young Virginia assemblyman and as a middle-aged U.S. Congressman, he developed an impatient mistrust of legislatures, with their inefficiencies and their bending to the winds of popular will. As one of the trio of envoys to France who were offered French bribes, in the so-called XYZ Affair, he developed a contempt for revolutionary democracy, which had there run riot. Outstanding among the few whole-hog Congressional supporters of President Adams's save-the-Federalist-Party policies, he was named Secretary of State (he had earlier turned down a Supreme Court Associate Justiceship) until Ellsworth's timely resignation gave Adams the chance to choose as Chief Justice the man who was to prove the doughtiest Federalist of them all.

The Court of which Marshall took command, a Court

which had been depreciated even below its original lowly status by Ellsworth's why-bother indifference to its operations and by Chase's rambunctious extra-judicial politicking, was regarded by most citizens with either apathy or scorn. The important thing was that Jefferson had been elected, the Republicans were in the saddle, and those federal judges who used to go around putting decent people in jail just for speaking their minds about politics would soon find out who was running the country now. Symbolic—and quite incredible today when the Court, in all its majestic dignity, meets in a marble temple that is one of the showplaces of Washington—was the fact that the architect of the new Capitol building had completely forgotten, or maybe deliberately failed, to provide a place for the Court to do its business. The great Chief Justice was sworn into office in a twenty-four-by-thirty-foot committee room in the Capitol basement, politely furnished by the Senate for the Court's use. In that tiny chamber, Marshall and his five associates began to hear the cases that were to raise the Court to prestige and preeminence.

Marshall's associates, at the start, were of course all fellow Federalists. But within a few years, deaths plus the addition of a seventh Justice gave the Republicans an expanding beachhead on the high tribunal; and by 1811, a decade after Marshall took charge, five of the seven Justices were Republican-appointed, with only Bushrod Washington, due to last another eighteen years, hanging on with his Chief from the old Federalist days. Still, the gradual filling of the Court with presumable opponents of Marshall's political and legal views did not shift, until near the very end of Marshall's long tenure, the course of

Supreme Court decisions. Indeed, except for William Johnson, the vastly underrated Justice who was Jefferson's first appointee and whose continuous if futile disagreement with many of Marshall's rulings made him the first great Court dissenter, and Joseph Story, the nominal Republican who immediately became Marshall's right-hand man, the other Justices of the Marshall era—forgotten names like Brockholst Livingston, Robert Trimble, Gabriel Duval— deserve scarcely so much as a passing mention in an account of the Court's history. Marshall *was* the Court—and they were his pawns, his puppets.

Stark statistics tell part of the story. During Marshall's whole incumbency, his Court gave the full treatment, meaning a decision plus an opinion explaining it, to 1,106 cases; in 519, or almost half of these, Marshall wrote the Court's opinion; (a Chief Justice does well today to write one-eighth of the Court's opinions, and Vinson, for instance, did not come close to this fraction). Of the 1,106 cases, 62 dealt with the "meaning" of the Constitution, thus embodying, one way or another, the most important facet of judicial review—and Marshall spoke for the Court 36 of the 62 times. How completely he guided his colleagues, even when he did not himself speak for them, is shown by the fact that he dissented from only 9 of all the 1,106 decisions—or in less than one per cent of the cases, a figure incredibly low when viewed against the habitually split Supreme Court of the mid-twentieth century.

Nor did Marshall waste any time taking full command over his seniors in service. Through the first four years of his Chief Justiceship, the Court, gathering momentum slowly, honored with formal opinions just twenty-six cases; and Marshall, who did not sit in two of them, delivered the Court's opinion in all of the other twenty-four—with not a single Justice dissenting from any of them. This, of course, was while the Court was still staffed, or stuffed, with hangover Federalists, only too glad to follow the lead of their new dynamic Chief and to let him do the dirty work of opinion-writing for them. As the first (and best) Republican Justice, Johnson, in a later letter to Jefferson, explained Marshall's monopoly as Court spokesman at the time Johnson joined the Court: "Cushing was incompetent, Chase could not be got to think or write—Paterson was a slow man and willingly declined the trouble, and the other two judges [*meaning Marshall himself and Bushrod Washington*] you know are commonly estimated as one judge."

But if it was a cinch for Marshall, at the beginning, to make a one-man show of a fully Federalist and either-unfit-or-lazy crew of colleagues, how did he manage to maintain effectively the same I-*am*-the-Court role in the face of the Court's early dilution and subsequent flooding with Republican appointees? By what Marshall magic did Federalist doctrine not wither but flourish as the law of the land, long after the electoral interment of the Federalist Party and the eventual extension of this shifted political sentiment to the judiciary? The answer lies partly—strange as it may sound—in the cozy living arrangements whereby the Justices, under an almost sacred ritual established by Marshall, were together not only at work but before and after working hours, in a pleasant routine that discouraged deep disagreement (Justices are human beings) and put a premium on friendly capitulation to the views of the most cogently articulate. The answer lies partly in the skill with which Marshall took advantage of this day-after-day intimacy to exploit, now patiently, now pointedly, his persuasive personality. The answer lies largely in that personality.

For Marshall made of his Court a sort of close-knit men's club, whose members lived and dined and wined with each other in the same Washington boarding house, wifeless while the Court was in session; and trudged together, through muddy or dusty streets, to and from their little courtroom in the Capitol basement; and did their most decisive work away from their official site of business, as legal discussion blended into political commentary or sheer social gossip and then drifted back to the cases, around the cogenial board. In such close and common quarters, even more than in the stiffness of the formal consultation chamber, Marshall's easy eloquence was at its best. Republicans might come and Federalists go, but Marshall stayed king of the cloister.

He did not stay king by throwing his weight around, by parading his Chiefship to his officially slightly inferiors, nor by sternness and severity of manner. By contrast to the oft-imagined picture of Marshall as austere, autocratic, coldly impressive—as a stronger John Jay, a tougher Charles Evans Huges—the man was a thoroughly likeable, approachable, outgoing and easy-going figure in his relationships with people, blessed with a gangling, rough-cut charm that made personal friends out of political enemies. Like so many innately powerful leaders, he wore his leadership casually and it needed no putting on of surface dignity. He could, as occasion called for, be shrewd or forthright, soft or bold, for the mind of a master strategist was always at work behind the genial front to achieve and secure, by whatever means, the ambitious aims to which his whole career was dedicated. In the intimate theater of the Court, his strategic talents masked by his effortless magnetism served to win to his purposes, one by one, almost every new Justice who was sent up to do him battle. On the larger stage of national politics, the same strategic genius came into play at a different level. He needed every ounce of it to wage successful war against his most outspoken major antagonist, President Jefferson—to whom, by the irony of events, he had administered the oath of office.

It was Jefferson who threw down the gauntlet in his first Presidential message, where he off-handedly presented "to the contemplation of Congress" the existing federal court system "and especially that portion of it recently enacted"—meaning, as was apparent to all, the Federalists' Judiciary Act of 1801, under which the new circuit judgeships had been hastily set up and manned with Federalist judges. Not that the Republican Congress needed any such reminder; they not only repealed the Act but, slightly worried that Marshall's Court would declare the repeal unconstitutional (because of the guarantee of lifetime tenure for all federal judges) they actually closed down the Supreme Court for a year under their constitutional power to make "such regulations." Marshall obeyed this edict and bided his time; his first big chance, or challenge, had come to him a short while before.

This challenge stemmed from another last-minute move of Adams's outgoing Administration, in which he had appointed no less than forty-two new justices of the peace for the District of Columbia but had done it so late that he had no time to make out their formal commissions. Jefferson, right after his inauguration, ordered his Secretary of State, James Madison, to withhold a batch of these commissions, and four of the would-be J.P.'s—headed by a William Marbury who thus made his name a byword in Supreme Court annals—asked the Court to order or, in the legal term, "mandamus" Madison to deliver their commissions to them. A preliminary order of Marshall's was contemptuously ignored by Madison, and when Congress shut down the Court for a year the whole affair was still unfinished business, waiting to be settled when the Justices reconvened.

The case of Marbury *v.* Madison, seen in retrospect, ranks as the most important decision in all Supreme Court history—judged by its potency as a legal precedent, a guiding authority, a basis for linking new decisions to old. Yet the actual ruling was of practically no contemporary consequence, since the term for which President Adams had named Mr. Marbury a D.C. J.P. (D.C. J.P.'s are not lifetime federal judges) had just about expired by the time the ruling was made. This fact did not stop Marshall— who thoroughly understood the implicitly fundamental challenge to the judiciary which fairly bristled from the Jefferson-Madison course of action—from turning a tiny and almost academic immediate issue into a mighty and abiding principle of constitutional law. To do so, however, he had to face and hurdle a dilemma which would have stymied a man less imaginatively bold.

Marshall was well aware that if the Court ordered the

delivery of the commissions to the Marbury quartet, the Administration would disregard this mandamus, leaving the Court helpless to enforce it and hence humiliated. He was also aware that if the Court bowed to the Administration by simply saying that Madison was within his rights in refusing the commissions, the judiciary would be publicly confessing its ignominious and perhaps irreparable submission to the executive. What Marshall did was a stroke of political genius, salted with lawyerly adroitness. He declared in ringing tones that Marbury and the rest were clearly entitled to their commissions; he excoriated Madison and especially Jefferson for not handing the commissions over; and then, in his master thrust, he held that the Supreme Court technically did not have the power to order the commissions delivered. To so hold, he had to take the audacious step that made Marbury *v.* Madison a milestone in the nation's history (though some might call it a millstone around the nation's neck). Speaking for a unanimous Court, he ruled that the section of the old, original Judiciary Act of 1789 (not of 1801) which said the Supreme Court could issue such orders or "writs of mandamus"—and which had stood unchallenged and been used regularly for years—was a violation of the Constitution and therefore completely void.

Here was the first exercise by the Supreme Court as a whole of its controversial veto power over Congress, of its full right of judicial review. John Marshall, by fastening on a petty point of proper legal procedure in an essentially insignificant case, by attacking a harmless bit of a statute that had been enacted not by Republicans but by Federalists, by handing his political opponents, with magnificent opportunism, a strictly Pyrrhic victory (Marbury never got his commission), established the supremacy of the judiciary over the rest of the federal government. That supremacy still holds today.

In touting Marshall's eloquent defense, in Marbury *v.* Madison, of constitutions *as read by judges* against laws passed by legislatures, the customary adulatory accounts frequently overlook a few other interesting facts:

In the first place, his argument was not precisely puncture-proof; with no authoritative precedent to fall back on (he was creating it, not following it) he had to resort to theory and logic to prove his point; his theory was often quite onesidedly inaccurate, as in his bland claim of universal agreement that constitutional words could automatically void legislative acts, a subject only recently hotly debated in the U.S. Congress; and his logic conveniently skipped the basic question whether judges were any better qualified than legislators or executives to interpret constitutions.

In the second place, Marshall's sincerity—or at least the depth of his conviction—was somewhat open to question. Only seven years earlier, in the course of arguing before the Supreme Court in defense of a Virginia statute which was under attack, he had insisted that "the judicial authority can have no right to question the validity of a law, unless such a jurisdiction is expressly given by the constitution"—and of course the U.S. Constitution nowhere expressly gives such a right. It can at least be doubted whether Marshall, a practical and politically knowledgeable man, would have asserted the right of judicial review as strongly as he did in Marbury *v.* Madison if a Federalist Congress and Administration had just taken over and the judiciary had been overwhelmingly Republican.

In the third place, Marshall's decision in Marbury *v.* Madison, for all its doctrinal boldness, was actually, when considered in its context, quite cautious and not terribly courageous. Marshall did not say to Congress: *You* may not do something yourselves—such as set up an income tax or prohibit child labor. All he said was: You may not authorize *us*, the Supreme Court, to do something— namely, issue writs of mandamus. Just as when the Justices of pre-Marshall days, acting then separately and not in a body, told Congress it could not turn them even temporarily into pension commissioners for veterans of the Revolution, so here, how could the Justices, now speaking through Marshall as a solid Court, be forced to do what they disowned the power to do? In this sense, Marshall's action was as safe as it was sensational—which merely adds another facet to its strategic brilliance.

Moreover, the less-than-bravery of Marbury *v.* Madison was underlined in a decision handed down within a week after the disposal of that celebrated case. The other case, Stuart *v.* Laird by name, gave the Court a wide-open opportunity to call the Republican repeal of the Federalists' 1801 Judiciary Act unconstitutional; indeed the Federalist press had been crowing, a bit prematurely, that this was precisely what Marshall's Court would do. Instead, the Court—with Marshall not sitting officially but clearly commanding his colleagues—decorously ducked the question of the repeal Act's constitutionality, in ruling that Supreme Court Justices could be made to sit in lower federal courts (the 1801 Judiciary Act had relieved them of this duty and the repeal Act had restored it) simply because they had been doing it for some fourteen previous years. Had precisely the same reasoning been used in Marbury *v.* Madison about the Court's power to issue writs of mandamus—which the Court had also been doing for several years—Marshall's most famous decision would have had to go the other way.

Thus, from every standpoint except immediate political expediency plus perhaps long-range political foresight, the great decision that nailed down Supreme Court dominance of the national government was a legal cripple. Lacking, perforce, any solid basis in precedent, vulnerable in theory and in logic, its central core of reasoning reversed within a week by another Court decision, Marbury *v.* Madison may seem scarcely worthy of the plaudits that have been heaped on it or the deference that has been paid it in the intervening century and a half. But both the plaudits and the deference, like the decision itself, and like every significant Supreme Court decision since, were and are rooted in politics, not in law. This only the ignorant would deny and only the naïve deplore.

Shortly after Marshall had clipped Jefferson from behind in Marbury *v.* Madison—with no official in a position to call any infraction of the rules—politics came even more pointedly to the Court in the impeachment of that old Federalist war-horse, Justice Chase. Although Chase's star had been eclipsed, as Court captain, by the luminosity of his new Chief, his open animosity to all things anti-Federalist had not abated but burgeoned with the advent of the Republicans to power. One angry harangue against

the Administration which Chase delivered before a grand
jury—of a sort that would have led him to ship its author
off to jail, had it been directed at President Adams's
regime a few years before—sparked the high-riding
Republicans into an effort to get Chase and thus teach the
rest of the Federalist judges a lesson. The House duly
voted Chase's impeachment (comparable to an indictment
in an ordinary case) but an intra-Party split among his
prosecutors, plus doubt whether the Constitution's "good
behavior" requirement called for criminal or merely un-
judicious conduct to unseat a judge, kept the Senate from
convicting him. Backhandedly vindicated, Chase kept his
seat—though he lost most of his influence—until his death
seven years later.

The most salient thing about the Chase impeachment
episode was the conduct of the great Chief Justice. Marshall, though in full sympathy with Chase's political views,
had never approved his slam-bang way of expressing
them; his attitude was much like that of many mid-
twentieth-century Republicans toward Senator McCarthy.
Aware of the threat to the Court's power and prestige
that was embodied in Chase's impeachment, concerned
for the future of the whole federal judiciary as a top force
in the nation's government if Chase should be convicted,
Marshall, for once in his triumphant career, was frightened
into ineffective ineptitude. Not only did he make a poor
and halting witness when called in Chase's behalf; he went
so far as to suggest, while the trial was in progress, that
the judiciary, to protect its personnel, should even give up
its governmental supremacy. "A reversal of those legal
opinions deemed unsound by the legislature," he wrote

to Chase, "would certainly better comport with the mild-
ness of our character than a removal of the judge who has
rendered them. . . . "

Whether or not Marshall was mainly worried about his
own judicial skin in making this astonishing suggestion
that Congress be empowered to overrule the Court, it
stands in stark contrast to the so recent swagger of his
Marbury *v.* Madison opinion. Once Chase was acquitted,
Marshall regained his old confidence, and in newly refreshed and strengthened measure. (If so blatantly unjudicial a Justice as Chase could not be convicted, how
could any other? Nor, in fact, has any other Justice ever
been so much as impeached.) But it is interesting to
speculate that, if Chase had been convicted, the man chiefly
responsible for judicial supremacy might also have been
chiefly responsible—through his judge-protecting proposal to let Congress reverse Court decisions—for killing
it shortly after it was born. Had this happened, the whole
of U.S. history, from the Dred Scott decision right up until
today, might have taken a quite different course.

Marshall's refurbished confidence soon led him into another patently political battle with Jefferson in the trial of
Aaron Burr for treason, over which trial Marshall presided
in person. Burr, though a nominal Republican who had
come close to wangling the Presidency away from Jefferson when they were elected together in 1800 (the confusion of equal votes for President and Vice-President,
with no preference stated, was cleared up afterward by the
Twelfth Amendment to the Constitution), had of late been
flirting with the Federalists, who were quite willing to
make the most of his personal pique against Jefferson.

When Burr was caught with an armed force, apparently preparing to start a revolt against the U.S. government with help from abroad, the Jefferson-hating Federalists tended to wink at this abortive undertaking and to side with Burr. Marshall sided with him in such a partisan way at his trial—tossing out evidence that might have convicted him, practically demanding his acquittal—that so conservative a Senator as John Quincy Adams more than hinted, in a later Senate report on the case, that Marshall ought to be impeached. But Marshall, after the Chase fiasco, was safely beyond any possibility of impeachment. His handling of the Burr case was in the nature of a cocky you-can't-touch-me-now gesture of contempt toward Jefferson.

Throughout these years, and especially after the Burr trial, all sorts of schemes were proposed in Congress with Administration backing to curb the power of the Justices—schemes ranging from an easy machinery for the removal of Justices without impeaching them to a limitation of their terms of office. None of these came to anything. Marshall, once he had survived the Chase impeachment scare, clearly bested Jefferson in their intra-governmental duel over judicial supremacy. But more than a decade after he left the White House, Jefferson—still smarting over his defeat at Marshall's hands, outraged that most of the Justices he had appointed had gone over to the enemy, battling away for his lifetime conviction that a last-word judicial autocracy was improper and evil—was still taking pot shots at the Court in general and John Marshall in particular. "An opinion," he wrote to a friend in 1820, "is huddled up in conclave, perhaps by a majority of one, delivered as if unanimous, and with the silent acquiescence of lazy or timid associates, by a crafty chief judge, who sophisticates the law to his mind, by the turn of his own reasoning."

But by this time the "crafty chief judge" and his Court —no longer the prime target of Presidential attack under the mild Administrations of Madison and Monroe—had turned their main attention to other matters. Outstanding among these was the slapping down of the sometimes rambunctiously democratic states—in the protection, as always, of the rights of private property.

Though important decisions dotted the whole of Marshall's Chief Justiceship, spreading across the Administrations of five U.S. Presidents, the three cases usually deemed the most momentous, after Marbury v. Madison, were bunched within a five-year span from 1819 to 1824. Each of the three threw out as unconstitutional an act of a state legislature. Each, either directly or by the broad grounds on which it was based, was a boon to commercial and financial interests, a shot in the arm to expanding U.S. capitalism. Each was essentially political; each still stands as good law today; and each in its own way has had a major effect on the nation's development. The three cases are known as the Dartmouth College case, McCulloch v. Maryland, and Gibbons v. Ogden or, as it is sometimes called, the steamboat case.

Many who have heard the almost tearfully emotional peroration of Daniel Webster's plea to the Court in the Dartmouth College case ("It is . . . a small college— and yet there are those who love it") have no notion what the crying was all about nor what the subsequent shouting was all about after Webster's pathos, far more than his legal arguments, won the decision for his client. Yet historian Charles Beard called the Dartmouth College decision "a spectacular event more important in American educational history than the founding of any single institution of higher learning"—including, presumably, Harvard and Yale. And the legal ripples of Marshall's ruling, which rested in part on making an imaginary individual out of a corporation, spread far beyond the educational world.

Dartmouth, under a charter granted by King George III in the mid-eighteenth century, was run—as were and are so many colleges and universities—by a self-perpetuating board of trustees. Being self-perpetuating, the board was still heavily overweighted with rather old-fogy Federalists long after the nation, and the state of New Hampshire, had gone Republican. Sparked by an insurgent Republican group within the college, the New Hampshire legislature passed a law to pack the board with new, politically appointed members, and so turn Dartmouth into a sort of state university. It was to stymie this purely political move that the equally political old trustees hired the spellbinding Webster to take their case to the Supreme Court.

In order to sustain his academic fellow Federalists, John Marshall had to rule that a charter was the same as a contract (this was brand-new legal doctrine); that the promises made by the British Crown in granting the charter were still binding, despite the Revolution, on the state of New Hampshire (this was also new); and that therefore the New Hampshire statute was unconstitutional because it "impaired the obligation of contracts." By such tortuous and unprecedented legal argumentation, with an assist from Webster's sentimentality, Marshall managed to hold the fort for Dartmouth's Federalist trustees. In doing so, he also set the stage for the permanent and practically unregulated control of U.S. higher education, especially in the East, by private "corporations"—and thus gave a tremendous boost both to academic conservatism on one side (only the wealthy can afford to endow colleges) and to academic freedom-from-direct-political-pressures on the other.

Furthermore, Marshall's new doctrines, once proclaimed as the law of the land, could scarcely be limited—and were not meant to be limited—to corporations that ran colleges. Many types of business corporations, especially transportation companies with their canals and turnpikes and ferries and bridges, operated under government-granted charters, which now became inviolable contracts. As Marshall's biographer, Beveridge, put it, the decision in the Dartmouth College case gave new hope and confidence to "investors in corporate securities" and to the whole of "the business world." And so did McCulloch *v.* Maryland, decided at the same Supreme Court term.

As a piece of political oratory turned by legal logic into enduring government principle, McCulloch *v.* Maryland is Marshall's most impressive opinion. It was here that he made his famous statement, whose appeal lies more in its sound than its sense: "We must never forget that it is a constitution we are expounding." It was here, too, that he simultaneously enlarged the power of the federal government to help private business, cut down the power of the states to interfere with such help, and created in almost off-hand fashion a tax-free sanctuary for wealthy investors which still gapes open, thanks to the broad strokes of Marshall's logic, in even more inviting measure than it did in Marshall's day.

The Bank of the United States, set up by Congress (for the second time) just after the War of 1812 to try to bring financial order out of the chaos of state-run banks, had been loaning money high-wide-and-handsomely to favored businesses and businessmen and then, as a depression came on, acting tough with smaller borrowers. Annoyed at this uneven-handedness, several states slapped heavy taxes on the branches of the U.S. Bank within their borders—taxes meant to drive the branches out, or out of business—and among these states was Maryland. The U.S. Bank's Baltimore branch, with a cashier named McCulloch, refused to pay the tax and Maryland sued to collect it. (McCulloch's name, like Marbury's, was thus legally immortalized; forgotten is the incidental fact that Mr. McCulloch was later convicted of misappropriating over $3,000,000 of the branch's funds.)

With Daniel Webster again arguing the right-wing side of the case (as chief counsel for the U.S. Bank over a long period of years, he never lost them a decision before the Supreme Court), Marshall and his colleagues backed the Bank, and branded the Maryland tax—and all other similar state taxes—unconstitutional. To do this, Marshall had to write into the Constitution two separate and reaching-beyond-the-horizon political principles that the Founding Fathers never saw fit, or dared, to put in the words of the document. Before calling the tax *un*constitutional, he had to make the Bank *constitutional*—for the list of Congress' powers nowhere includes the power to set up banks. What he did was to *infer* this unspecified power from Congress's specified control of U.S. currency, plus a couple of other clauses of the Constitution. He thus gave to the nation's charter of government a so-called "broad" interpretation and gave to the Congress a far-flung and flexible judicial benediction to go ahead with whatever extras it deemed necessary to supplement its narrowly listed powers—a slant toward the Constitution and toward Congress which men of Marshall's political stripe were to bitterly denounce when the New Deal rolled around more than a century later.

But granted the U.S. Bank was proper, what was improper about state taxes on its branches—inasmuch as the Constitution, though forbidding some kinds of state taxes, says nothing about these? Here Marshall pulled out of his judicial hat a fat new rule of government which was not even hung from some other rule written in the Constitution. He said, in effect, that since the Constitution creates a dual sovereignty—federal and state—it *must* mean that neither sovereign may destroy the legitimate activities of the other; and since, in the tricky key phrase of the whole decision, "the power to tax involves the power to destroy," therefore any state tax on any legitimate U.S. activity was unconstitutional. It was this flat black-or-white logic (instead of a sensible recognition that, whereas some taxes may "destroy," others may not) that made all the federal government's operations completely untouchable by state taxes and vice versa—to the point where, until quite recently, an oil company that leased oil lands from Indians went scot-free from state taxes on its private profits, because Indians are "wards" of the United States; and state employees, from governors on down, paid no federal income taxes on their salaries. It is that same flat Marshallian logic that, even today, exempts the interest on state and city bonds from federal income taxes, and so makes those bonds a favorite investing refuge for the really rich. By saying far more than he had to say to decide the case, Marshall made of McCulloch *v.* Maryland the birthplace of two major principles of American law and government, both of them politically inspired and both of them full of political vitality ever since.

As in McCulloch *v.* Maryland, so too in Gibbons *v.* Ogden, five years later, Marshall expanded the powers of the federal government by reading what he wanted to read into the Constitution—and he did it again at the expense of the states. But whereas in the earlier case his talk of dual sovereignty had at least implied something resembling equality for the states, though the decision had of course gone against them, in Gibbons *v.* Ogden he denied any such equality and proclaimed clear and full supremacy for the federal government wherever it had the power to act at all. Since there were few realms where Marshall would have denied that power, the logic of his opinion here was perhaps the strongest blow he ever struck against the popularly run state governments with their soak-the-rich-and-help-the-poor political philosophies—although, paradoxically, the actual decision was one of the few he ever handed down that was greeted with popular cheers.

Gibbons *v.* Ogden is also called the steamboat case: Ogden had bought an interest in Robert Fulton's old steamboat company, which years before had been given by the New York legislature a monopoly to run steamboats in the state, and Gibbons was ignoring this state grant and running a rival service in and out of New York City. Ogden sued to have Gibbons's boats permanently beached. (The names of Supreme Court cases always list first the man who took the case to the Court, meaning the one who lost in the lower court, regardless of whether he started the case originally.) By the logic of the Dartmouth College decision, it might seem that Marshall would have called the state-granted monopoly a contract, like Dartmouth's charter, and upheld Ogden's plea. But among other factors here was the poor and quite inadequate service provided by the monopoly, so that the commercial growth of New York City was being hindered, and not only the general public but almost all business interests wanted more and competitive steamboat lines.

Marshall satisfied everyone save Ogden and his friends by turning to the clause of the Constitution that gives Congress power to "regulate commerce . . . among the several states" and endowing it with a meaning that is scarcely in its words. Since Gibbons's steamboat service hit several New Jersey ports, it clearly involved commerce among the several states or, as it has come to be called, interstate commerce. What Marshall held was that the Constitution's grant to Congress of power to regulate interstate commerce withdrew all such power, by implication, from the states—even when Congress was not doing any regulating. Therefore, the steamboat monopoly had been an attempt on New York's part to poach on the federal government's preserves and, as such, was unconstitutional. Gibbons could keep right on running his steamboat line and so could anyone else who wanted to start another one. But infinitely more significantly, it was written into the law of the land that wherever Congress has specific power, the states have none (or, as Courts since Marshall's have slightly modified it, practically none), despite the absence of any such exclusive rule from the words of the Constitution itself.

Before, during, and after this trio of memorable decisions, Marshall's Court indulged in some considerably less admirable judicial work, where the protection and fostering of property and business interests could hardly be linked in any way to the future development of the nation. There were, for instance, the Yazoo land claims, arising from the same crooked real estate deal that had kept James Wilson from the Chief Justiceship, and coming up to the Court for a direct decision a dozen years after Wilson's death. Despite the fact that the claims were based on the cheap "sale" of millions of acres of land by a Georgia legislature that was indubitably and confessedly bribed to sell it, despite the quick repudiation of this "sale" by a subsequent and honest legislature, despite the fact that the claims had been bought up by speculators, mostly from New England, who counted on political influence to bring them a fast profit—despite all this, Marshall's Court ruled that the claims, though concededly conceived in fraud, were still perfectly valid and that the state of Georgia had to honor them. The get-rich-quick gamblers eventually collected close to five million dollars. U.S. law collected a new principle: that judges were to take for granted the lily-white nature of government financial transactions even though thoroughly aware that the trans-

116661

actions were fraudulent. As an obvious aftermath of this decision by the great Chief Justice, unscrupulous operators were encouraged for scores of years to take their chances on the mild criminal penalties they might remotely incur in acquiring state grants, state lands, state franchises, by bribing or buying state legislators. There were no real railroads in Marshall's day, but the railroad "robber barons" of the second half of the century had him to thank for the success of much of their political chicanery.

It was also under Marshall's aegis that the Court began to uphold—in a series of cases that came to total more than ninety—all sorts of patently phony claims to Florida or Louisiana land, based on forged "copies" or copies of "copies" of alleged grants from Spanish authorities just before the U.S. acquired these territories. That the juiciest of these claims were always, like the Yazoo claims, in the hands of Northern speculators by the time they reached the Court, and that the speculators were often well enough fixed to hire the doughty Daniel Webster to represent them, did not stop Marshall (indeed, *au contraire*) from shrugging off as irrelevant their fraudulent character— this time because of the sanctity not of government grants but of foreign treaties. It was under Marshall's aegis, too, after gold was discovered on Cherokee Indian land and Georgia whites tried to grab it by fair means or, for the most part, foul, that the Court in a trio of cases backed and filled, ducked the biggest and toughest problem, and ended up with the decision that led Andrew Jackson to invite Marshall to enforce it himself. So raw was the treatment of the Cherokees which Marshall blandly countenanced that his almost *alter ego*, Justice Story, after a rare dissent from a Marshall holding, blurted out in a letter to a friend: "Depend on it, there is a depth of degradation in our national conduct. . . . There will be, in God's Providence, a retribution for unholy deeds, first or last."

It was likewise under Marshall's aegis that the Court began its long and sorry history, only very recently corrected in some part, of winking at, if not actively blessing, the illegal and often inhuman treatment of Negroes in the South. A slave-owner himself, Marshall used all manner of technical, legalistic word-tricks to evade real enforcement of the Congressional outlawing of the slave trade; here, for once, he was not so anxious to uphold Congress's hand, presumably because he saw it as a threat, not a boon, to one well-propertied class. And when a couple of Southern states passed laws banning free Northern Negroes from crossing their borders, Marshall's passionate concern for exclusively federal control of interstate commerce did not carry over to this form of interstate movement. Justice Johnson, the one Court Republican who stood up against Marshall from the beginning, courageously branded one of these laws unconstitutional—as it clearly was—when it came before Johnson in a circuit court. Marshall not only declined to back up his colleague but wrote to Story in tremendously revealing vein: "Our brother Johnson, I perceive, has hung himself on a democratic snag in a hedge composed entirely of thorny State-Rights in South Carolina. . . . You have, it is said, some laws in Massachusetts, not very unlike in principles to that which our brother had declared unconstitutional. We have its twin brother in Virginia; a case has been brought before me in which I might have considered its constitutionality, had I chosen to do so; but it was not absolutely necessary, and as I am not fond of butting against a wall in sport, I escaped on the construction of the act." This, be it remembered, was the great "expounder of the Constitution," who was "escaping"—where human rights, not property rights, were at stake—from expounding it.

No such timidity—or disinterest—inhibited Marshall when state bankruptcy laws came within his ken. These were precisely the type of leveling laws (though of a rather mild variety, helping debtors at the probable expense of creditors) which all the Federalists, from the Founding Fathers on, had viewed with alarm. So Marshall did not try to "escape" from declaring a New York bankruptcy law unconstitutional in a decision (Sturges *v.* Crowninshield) that one historian has called "the principal cause of the Jacksonian Revolution"—even though, in order to get a unanimous Court behind him, he had to base his holding on a far narrower ground than was his wont, in one of the muddiest opinions he ever wrote. It was the compromised ambiguity of this opinion that opened the way for the only major defeat Marshall ever suffered as Chief Justice, when a bare four-to-three majority of his Court later ruled, over his dissenting protest, that state bankruptcy laws were not all automatically unconstitutional.

This defeat of Marshall on an issue dear to his heart and his politics took place in 1827, the year before Andrew Jackson was elected President in a popular uprising against not only John Quincy Adams's conservative regime but John Marshall's judicial attitude toward such things as

U.S. Banks and state bankruptcy laws. That a new and less Federalist slant had begun to seep into Supreme Court thinking, that the doom of the dominance of Marshall's philosophy was presaged even eight years before his death, was indicated not so much by the anti-Marshall decision itself as by the tone of Justice Johnson's opinion for the majority. "It is among the duties of society to enforce the rights of humanity," wrote Johnson in strange-sounding words to come from that citadel of conservatism, the Court, "and both the debtor and the society have their interests in the administration of justice, and in the general good, interests which must not be swallowed up and lost sight of while yielding attention to the claim of the creditor. The debtor may plead the visitations of Providence, and the society has an interest in preserving every member of the community from despondency—in relieving him from a hopeless state of prostration in which he would be useless to himself, his family, and the community. When that state of things has arrived, in which the community has fairly and fully discharged its duties to the creditor, and in which, pursuing the debtor any longer would destroy the one without benefiting the other, must always be a question to be determined by the common guardian of the rights of both; and in this originates the power exercised by governments in favor of insolvents." It was from this humanitarian view that Marshall dissented.

But the situation was far more frequently the other way around during the twenty-nine years of Johnson's sometimes subtle, sometimes sharp heckling of his Chief. From 1805 through 1833—the period of Johnson's Justiceship— only 74 dissenting opinions were written into the records of the Court (there are usually more in a single term today); of these, 6 were Marshall's own whereas 34, or close to half, were the products of Justice Johnson's firm and unseducible anti-Federalism. Alone of the Republican-appointed Justices, the sturdy South Carolinian, who was one of the two youngest men ever named to the Court (he was barely thirty-two when nominated), stuck to his Jeffersonian political creed, with only a few lapses, in the face of Marshall's power and personal charm. Indeed, if past Supreme Court history had been written by men less partial to Marshall's views and hence less loadedly kind to the great Chief Justice, Johnson might well be currently rated much as Holmes, the great dissenter of a century later, is rated—as the voice of the nation's democratic conscience, even though it usually spoke ineffectively, because in dissent.

By contrast to Johnson, the only other man worth mention on Marshall's Court was the product and tool of conformity rather than conscience. Joseph Story, who came to the Court, like Johnson, at the ripe young age of thirty-two, was the epitome of the proper Bostonian—high-born and Harvard-educated, witty and well-to-do, a gentleman lawyer, banker, and dabbler in politics. Though formally a Republican, he was so socially surrounded by Federalists, from his forebears to his business associates, that ex-President Jefferson shrewdly but futilely warned his White House successor, James Madison, not to appoint Story; but Madison, impressed by the young man's brilliant legal record, fell back on him as a fourth choice after two other New Englanders had declined the job and a third had been turned down by the Senate. Like so many subsequent

Presidents who have misjudged beforehand their Supreme Court nominees, Madison soon regretted the appointment; Story was fast taken over, lock, stock, and basic conservatism, by Marshall, so that he became, for more than a score of years, the only Justice whom Marshall really trusted to write an occasional important opinion in his stead. (In none but the Negro cases, where Story's Northern anti-slavery sentiments stood fast against his Southern Chief, did the disciple disappoint his master.) For this reason, plus such scholarly activities as teaching law at Harvard and writing voluminous legal textbooks, Story is as celebrated in lawyers' conventional Supreme Court legend as the more imaginative, independent, and ahead-of-his-time Johnson is generally ignored.

Or perhaps it would be more accurate to say that Justice Johnson, like so few Supreme Court members before or since, was in step with his political time, whereas Marshall, Story and their carbon-copy colleagues lagged increasingly behind. Because of this lag and because of the steady accretion of top government power in the judiciary under Marshall's benevolent despotism, sporadic efforts were made from Jefferson's Administration through Jackson's to cut the Justices down to democratic size. Proposals included limiting the terms of the Justices (Jefferson once suggested six years as enough), packing the Court with new members, giving the last word on constitutional issues to the Senate instead of the Court, requiring a five-out-of-seven vote to call a law unconstitutional, and the outright repeal of Section 25 of the Federalists' old 1789 Judiciary Act under which the Court had first taken on, and under which, technically, it was still exercising, the right of judicial review. That all these Court-hobbling schemes came to naught, despite Presidential backing for several of them, was due in large measure to Marshall's masterly over-all long-range strategy.

For Marshall, after his initial announcement of the Court's supremacy over Congress in Marbury *v.* Madison —a decision which actually reduced in a minor way the Court's own power, not Congress's—never again called a Congressional act unconstitutional. On the contrary, thirty-odd years' worth of his subsequent significant rulings tended toward enlarging the powers of Congress at the expense of the powers of the states. Why, then, should Congress want to restrict, by either simple statute or constitutional amendment, the very Court that was always championing and expanding Congress's own powers? For all the political hostility of most Congressmen and Senators, individually, to what Marshall and his Court were really doing in the regular and often ruthless protection of property rights, they were lulled or flattered into inaction against the Court by the protection-of-Congress phrases in which he cloaked his more immediate and more specific purposes. By the time later Congresses finally caught on to what Marshall had so dexterously done in his politico-economic shell game (the pea of top government power was under the Supreme Court shell, not the Congressional shell, all the while), later Supreme Courts had built so solidly and sonorously on Marshall's words that all efforts to override or undercut judicial supremacy were considered akin to treason.

This judicial supremacy, this rule by judges, was Marshall's major and most fundamental contribution to the

American scheme of government—not that he created or first invented it, for he did not, but that he established it, emblazoned it into the unwritten Constitution, for the use of generations of Justices to come. Even more than his go-right-ahead encouragements to Congress and his stop-right-there strictures to state legislatures, the assured audacity with which he lifted his own branch of the federal government from neglect and contumely to respect and power helped fashion a cohesive, consolidated nation. But to say all this is neither to ignore nor to applaud Marshall's own chief motive, his propulsive purpose; in a sense, his achievements, however great, were fortunate by-products of his immediate and constant concern for the interests of private property. To be seen straight, the famous decisions, the cases that wrote new chapters into the law of the land, must be looked at as part of a larger pattern, which covers the infamous decisions too, such as the protection of unscrupulous speculators and slave-traders and the denials of protection to Negroes and Indians as well as to bankrupts and debtors—and indeed to whatever minorities, or majorities, seemed to stand in the road of Marshall's dream of a nation run by and for men of wealth, no matter how they acquired it. The average citizen's concept of equal justice for rich and poor did not rank high in Marshall's judicial guidebook.

But some such concept—of justice, of humanitarianism, of democracy with a small "d"—was rampant in the land by the time Marshall died. It had helped elect and re-elect Andrew Jackson to the Presidency; now, in 1835, it was to get its first chance at the helm of the Supreme Court. For thirty-four long years, John Marshall, at political odds

with every Administration since his appointment save
perhaps John Quincy Adams's, had braved and bested the
growing forces of liberal democracy, had blended boldness
and subtlety, force and charm, selective logic and a sort of
home-baked law, to stand his ground for the brand of
conservative and essentially autocratic government in
which he so deeply believed. To replace him and to use for
all of the people the power that mighty Marshall, last of
the great Federalists, had won for the Supreme Court,
President Jackson picked Roger Brooke Taney of Maryland—and of subsequent Dred Scott ill fame. No Chief
Justice has ever had so bad a historical press as Taney,
and, except for his one most egregious error, deserved it so
little.

CHAPTER 4

Not States Against Nation but South Against North as the Court Leads on to War

JUST AS JOHN MARSHALL is known as the great judical advocate of a strong central government, so Roger Brooke Taney is commonly catalogued as the Chief Justice who, above all others, championed against federal engulfment the rights of the separate states. Just as Marshall is praised for a benign and farsighted statesmanship that helped weld the union together, so Taney is damned for a cantankerous if not malevolent divisiveness that, except for Lincoln and the force of arms, might have rent the nation permanently asunder. The more Marshall

111

has been pictured as history's hero, the more Taney has
become her convenient villain. History—and the explanation of events—is always so easy, so elementary, to those
whose intellectual spectrums skip from black to white and
back again, insensitive to factual shades of gray.

Yet it was no deep difference over theories of government, no disagreement about what might be abstractly
best for the nation, that really distinguished Marshall
from Taney in the context of their own times—no matter
how hindsight may invent such a doctrinal dispute, for the
satisfaction of those who like easy answers. Nor was it for
any such conceptual reason—states' rights against national
power—that Daniel Webster gloomily lamented, con-
cerning Taney's appointment, "Judge Story thinks the
Supreme Court is *gone*, and I think so too." What dismayed
Webster and Story was precisely what dismayed people of
their political ilk when Jefferson, or Jackson, or Franklin
Roosevelt was elected President. It was the accession to
top political power of a man whose slant, not toward so
dull and recondite a matter as dual sovereignty but toward
the bread-and-butter problems of day-to-day government
—who gets favored and who gets hurt—was obviously at
radical odds with their own.

True, Taney had recently said of judicial supremacy:
"The opinion of the judges has no more authority over
Congress than the opinion of Congress has over the judges,
and on that point the President is independent of both.
. . . Each public official who takes an oath to support the
Constitution swears to support it as he understands it, and
not as it is understood by others." And this might con-
ceivably have been read by Webster and Story—on the

most unlikely assumption that they were so naïve as to so read it—as presaging an abdication of the right of judicial review by a Court headed by Taney, so that *their* idea of a Supreme Court would indeed be *"gone."* But Taney had expressed this view as a high official in Jackson's Administration in the course of one of its quarrels with the Marshall Court; to suppose that he was going to hold to this position as Chief Justice and commit a sort of authoritarian hara-kiri would have been absurd; nor did he do so, nor could Webster and Story have really expected that he would.

On the contrary, they were afraid—and with considerable reason—that Taney would use the exact same powers that their comrade-in-conservatism, Marshall, had used, but toward quite different ends; for, in the words of the Supreme Court's most orthodox historian, Charles Warren, it seemed "evident that Taney would approach a case from the human . . . standpoint." Warren also opines, after stressing and restressing all the abstract business of Taney's preference for states' rights over federal dominance, that a "change of emphasis from vested, individual property rights to the personal rights and welfare of the general community . . . characterized Chief Justice Taney's court"; and just such a "change of emphasis"— not any forthcoming shift of supremacy from the nation to the states or any possible self-demotion on the part of the Court—was what Webster and Story and all the rest of the commercial-creditor class along with their advocates and sympathizers apprehensively deplored in advance when Taney replaced Marshall. To put it plainly, they feared that the new Court was going to look out for people, as people, instead of continuing Marshall-wise to bend every effort and twist every law to look out for property, as property, and for the special interests of those who owned a lot of it.

Strangely, these prophets of impending doom and disaster for propertied folk were proved in the long run wrong, or at least half-wrong—just as Warren, though judging Taney's Court backward instead of forward through time, is essentially wrong in stressing states' rights and human rights as the keys to Taney's judicial philosophy. The error was and is an easy one to make. Because most of the big cases that hit Taney's Court for the first twenty years had to do with the special privileges of one type of property-owner, because Taney did not share Marshall's solicitude for the banker-investor-merchant group of the North and East, because Taney therefore overrode or modified some of Marshall's more extreme holdings in the realm of banking and bankruptcy and business monopolies, Taney seemed to be, and to a substantial degree actually was, a sort of defender of the people against flagrant financial exploitation backed by legal authority.

But there was another type of property than paper stocks and bonds and notes and credits in a ledger, and for this other type of property Taney had a far more protective feeling. This was the property of the agrarians, the planters, the farm bloc of Taney's time, whose wealth was almost exclusively in two things—land and the slaves who worked the land. When it eventually came to dealing with this kind of property in behalf of the landed aristocracy of the South and the growing West, Taney proved as staunch a champion of vested rights as Marshall had been before him. Indeed, whereas Marshall's economic and political slant had been much like that of the twentieth century's Eastern or Wall Street Republicans, Taney was far less a precursor of today's up-the-little-man Democrats than of Midwest Republicans and Southern Democrats rolled, as it were, into one. The gloss of liberalism that shines from Taney's first two decades as Chief Justice was the limited if still useful liberalism of the big-time farmer who mistrusts city slickers—and even so limited a liberalism was refreshing when first effectively expressed in Supreme Court decisions. But the inevitable reversion to sectional self-interest, to the protection of property rights at all human cost once the ox that was threatened with goring was agricultural, not commercial, could and should have been foreseen long beforehand and ought to be far better understood today. That Taney's judicial career culminated, though it did not end, in the Dred Scott catastrophe was his great misfortune; had he died eight years before he did die, he might have gone down in history—half deservingly, half by happenstance—as the most liberal Chief Justice of them all.

If this seems a paradox, it is only so because "liberalism" and "conservatism" are rough and relative terms; the statesman or the judge who is found "on the people's side" against the economically strong and better favored may be there on one issue out of ten or nine out of ten; further, his liberal or conservative reputation is almost bound to rest on the chancy business of how many instances involving this basic issue, how many involving that, he has to deal with in the course of his career. By contrast to Marshall, who plumped for property rights in every instance and on every issue, no matter whether Northern businessmen or Southern slave-holders were pleading for judicial help (and so was that comparatively rare species, the complete economic conservative), Taney for years looked like a leftist because the problems he faced were all of a pattern to invite from him a popular instead of a property-protecting response. When the pattern and the problems and the kind of property that was asking for protection finally changed, Taney ran true to his slave-tended-plantations-and-mansions-and-magnolias form—and it is for this rather than his long previous record that he is chiefly and disparagingly remembered.

But there is even greater paradox—and greater poppy-cock too—in the stubborn and lasting legend that Taney, by contrast to the nationalist Marshall, was a dedicated devotee and defender of states' rights, *as such*. And this legend stems from a sweeping misconception of the whole supposed role of political theory in the very real and un-theoretical political battles of Marshall's and Taney's times—plus a flat misreading or twisting of history. As the story goes, the Federalists, including of course Marshall, had been strong for the central government, and the anti-Federalists or Republicans had been equally strong against it (and so much is superficially true); when the Federalist Party became, by and large, the Whig Party and the old Republicans changed their name to Democrats —which happened around Jackson's time—the same basic federal-power-against-state-power split continued to char-acterize the two; this deep doctrinal disagreement kept constantly on until it was bloodily resolved by the Civil

War (by which time the old Whigs were the new Republicans), with the Federalist-Whig-Republican group battling consistently through the years, and eventually victoriously, for the principle of federal supremacy, and the Republican-into-Democratic group fighting faithfully and single-mindedly, on every level including the judicial under Taney, for the principle of states' rights and state autonomy. The story is nonsense.

It was not federal supremacy against states' rights but the commercial interests of the North and East against the agricultural interests of the South and West that sparked and finally brought to flame the hostility between the two political parties—their spokesmen on the Supreme Court not excepted. When Marshall regularly upheld the national government and extended its regulatory reach while laying low state "leveling laws," particularly in the South, his eye was not on the niceties of political theory but on the practicalities of financial prosperity for business —no matter in what grandiloquent and high-sounding legalisms he may have formally justified what he did. When the states, especially in the South, defied the federal government, including sometimes Marshall's Court, on banks or bankruptcies or tariffs (South Carolina tried to "nullify" a Northerners' tariff act in 1833), their eyes were not on states' rights *in principle*, regardless of their state-proud protestations, but on the immediate and sectional economic welfare of their citizens. And when Taney's Court, for quite a time, turned the tenor of high judicial rulings in favor of the states, under a novel extension of something called "state police power," it was not because of any bookish notion about past federal

encroachment on states' rights; it was because of a com-
placent unconcern about state action that might hit or
hurt Northern and Eastern merchants or investors, so
long as such action did not threaten the pocketbook interests of Southern and Western agrarians, planters,
farmers.

The tip-off on the fundamental foolishness of all the
eloquence, judicial and otherwise, about states'-rights-
against-national-power came in the decade before the
Civil War, when national power was used, for a change, in
behalf of the South, as the federal government sought to
enforce the fugitive slave law. Now it was the former
"states' righters" who touted the central authority to the
skies while it worked to return to them their northward-
fleeing slaves; now it was the sanctity of national supremacy, not the state police power, that Taney's judiciary
preached and practiced; and now it was the Northern states,
almost all of them, who flouted, both officially and sur-
reptitiously, the government of the United States and
claimed the rebel right to run themselves. The Wisconsin
legislature, for instance, solemnly resolved "that the
several states . . . being sovereign and independent,
have the unquestionable right to judge of its [*the Constitution's*] infraction and that a positive defiance by those
sovereignties of all unauthorized acts . . . is the rightful
remedy." This reversal of roles, with the South for the
union and the North for nullification—a reversal always
glossed over by the easy-answer historians—came to a
head in 1857 with the announcement of the pro-slavery
Dred Scott decision by Taney's Court, since the Court was,
of course, a branch of the federal government. Until that

government, four years later, changed sides on the issue of slavery, the Democratic agrarian South was the union's lusty champion, while the Republican commercial North blazed with states' rights stuff. Then with Lincoln and war came a sudden reshifting of the mouthed political principles that camouflage, and have always camouflaged, what men really want and mean. Among the men who wanted and meant something other than what they nobly said, on the empty issue of states' rights, in the 1830's and '40's and '50's, were the honorable Justices of the Supreme Court, led by Roger Brooke Taney.

Except on the absurd if orthodox assumption that what Justices, or at least Chief Justices, think and do must be explained on some lofty level of government theory, of unearthly and infinite logic, involving such high-sounding matters as state sovereignty, national supremacy, and the proper postulates of federalism, the truth about Taney is, perhaps surprisingly, simple. He was a brilliant lawyer— which means, among other things, that he could weave a spell of impressive words about any argument toward any end that, as attorney or judge, he wanted to achieve. As counsel in one case, he orated: "A hard necessity, indeed, compels us to endure the evil of slavery for a time . . . while it continues it is a blot on our national character, and every real lover of freedom confidently hopes that it will be effectually, though it must be gradually, wiped away; . . . until the time shall come when we can point without a blush to the language held in the Declaration of Independence, every friend of humanity will seek to lighten the galling chain of slavery. . . ." But these in-inspiring sentiments, expressed in the course of litigation, did not keep him, shortly after, from defending a noisome character who had been charged, quite accurately, with the crime of slave-trading. Nor did they keep him from insisting as attorney in another case: "The African race in the United States, even when free, are everywhere a degraded class. . . . The privileges they are allowed to enjoy are accorded to them as a matter of kindness and benevolence rather than of right."

Taney was also a shrewd politician whose shrewdness was masked by the air of tremendous personal sincerity that emanated from his ugly and unprepossessing person. An ardent Federalist until he was well over forty, and a leader of that party in Maryland who served it well in the state legislature and out, he turned Democrat to support Andrew Jackson, whose bitter opposition to the U.S. Bank and whose sympathies for the South as against the North, for the planters against the traders, Taney almost automatically shared. Both the lawyer and the politican in Taney are apparent in his Court opinions.

But above all else—and explaining in obvious and meaningful fashion his whole judicial philosophy—Taney was a Southern gentleman, a straight political representative of what historian Charles Beard used to call "the slavocracy." Though descended, generations back, from an indentured servant who thus got to the New World, Taney was born into a wealthy, slave-owning family of tobacco planters. There is not one of his decisions as Chief Justice —from his years of nipping at the Marshall-nurtured rights of Northern capitalists to his ill-fated last-ditch effort to hold the dike for slavery—but can be traced, directly or indirectly, to his big-plantation birth and background. No states'-rights nonsense distorted to fit a hypothetical pattern, no liberalism turned either suddenly or gradually to conservatism, makes the slightest sense about Taney. From first to last, he was simply the judicial spokesman of the old South.

When Taney took over the captaincy of the Supreme Court in 1836—after a slightly anti-Jackson Senate had rejected him as an Associate Justice a couple of years before, and after a somewhat pro-Jackson Senate debated his fitness for ten weeks before confirming him for the Chief-ship—he found himself flanked on the high bench by four other Jackson appointees plus only two survivors from pre-Jackson days. With a Court thus loaded, five to two, for Democratic agrarianism, and with Marshall's old Federalist magic finally gone, Taney had no trouble making of the Court—and of the Constitution as read by the Court—the tool of a different political clique from the one that had run the judicial show for almost half a century. Those who persist in thinking of constitutional law and its top expounders as above politics might contemplate with profit, if with disillusion, a decision made by Taney's Court during his very first term as Chief. A few years earlier, Marshall's septet had blasted as utterly unconstitutional Missouri's issuance of paper money backed by the credit of the state, and had gone so far as to tell a debtor who had borrowed from the state in this paper money, and then spent it, that he need not repay it. Now Taney's tribunal gave constitutional benediction to a Kentucky law that achieved precisely the same practical purpose—that of putting easy money in the hands of the hard-pressed, especially farmers—in a slightly different formal manner; what Kentucky did was to set up and completely run a state bank which made loans in the form of bank notes, technically not issued on the credit of the state but on the credit of the state bank; perfectly proper, said Jackson's farmer-minded Justices. It did not matter that Justice Story almost sobbed his disapproval in a dissent in which he presumed to talk for his old mentor, Marshall, as well—probably the only time that a deceased Justice has joined in a Supreme Court opinion. Nor did it matter that the words of the Constitution, forbidding states to "emit bills of credit," had not changed. What had changed was the one all-important determinant of judicial decisions about government matters: the personnel of the Court and the politics of a majority of its members.

So too, during Taney's first term at the helm, one of Marshall's great legal landmarks, the Dartmouth College decision, was whittled down to size in the Charles River Bridge case. A toll bridge across the Charles River, operating under a charter granted by Massachusetts fifty years before, had been making such fantastic profits out of its monopoly on traffic between Boston and Charlestown, the easiest route to the West, that shares of stock in the bridge company had gone up from $100 to over $2,000, when the state legislature authorized a rival bridge. Against the claim of the profiteering monopolists that the new charter was unconstitutional as an "impairment of the obligation of contracts"—a claim thoroughly in line with Marshall's Dartmouth College ruling—Taney and his four fellow Jacksonians upheld the state and its new bridge, on the ground that the old bridge's charter, while still inviolable, nowhere forbade in so many words another bridge across the Charles at another place. Moreover Taney, though talking mostly legal language, gave away at the end of his opinion the fact that it was economics, not constitutional law, that dictated the decision: "If this Court should establish the principles now contended for, what is to become of the numerous railroads established on the same line of travel with turnpike companies? . . . The millions of property which have been invested in railroads and canals, upon lines of travel which had been before occupied by turnpike corporations, will be put in jeopardy. . . . This Court is not prepared to sanction principles which must lead to such results."

Neither Taney's legal principles nor his economics appealed to the more monopoly-minded relics on the Court from Marshall's day. Bemoaned Justice Story, in a long dissent that undoubtedly indicated how the case would have gone under Marshall, "I stand upon the old law, upon law established more than three centuries ago"—a slight overstatement, since the unprecedented Dartmouth College decision was only eighteen years old and the U.S. Constitution only fifty, and ancient Brisith law, to which Story referred, could scarcely control a case arising directly under the words of the American charter of government. But Story was quite accurate in his off-the-Court comment that "a great majority of our ablest lawyers are against the decision of the Court." He was not so accurate in predicting: "There will not, I fear, ever in our day, be any case in which a law of a State or of Congress will be declared unconstitutional." The "I fear" is immensely revealing of the politico-economic role that Story and the commercial-

creditor group wanted the Court to keep on playing—
under any legal principles that might come in handy.

For twenty years, Taney's Court continued to cut
down—little by little, now here, now there—the supposedly vested rights of investors. Corporations set up in
one state were denied the privilege of doing business as
they pleased in any other state, if the other state chose to
restrict them severely or even to keep them out entirely.
The unruly liquor industry was made subject to state
control by licensing laws, regulating the sale of liquor and
amounting to the first mild form of prohibition. These and
other similar rulings were said to be based on a fuzzy
concept called "state police power"—and Taney's frequent
use of the term is one reason why he is conventionally
classified as an anti-nationalist. But his efforts to explain
what he meant by it were so circular and question-begging
than any whole-hog nationalist might well have sub-
scribed to his words: "What are the police powers of the
state? They are nothing more or less than the powers of
government inherent in every sovereignty to the extent
of its dominions . . . its authority to make regulations of
commerce is as absolute as its power to pass health laws,
except in so far as it has been restricted by the Constitution of the United States." In view of the "except," how
could even Marshall have taken exception?

What "state police power" really meant in Taney's day
and has meant ever since is the use of state laws to do
things that a majority of the Justices, at any given time,
do not strongly disapprove of the state's doing—nothing
more, nothing less. For all Taney's comparative indifference to property rights of a commercial kind when they

came in conflict with state laws, it was something else
again when the kind of property or the kind of rights in
question were dearer to Taney's agrarian heart. And so he
upheld land grants, especially in California, as patently
forged and fraudulent as any Marshall had upheld before
him—and frequently had to do it over the shocked dissent
of two or three of his brother Jacksonians, who loved the
land-owning group as much as he but tolerated barefaced
dishonesty less. Here was the sort of case where the
essentially disparate judicial philosophies of Marshall and
Taney—one forever protecting the rich no matter what
their riches, the other forever protecting farmers and
land-owners, rich or poor—completely coincided.

Not so where banking was concerned. As Marshall,
most mightily in McCulloch v. Maryland, championed the
U.S. Bank with its policy of coddling the commercially
wealthy, so Taney was all for state banks with their more
liberal loans to local farmers, large or small—and his
violent hatred of the U.S. Bank was his most unwavering
political passion. This hatred stemmed originally, in
considerable part, from an experience that involved,
strangely, both Mr. McCulloch and Chief Justice Marshall:
the Bank's Baltimore branch had concealed McCulloch's
$3,000,000-plus defalcation to try to save itself some of
the loss by a subsequent insurance scheme, and Taney
argued the case against the Bank before Marshall's Court.
When Marshall ruled for the Bank on the bland—and
false—assumption that the Bank officials must be honorable men, he unwittingly chose his own successor as Chief
Justice. For Taney's resultant bitter hostility to the Bank
led in turn to his joining up with the Jackson Democrats,

to his appointment to Jackson's Cabinet, first as Attorney-General, then as Secretary of the Treasury (for the specific purpose of handling at each stage Jackson's battle with the Bank) and finally to Taney's reward in his elevation to the Court Chiefship. Of such little incidents is the supreme law of the land later born.

Along with his antipathy to the U.S. Bank, Taney retained an oversolicitous tenderness for state banks—so when a case came before his Court where Ohio had given its banks a boon, in the form of taxes lower than other corporations paid, and a later legislature had tried to take it back, Taney's reaction was all but automatic. Sounding exactly like Marshall, he berated the state for attempting to welch on its "contract," and declared the repeal of the tax boon unconstitutional; somehow, the vaunted "police power" here got lost in the shuffle when a state tried to use it in a way that offended the prejudices of its greatest exponent. But three of Taney's Democratic colleagues violently dissented against their Chief's apparently aberrational veto of a state law in order to protect vested rights of a non-agrarian kind—and in doing so, they gave "state police power," as they would have applied it here, a more trenchant meaning than Taney ever gave it. They asked: "What remedy have the people" against such "vicious legislation" as tax favors conferred by past legislatures on special groups, like state banks. "Under the doctrines of this court none is to be found . . . if the wrong has taken the form of a contract. The most deliberate and solemn acts of the people would not serve to redress the injustice, and the overreaching speculator upon the facility or corruption of their legislature would be protected by the powers of this court in the profits of his bargain."

The author of these strong words in dissenting defense of state governments against special privileges for property was Justice John Campbell of Alabama, a high-minded plantation-owner who had freed all his slaves when named to the Court but who later resigned his Justiceship to join the Confederacy, as a matter of principle, and survived the Civil War for almost a quarter of a century as one of the leading lawyers of the South. Campbell, along with Justices Daniel of Virginia and Catron of Tennessee, formed a rather radical and frequently dissenting trio on Taney's Court as Taney's Chiefship drew toward its Dred Scott climax. It was Daniel who—of course in dissent—questioned the whole doctrine of judicial supremacy as scathingly as it has ever been questioned, on the Court or off: "I ask upon what foundation the courts of the United States, limited and circumscribed as they are by the Constitution and by the laws which have created them and defined their jurisdiction, can, upon any speculation of public policy, assume to themselves the authority and functions of the legislative department of the government, alone clothed with those functions by the Constitution and laws. . . ." And Daniel added that the particular decision from which he was then dissenting was, on the part of the Court, "an act of usurpation."

But it was no judicial usurpation of the lawmakers' job to Daniel, nor to any of the other Southern Justices, when the big political question that was already rending the country in half—the question of Negro slavery, on which the South's whole economy was built—was finally thrown at the Court in a potentially farther-reaching fashion than had been involved in the sporadic upholding of fugitive-slave laws by the federal judiciary. This was in 1856; and the Court now had nine members, just as it has today, the extra two having been added to handle the new Western and Southwestern circuits shortly after Taney took over. Five of the nine were Southerners—Taney, Campbell, Catron, Daniel, and Justice Wayne of Georgia; the other four—McLean of Ohio, Curtis of Massachusetts, Nelson of New York, and Grier of Pennsylvania—represented (and the verb is accurate) the North. To these nine men fell the task of deciding *or of not deciding* the explosive political problems posed in the name of an illiterate and comparatively disinterested Negro by means of a cooked-up case—a case that made the Negro's name even more familiar in U.S. legal annals than those of Marbury and McCulloch, a case whose dramatic short-range impact made it the most famous, or infamous, in all Supreme Court history.

Dred Scott had been taken by his master, some twenty-odd years before, from the slave state of Missouri through the free state of Illinois into Wisconsin Territory, where slavery was outlawed by the Missouri Compromise. Later brought back to Missouri, he was induced to go to court to try to establish his status as a free man, since he had been free for years while living in the North. The Missouri courts ruled—in accordance with an almost forgotten Supreme Court decision of 1851 (where the slave's residence on free soil was, however, much shorter)—that Scott had gone back to bondage the second he crossed the Missouri border. To get the case into the federal courts and up to the Supreme Court, Scott was technically "sold" to a New Yorker named Sandford, who promised to free him and his family (and did so) no matter which way the decision went. As in so many momentous Supreme Court decisions, from Marbury *v.* Madison until last Monday's headlined ukase, the effect of the Court's action on the actual litigants was negligible; what the Justices were doing, for all their huffy denials that they ever do so, was not to settle a real and narrowed-to-its-facts dispute between two "parties" to a lawsuit, but to slap on, with broad strokes of the judicial brush, a major rule of government.

Nor need they have done so. To resolve the issue of Dred Scott's status, which was what they were supposed to be doing, the Justices need only have said—and could have said in a couple of sentences—that whether Scott, once back in Missouri, was a slave or a free man was Missouri's business, not the business of the federal government; and Scott *v.* Sandford (the case's technical name) would have dropped into oblivion. Indeed, this is precisely what the Justices planned to do after they first heard the case, with two of the Northerners prepared to join their Southern brethren in upholding Missouri—and re-enslaving Dred Scott—on this narrow and uninflammatory ground.

Then politics flooded into the case from every direction —just as politics has always flooded, seeped, or trickled into every really important Supreme Court case. Justice McLean, whose consuming ambition to become President was common knowledge, let it be known that he was going to tear the case wide open in a dissent which would amount to a long, learned, but fiery tract against slavery—plus a blast at his colleagues for supporting slavery, even by indirection. Georgia's Justice Wayne threatened a half-dissenting pro-slavery treatise that would deplore the Court's ducking of the big issues, and Justice Curtis of abolitionist Massachusetts got ready to rip into Wayne with another dissent that would supplement McLean's. One of the main thrusts intended by both McLean and Curtis was a fighting defense of the Missouri Compromise, under which Wisconsin Territory had been designated as free soil, and on which Dred Scott's claim to freedom was therefore founded. And this despite, or more realistically, because of, the fact that the Missouri Compromise had been repealed by a pro-slavery Congress a couple of years before. What McLean especially, and Wayne and Curtis to a lesser degree, planned to deliver were political speeches for or against slavery from the platform of the Supreme Court.

Faced with this forensic free-for-all, the other Justices decided to hear and discuss the case again. Meanwhile James Buchanan, who, though a Pennsylvanian, was mildly sympathetic to the South, had been elected President; and with the federal executive as well as the legislature thus safe for slavery, at least for a time, the Southern Justices were encouraged to put their third branch of the government in the same camp in a more substantial way than they had at first intended. The result was the full-blown Dred Scott decision, in which the Supreme Court, for the first time since Marshall did it more than half a century before, and so for the second time in its history, branded an Act of Congress—the old and recently repealed Missouri Compromise—as unconstitutional.

The Court's pronunciamento that the Missouri Compromise had been invalid and void from the beginning was based on the broad, flat declaration that Congress had no power to ban slavery in any of the Western territories (as the Compromise had done, north of an agreed line)—and this in the face of the Constitution's grant to Congress of "power to . . . make all needful rules and regulations respecting the territory . . . belonging to the United States." What this meant was that not even any future anti-slavery Congress could re-establish something like the Missouri Compromise or designate any U.S. territory as free soil, that the institution of slavery was at liberty to spread wherever it could or it pleased, unless and until the Court's decision should be reversed by the Court itself, by constitutional amendment, or by force of arms. In effect, the Court told the fast-growing Republican Party to stop wasting its energy and its oratory on efforts to restrict slavery by federal law.

Not only the decision but the preparatory manipulation of its manner and its timing was pungent of politics. When President Buchanan, in his inaugural address, adjured the nation, North and South, to accept the Court's judgment in the by-then-well-publicized Dred Scott case, regardless of how it might go—and did it with a deliberate air of innocent impartiality—he had already been told exactly what the Court had decided, how the Justices were lined up, and when the decision would be announced (which date, by purposeful postponement, was two days after

Buchanan's inauguration). More than that, Buchanan, at the request of Southern Justice Catron, had actually written some days earlier to his fellow Pennsylvanian, Justice Grier, to urge him to vote with the five Southerners so that the ruling would not be by a bare five-to-four majority along strictly sectional lines; and when the Court's action was made public, it was indeed a six-to-three decision with Grier adding his weight to the advocates of slavery.

That the decision, including its substance, was the fruit of a collusive and carefully conceived plot between the President-elect and the Court majority, as many incensed Republicans, led by Senator Seward, charged, is a considerable exaggeration; that there was shocking impropriety in the prior revelation of the ruling to Buchanan, as lawyers and other Court-worshippers have felt ever since the facts came to light more than fifty years later, is a naïve notion, stemming from the myth that Justices are, and ought to behave like, high priests rather than political functionaries; but that Buchanan's comment in his inaugural was loaded with hypocrisy and deceit is beyond question, and that the whole case was shot through, as are all big Supreme Court cases, with plain partisan politics is as obvious as it should be unsurprising.

Like the meat of the Court's ruling and the contrived circumstances surrounding its issuance, the opinions of the Justices—and each of the nine said his separate say—were, with one exception, political to the teeth. (The exception was Nelson's; he alone stuck to the narrow point on which the Court had first hoped to dispose of the case, and refused to take part in the bitter bigger debate.) And in all the pseudo-judicial speechmaking, Chief Justice Taney, delivering the main opinion for the majority, stood out as the most patently political of the lot, as he more than matched the McLean dissent which had originally sparked the fireworks. Not content to label the Missouri Compromise unconstitutional and let the decision rest on that, he held that no Negro could be a U.S. citizen, so that Scott had no right to bring suit in a federal court in the first place—a holding which, by regular legal procedure, should have stopped the Court from so much as considering the constitutionality of the Compromise, since the case was over, there was no case left, once it was ruled that the plaintiff had no right to sue. But Taney, backed by five of his fellows, was not to be stopped.

With evident relish, he flayed the holier-than-thou attitude of the North, "where the labor of the Negro race was found to be unsuited to the climate and unprofitable to the master," and he jabbed and twitted New England for its pious protestations of concern for the Negro while its ship-owners grew rich "in the slave trade, procuring cargoes on the coast of Africa and transporting them for sale" to the South. No opinion could have revealed more clearly the economic and emotional roots of Taney's judicial credo; what had passed, for two decades, as a humanitarian concern for the poor against their commercial exploiters, and a consequent championing of regulatory state laws, was now illumined as, in large part, an almost envious competitive sectionalism, a loyalty to the South which encompassed a scorn for the North. Nor could any opinion have been better calculated to enrage the opponents of Negro slavery—and to wreck its author's judicial reputation, once his side lost the war that his opinion helped bring on.

Among those who were enraged by Taney's treatment of the Dred Scott case—although his was a slow boil—was Abraham Lincoln of Illinois. One of his earlier and milder statements, in which he counseled acceptance of the decision until it should be—as he thought it properly could be —reversed by Congress, went on to the trenchant and timeless comment that "our judges are as honest as other men and not more so. They have, with others, the same passions for party, for power, and the privilege of their corps. . . . Their power is the more dangerous as they are in office for life, and not responsible, as the other functionaries are, to the elective control." But eventually, Lincoln's seething indignation burst into belligerence: "Familiarize yourselves with the chains of bondage and you prepare your own limbs to wear them. Accustomed to trample on the rights of others, you have lost the genius of your own independence. . . . And let me tell you, that all these things are prepared for you by the teachings of history, if the elections shall promise that the next Dred Scott decision and all future decisions will be quietly acquiesced in by the people."

Despite Lincoln's dire forebodings, what might be classed as "the next Dred Scott decision" was conspicuously not "quietly acquiesced in by the people." In 1859, in a case arising out of the flagrant flouting of the federal fugitive-slave law by a Wisconsin abolitionist, the Court, now riding high, put its stamp of approval on the slave-catching statute—which clearly violated several sections of the constitutional Bill of Rights—and ordered it obeyed. Taney, in ringing words that would have stirred John

Marshall to pride in his successor, spoke out for national supremacy over the states and judicial supremacy over all; of the Supreme Court he said: "If such an arbiter had not been provided in our complicated system of government, internal tranquility could not have been preserved and if such controversies were left to the arbitrament of physical force, our Government, State and National, would cease to be a government of laws, and revolution by force of arms would take the place of courts of justice and judicial decisions." To all this sonorous self-defense the state of Wisconsin responded by calling Taney's decision itself unconstitutional, and encouraging—not that such encouragement was needed in any of the anti-slavery states—disobedience of the federal law. Now was the time when Southern support of the national government, including especially the Court, was at its crest, and state sovereignty was the watchword of the North. Little more than a year later, Lincoln was in the White House and Southern states were seceding from the Union that Northern soldiers were going to war to defend.

The Republicans went to Washington, war came to the nation, and the windy slogans that men use to lend a false dignity to their deep and human allegiances veered 180 degrees—but Taney and his Court stayed on; as so often, the Court became a mourners' bench for an old order that had passed. Inevitably, conflict between Lincoln and Taney soon boiled into an immediate and specific issue, but the odds against the Chief Justice—by contrast to those Marshall faced in his early challenge of Jefferson —were overwhelming in that Taney was now well over eighty years old, a war was on, and the issue was con-

siderably more vital than the commissioning of a justice of
the peace for the District of Columbia. Lincoln, especially
anxious to keep Maryland under control and out of the
Confederacy, had suspended the "writ of habeas corpus"
(under which men summarily arrested and imprisoned can
demand their temporary release for a fair trial); a Marylander named Merryman, suspected of rebellious activities,
had been whisked to jail by the local commanding general
and was being held for obvious conviction by a military
court; Taney, sitting as a circuit judge, heard Merryman's
plea for a habeas corpus writ and issued one; the general,
naturally obeying his commander-in-chief instead of
Taney, paid no attention to the writ; whereupon Taney
quixotically ordered the general arrested for contempt of
court.

In the course of declaring that only Congress, not the
President, could constitutionally suspend the writ, Taney
proclaimed that if judicial authority could thus be "usurped
by the military power at its discretion, the people of the
United States are no longer living under a government of
laws [again, *that ancient chestnut*] but every citizen holds
life, liberty, and property at the will and pleasure of the
army officer in whose military district he may happen to
be found." Both the general and Lincoln, to whom Taney
sent a copy of his opinion, shrugged and went on with the
war, Merryman stayed in prison, and the writ of habeas
corpus remained suspended—unused and useless—until
the war was over. Yet Taney, who was thoroughly prepared to be imprisoned himself for his brashness (Lincoln
was of course too intelligent and too gentle to make any
such move), had struck a brave blow for individual liberties

which, however futile, was a rare gesture for a Supreme Court Justice. That Taney's motive may well have been hostility toward Lincoln, the North, the war, and the new order—rather than a passion for civil rights (would he have ruled the same way against Jefferson Davis?)—does not detract from the courage of what the old man did.

Around this time, and all within two years, Taney's three ablest colleagues—Campbell, Daniel, and McLean—either resigned or died. In replacing them, no more than any other President did Lincoln look to merit alone; indeed, his first appointment was one of the worst ever made to the Court, for Noah Swayne of Ohio—named as a barefaced sop to certain business interests who were supporting the war for less than idealistic reasons—was a corporation lawyer, as successful as he was callously unethical, who was not to change his spots or his spottiness throughout his long judicial career. Lincoln's other two selections were happier; David Davis of Illinois, though chosen, like Washington's Justice Blair, because he was an intimate personal friend, soon demonstrated his high caliber (as Blair did not); Samuel Miller of Iowa, humanitarian and unlegalistic realist, became, despite the fact that history has largely overlooked him, one of the Court's few top-flight Justices. But bad or good, each of the three had politics to thank, in part, for his appointment—and the first big case that came before them italicized the importance, both to them and to the President, of the political factor which underlay their choice.

In the normal course of the war, the North had been blockading Southern ports and seizing ships and cargoes headed not only for coastal trade but abroad; under international law, the legality of these seizures was highly questionable, since Congress had never formally declared war but merely authorized the President to suppress an insurrection; this technicality—somewhat suggestive of President Truman's twentieth-century "police action" in Korea—brought the problem before the Justices. That the blockade was given legal blessing by a bare five-to-four majority is less significant than that Lincoln's three brand-new nominees were among the prevailing five; without their presence, the decision would almost surely have gone the other way. Not that this would have affected Lincoln's conduct of the war or stopped the blockade, for a contrary ruling would doubtless have been treated as was Taney's judicial demand that Merryman be released under a writ of habeas corpus, a couple of years before. In fact, what Lincoln's Justices achieved was less a substantial boost to the Union cause than a saving of face for the Court itself—which would otherwise have seen its solemn decree ignored, its last-word superiority brushed aside, and its very existence as a governmental force seriously threatened.

But to Taney, who was, of course, among the four dissenters, this was the end. Court prestige or no Court prestige, he could not stand to see the hated hordes of the North given the highest judicial sanction as they rampaged against his beloved South. At his venerable insistence, the Justices politely ducked, as only they, among top government servants have power to do, the two or three other major wartime issues thrust before them, and for the duration of the hostilities, the Court remained quiescent—and safe.

Embittered, impoverished, estranged from the new

people as well as the new policies that now surrounded him at the seat of the national government, Taney died just six months before the assassination of his arch-nemesis, Abraham Lincoln. Like so many heads of the Court, from John Marshall to Harlan Stone, he had, in his heyday, made his enduring imprint on the nation and its laws— and then had lived too long. The political beliefs he was born to and to which he dedicated his career were neither wholly bad nor wholly good, and although he saw them rudely crushed, many of their remnants and ramifications survived to grow again. The legal principles he planted or cultivated still crop up in Court opinions, although often as hybrids that he himself would disown. The culture he championed—the agrarian culture of the old slave-owning South—was on its deathbed when Taney died, although elements of it were to rise, phoenix-like, from its ashes decades later. He might have died a little happier had he known that in the era just ahead—the era of ruthless "reconstruction" and rampant capitalism and expansion high-wide-and-not-always-handsome—there would be no Chief Justice for almost fifty years who could hold a candle to Roger Brooke Taney.

CHAPTER 5

The Court Rides Back
to Power on the Nation's
Surge to the West

THE THREE DECADES following Appomattox and the death of Lincoln are perhaps the most neglected and underrated in all U.S. history. There were no wars; there were no great Presidents nor even, save only Cleveland, any very good ones; there was none of the stuff of which conventionally name-and-date-conscious history is made. Yet the nation grew more rapidly and rambunctiously during the last third of the nineteenth century than at any other time—riding westward with the railroads, spreading across the continent with the shoulder-swinging confidence

141

of young manhood on the make. And in this coming of age of American capitalism, the Supreme Court, like an admiring and encouraging uncle, played—now unobtrusively, now boldly—a major part.

Nor was this any mean accomplishment on the part of the Justices. After the Dred Scott debacle, after the wartime caution which verged on cowardice and which was to continue into the early Reconstruction years, the Court's prestige and its consequent power were at a nadir unprecedented since Marshall had made of it a potent government force. There was no public outcry, such as greeted years later Franklin Roosevelt's "Court-packing" plan, when Congress calmly, within the short span of seven years, first raised the number of Justices to ten, then lowered it to seven (it never actually got below eight, since a couple of Taneyan relics refused to resign or die), then restored it to nine—although all three of these shifts were barefaced political moves, each dependent on the current occupant of the White House and dictated by a bland before-the-fact taking for granted that any appointment made by him would be acceptable (in the case of Lincoln and Grant) or unacceptable (in the case of Andrew Johnson) to Congress.

Moreover, after the long and lusty incumbencies of Marshall and Taney in the Chief Justiceship, the Court was headed for the remainder of the century by a trio of poor-to-middling jurists, none of whom had the personal or intellectual fire to lead, much less dominate, his own Court; even lawyers asked to list the Court's past Chiefs are apt to forget Salmon P. Chase, Morrison R. Waite, and Melville W. Fuller. All three were outshone and overshadowed by a series of higher-calibered associates—from Samuel Miller, whom Chief Justice Chase himself had the grace to call "beyond question the dominant personality . . . upon the bench," to John Harlan, the brilliant precursor in liberalism and in dissent of Justice Holmes. All three were swept along—sometimes willing, sometimes protesting—as their crews kept the Supreme Court's craft pretty squarely in the current of the inexorably expansionist times.

Not that those crews kept smoothly in stroke; few of the telling Supreme Court decisions of the late nineteenth century were unanimous and many were five-to-four; as the Court's membership shifted, as new Presidents named new and politically sympathetic Justices, confessed or *sub rosa* reversals of recent rulings became the regular order of many a decision day. But neither the reversals nor the narrow margin by which they were often effected delayed for long the renaissance of a refreshed and refurbished Court prestige. Between the Civil War and the Spanish-American War, while the Court's personnel was in constant flux and no strong hand was ever at the helm, a majority of the Justices managed to ride the crest of the times back to power such as Marshall had never known.

This resurgence of the judiciary from impotence to dominance is best italicized by contrasting what the Court did not do in the late 1860's with what it did in the middle 1890's. Soon after the Civil War, in a series of dull cases dealing technically with state bonds and state debt-limits, dealing actually with the westward reach of the rampaging railroads, dealing legally with the right of state courts to change their minds and their decisions, the Justices spanked

the state courts of Iowa; then saw their orders disobeyed
and flouted; and eventually surrendered officially, if reluctantly. Nobody protested or even clucked at Iowa's successful defiance of the Supreme Court of the United States.
At about the same time, Congress practically dared the
Court majority, still sympathetic to the South, to declare
the ruthless Reconstruction Acts, passed over President
Johnson's veto, unconstitutional; the Court ducked this
opportunity so obviously that a Cabinet member commented: "The Judges of the Supreme Court have caved in,
fallen through, failed. . . ."

But a little less than thirty years later, the Court's self-
confidence, indeed its cockiness, was such that in a single
year, 1895, it made, and saw upheld, three of the most
politically important decisions in its entire history, each
of them in its separate way an almost insolent flaunting of
judicial supremacy over Congress and over the government
of the nation. One of these three was the Pollock decision,
branding the Democratic-Populist income tax unconstitutional by a bare 5–4 vote, and so postponing until the
Sixteenth Amendment was adopted, after a lag of eighteen
years, what soon became the most fruitful (and, by different
lights, the fairest or most unfair) source of federal revenue.
One was the Knight decision, in which the high-riding
Justices, instead of calling the new Sherman Anti-Trust
Act invalid under the Constitution, so emasculated it, in
the course of "interpreting" its meaning, that it has never
since recovered its virility. The third was the Debs decision, where the Court took it upon itself, in the utter absence of any Congressional law calling for judicial action, to
regulate interstate commerce on its own—though the

Constitution gives that power only to Congress—by blessing the order of a lower federal judge which sent the leader of a railroad strike to jail. Thus, through the veto of one Congressional statute in the name of the Constitution, through the near-veto of another in the guise of "interpretation," and through assumption of one of the powers of Congress where there was no statute at all, the Justices announced to all but the politically astigmatic that they were governmentally supreme in more than name.

Less than three decades earlier, a retired Justice, Curtis, had said: "Congress, with the acquiescence of the country, has subdued the Supreme Court. . . ." Six decades later, a sitting Justice, Douglas, was to say, specifically of the Debs decision but, by implication, of the Court's whole attitude, plus the nation's tolerance of that attitude, back in 1895: "No greater claim to judicial supremacy has ever been made. . . ." Here, in the words of two of its members, speaking almost a century apart, is highlighted the Court's quick rise from the subjugation of post-Civil War days to the proud government primacy that, once reachieved, it has held for itself ever since. How was this rapid resurgence accomplished? There is at least a clue in the second half of Justice Douglas's comment on the Debs case: ". . . and significantly it [*the "claim to judicial supremacy"*] was made on behalf of vested interests that were callous to human rights."

It was indeed vested interests, property interests, the protection of accumulated and accumulating wealth, that dominated the philosophy and the decisions of most of the Justices during those years when the Court was regaining its power. Not that this was any judicial innovation; Marshall's Court, and Taney's too, had read the law at a slant to safeguard now this, now that, kind of property or wealth. Nor was this new-era Court—at least at the start—out of tune with the timbre of its own times; those were the days of the robber barons, but more revealing is the fact that they were not known as robber barons then; they were rather the swashbuckling risk-taking leaders of America's surge to the west—for all their financial finagling, more adventurers than exploiters—and the railroads that were their wealth and their life were the nation's life as well. Hence, it is neither surprising nor necessarily sinister that most of the men appointed to the Court in the late nineteenth century, including two Chief Justices, Waite and Fuller, had made their names and their legal reputations primarily as railroad lawyers.

But when many, though not all, of these former railroad lawyers began to twist the law unduly in favor of the railroads and of other closely connected corporations, plain-speaking Justice Miller was moved to blurt out, after a Court conference in which his somewhat more objective views had been voted down: "It is vain to contend with judges who have been, at the bar, the advocates of railroad companies, and all the forms of associated capital, when they are called upon to decide cases where such interests are in contest. All their training, all their feelings are from the start in favor of those who need no such influence." And when Justices who had leaned toward the railroads when the railroads represented, in the true sense, free enterprise, continued to lean toward them as they grew fat and not so free, sentiments like Justice Miller's spread far and wide beyond the confines of the Court and contributed to the growing Populist movement. But by this time the Court, having unobtrusively regained its power, was ready to resist, in its own right, any would-be inroads on the course of capitalism flamboyant. As its chief weapon in judicial defense of an economy untrammeled by bothersome restrictive laws, it chose, and gradually fashioned to its purpose, one-third of one sentence of the long, new Fourteenth Amendment to the Constitution.

The Fourteenth was one of three amendments adopted soon after the Civil War and designed, according to all obvious intents and announced purposes, to guarantee the rights of the newly freed Negroes. As such, it was crammed down the reluctant craw of the defeated South by a law that banned any seceding state from re-admission to the Union until it had ratified the Amendment. In the middle of a sentence, in one of five sections of the Amendment, appears the phrase: "nor shall any state deprive any person of life, liberty, or property, without due process of law." The phrase was clearly copied from the Fifth Amendment, a bulwark of the Bill of Rights, which forbids the *federal* government to deprive any person of "life, liberty, or property, without due process of law." As originally written in the Fifth Amendment, it was no more than a roundabout and melodious way of saying that no one suspected or accused of crime could be hanged, jailed, or fined without fair and legal treatment, before and during trial.

But the Fourteenth Amendment's "due process clause" —as it is commonly called—(and even the Fifth Amendment's too) has come to mean something quite different today. Without so much as a close competitor it has become, to lawyers, the most familiar and useful phrase of

the entire Constitution; indeed, well over a thousand of
the Supreme Court's full-dress decisions have revolved
around the little due process clause. These decisions have
rarely dealt with Negroes, or with people of any color,
accused of crime. They have dealt instead with corporations
or, less often, with real (not corporate) "persons" who
claimed through their lawyers that some duly enacted and
fairly administered state law, taxing them or regulating
their business activities, "deprived" them of property
"without due process of law." In sum, the Fourteenth
Amendment's due process clause has become the last, and
quite often successful, resort of men or companies who
stand to lose money through the normal working of some
state law, properly passed by a properly elected legislature,
properly signed by a properly elected governor, and properly put into effect by properly chosen state officials, including judges—some law that perhaps clamps down on
sweatshops, or taxes big fortunes handed on at death, or
orders a monopoly like an electric company not to charge
so much. And this legal legerdemain, by which an old
Bill of Rights phrase has been inflated into a semantic
excuse for the judicial veto of state laws of any and all
varieties, was first perpetrated, toward the end of the
nineteenth century, by a Supreme Court hell-bent to guard
the business interests that had sparked the nation's westward growth, against what the Founding Fathers would
have called "leveling laws"—no matter that those laws
reflected the democratic will.

Although the pro-business perversion of the plain meaning of the due process clause (Justice Holmes once snorted
in disgust, and in dissent: "Of course, the words 'due

process of law' if taken in their literal meaning have no application to this case. . . .") came to effective life only after the Justices gave it their official benediction, the twist had been anticipated, ardently urged, and perhaps even plotted long before. At least, two members of the congressional committee that drafted the Fourteenth Amendment later insisted that they had planned it that way. John Bingham, a shrewd and successful railroad attorney, said so in a speech to Congress; and Roscoe Conkling, another prominent corporation lawyer, remarked before the Supreme Court, while trying to argue a railway client out of paying a state tax: "Those who devised the Fourteenth Amendment . . . planted in the Constitution a monumental truth to stand four square to whatever wind might blow. That truth is but the golden rule, so entrenched as to curb the many who would do to the few as they would not have the few do to them." In context, it was clear that Conkling's "many" were any democratic majority and his "few" any businesses or businessmen financially hit or hampered by a state law.

Regardless of whether Bingham and Conkling were indulging in accurate revelation or, perhaps, in clever and purposeful afterthought, it is a nice question whether the "intent" of the drafters of a constitutional phrase, or of a statute, should prevail if that "intent" has not been fully revealed to those who adopt, or enact, the words into law. Should a court say that a piece of legal language means what the man who wrote it wanted it to mean, or what other men understood it to mean when their votes gave it governmental sanction and force? The problem—characteristically legal in its potential convolutions and its essential irrelevance (judges use either answer as an excuse for reaching whatever decision they want)—is the basis of many an inconclusive court argument in many a case of constitutional or statutory "interpretation"; but it is a dead problem today so far as the due process clause is concerned. Despite the fact that practically every legislator, state or federal, who had a hand in putting the Fourteenth Amendment into the Constitution thought he was helping insure the civil rights of the Negroes—and had no notion that he was sheltering corporate and other businesses, way into the indefinite future, from vexatious state regulations and taxes—the legal clan eventually saw to it that the Bingham-Conkling "intent" held sway. As Charles Beard describes this lawyers' crusade: "In learned briefs and prolix arguments, counsel for these harassed concerns warned the Supreme Court with emphatic repetition against the oncoming hosts of communism and anarchy . . . and demanded that the Court stem the tide by assuming the function of passing upon the reasonableness of all menacing legislation."

The Court did not capitulate immediately. But as it regained its confidence after its near-hibernation of Civil War and early Reconstruction days, as Northern Republican railroad lawyers replaced Jacksonian agrarians on the high bench, the Bingham-Conkling vision of the due process clause, with its vast political potential, gained gradual acceptance among the Justices—first in dissenting opinions, then in half-concessions by a Court majority—until in 1890, a quarter-century after the war ended, it was first made the basis of a full-fledged and far-reaching Court decision. By that momentous decision, to quote Beard again, "every act of every state and local government which touched adversely the rights of persons and property was made subject to review and liable to annulment by the Supreme Court at Washington, appointed by the President and Senate for life and far removed from local feelings and prejudices." Five years later, in the income-tax and anti-trust and railway-strike decisions, the Court was spectacularly riding herd on Congress too. Within three decades, the Justices had climbed back from the depths to the heights of sheer political power.

The man who, at Taney's death, took over the Chief-ship of a Supreme Court deep in disrepute—and who, during his brief nine-year tenure, did little himself to repair the Court's prestige—is better known as Lincoln's brilliant but unruly Secretary of the Treasury and as an unabashed seeker after the Presidency, so persistent, if perennially unsuccessful, that he alternately wooed the Republicans, the Democrats, and the Liberal Republicans in his hunger for a nomination he never won. Salmon P. Chase of Ohio, so conventionally handsome that he was once called "a sculptor's ideal of a President," had been named to Lincoln's Cabinet from the U.S. Senate, largely as a reward for his legal and political record as an all-out abolitionist—a record which had earned him the sobriquet of "attorney-general for fugitive slaves." And it was for even more pointedly political reasons that Lincoln chose Chase to replace Taney at the head of the Court—however this fact may offend ingenuous idolators of the Court or of Lincoln. As the great President himself put it, in a blend of blunt-ness and shrewdness, "we wish for a Chief Justice who will sustain what has been done in regard to emancipation and the legal tenders [*the paper money of questionable validity, issued during Chase's Secretaryship of the Treasury to help pay for the Civil War*]. We cannot ask a man what he will do, and if we should, and he should answer us, we should despise him for it. Therefore we must take a man whose opinions are known." Had Lincoln lived he would have learned, as have other Presidents, that no amount of political shrewdness in naming a new Justice can keep that Justice—especially if he is ambitious—from changing his "known" opinions after he has donned the security of a robe.

While the legality of the Emancipation Proclamation never came before the Court, since slavery was abolished by the Thirteenth Amendment soon after Lincoln's death, the legality of the Civil War paper money was litigated to the teeth—and the most vocal and violent judicial contemnor of the paper-money laws he had helped to plan and put into effect was Chief Justice Chase, now out to swing for himself a Presidential nomination on some other ticket than the Republican. But before the Legal Tender Acts, as lawyers still call them, came up for constitutional review, Chase and his colleagues were faced with some other big government problems and managed to flub or flee them all—with one exception. The exception looms large only in the perspective of retrospect; it seemed singularly insignificant at the time and hence is paid little attention by most Court historians. What the Court did, and did admirably, though by a bare 5–4 vote, was to declare unconstitutional an Act of Congress requiring a loyalty oath from lawyers (and directed, just after the Civil War, against Confederates, not Communists); but the reason this decision stands out in the panorama of time is because it is one of three instances in the Court's entire history where the ultimate power of judicial review, in the veto of a Congressional law, has been clearly and significantly used in behalf of civil liberties. This case aside, the Chase Court did itself less than proud, and Chase's own record stands as a monument to the potential fallibility of even the best of Presidents in choosing Chief Justices wisely.

There was the Court's running battle with the state of Iowa over Iowa's financial magnanimity in trying to lure the railroads through its corn fields and into its cities—a battle notable on three scores. It was notable because—in stark contrast to what was shortly to come—the legislature of a farm state had sparked a legal tussle by taking official action for, not agin, the then-fledgling railroads. It was notable because of the vitriolic vigor of Justice Miller's dissent, in the first of several cases, not only against the Court's pro-railroad decision as rationalized by his fellow Justice, ex-railroad-lawyer Swayne (in reversing the Iowa Supreme Court's anti-railroad ruling) but also against "language as unsuited to the dispassionate dignity of this court as it is disrespectful to another court of at least concurrent jurisdiction over the matter. . . ." And it was notable because, in accord with Miller's dissenting doubt that the Justices could "induce the Supreme Court of Iowa to conform its rulings to suit our dictation," the Iowa court did indeed disregard the U.S. Supreme Court's orders in three consecutive cases until it forced the high tribunal, devoid at that time of the prestige that underlies its power, to ignominiously back down.

There was also the Chase Court's strategic retreat from battle with a revengeful Republican Congress, bent on beating down the defeated South with the misnamed Reconstruction Acts that in many ways defied all decent concepts of constitutional propriety. Paradoxically, this retreat came hard on the heels of a ringing declaration by the Justices in behalf of human rights, in a case called *ex parte* Milligan—a case much celebrated in legal annals but presumably celebrated rather for its language than for its beneficent impact on events, which was practically nil. Milligan, a Copperhead or pro-Southern Northerner, had been sentenced to be hanged by one of Lincoln's military courts, shortly before the war ended. In releasing him under a writ of habeas corpus—the same writ that old Taney had used in his gallant but futile gesture for Merryman, and that the Court as a whole had timorously backed away from using while the war was on—the unanimous Justices proclaimed through Justice Davis: "The Constitution of the United States is a law for rulers and people, equally in war and in peace. . . . No doctrine involving more pernicious consequences was ever invented by the wit of man than that any of its provisions can be suspended during any of the great exigencies of government." Noble words but scarcely brave ones, since the Court conspicuously failed to speak them—or, more importantly, to act on them—until the war was over.

Indeed, the real and immediate impact of the Milligan case was anything but beneficent. While the whole Court agreed that a *President* could not replace functioning civil courts with military courts, a five-man majority of the Justices went further and denied the same power to Congress. But the Reconstruction Congress was at that moment gleefully setting up military courts below the Mason-Dixon Line to help subjugate the beaten South. In no mood to be cowed by a Court it held in contempt, Congress forthwith reduced the Court's membership from ten to seven as any sitting Justices should resign or die (lifetime tenure prevented unseating them, but two of the five-man majority were well over seventy)—and thus automatically disposed, as well, of President Johnson's unconfirmed nominee to fill the seat of Justice Catron, who had died before the Milligan decision.

If the rampaging Republican Congress was not cowed by an unsympathetic Court (nor by an unsympathetic President), it was soon clear that the Court was now cowed by Congress. In the first suit brought to test the constitutionality of the Reconstruction Acts—technically, a plea that the Court enjoin the President from administering them—the Justices bowed themselves out by denying that they had any right, under the doctrine of separation of powers, to give orders directly to a President. In the next suit the President was not directly involved but two of his highest subordinates, Secretary of War Stanton and General Grant, were; this time the Court's excuse for ducking was one that has since acquired a familiar and tired ring; the issue was not "legal," it was "political"—and as such was none of the Justices' business. Then along came a suit, by a Mississippi editor named McCardle, challenging head-on the authority of the military tribunals set up by Congress in the South; the membership of the Court had not changed by one man since the proud pronouncement of the Milligan case.

As the publicized McCardle case went up to the Court for argument, with the legal rightness-or-wrongness of the whole Reconstruction scheme potentially hanging on the decision, Congress—for all its self-assurance, not anxious to face the dilemma of either disobeying, flatly and arrogantly, a specific Supreme Court order or else submitting, meekly and weakly, to the order it anticipated—took fast action. Under its constitutional control of the Court's right to hear cases appealed from lower courts, it feverishly prepared a bill to prohibit the Court from going any further with the McCardle case (appealed from a federal circuit court) or from entertaining any others like it. Time was now, as lawyers say, of the essence. Before the bill could be perfected and pushed through, the Justices had finished hearing the McCardle pleadings—and they were well aware of what Congress was fashioning to handcuff them. But instead of announcing a quick and easily curt decision reaffirming—this time in cold fact, not just in warm oratory—the majestic Milligan manifesto of only two years before, they stayed their judicial hands until the Congressional handcuffs were welded into law. Then, in an opinion penned by Chief Justice Chase and redolent of sadly self-righteous abnegation in the face of the inevitable —which had not been inevitable—the Justices submitted to Congress's command and dropped the case. In popular esteem as in political power, the Court had hit rock bottom.

Comparative cowardice soon gave way to almost equally unimpressive confusion, as the Court finally tangled with the Legal Tender Acts that had led Lincoln to name their Cabinet sponsor to the Chiefship. Including Chase, the Court in 1869 numbered five Lincoln appointees out of eight members, the other four being Swayne, Davis, Miller, and Stephen J. Field of California—who had been chosen as a tenth Justice in 1863 to represent a new federal court circuit in the far West, who was an intimate and a protégé of Leland Stanford (better known in the nineteenth century for the political machinations of his Central Pacific Railroad than for the university he founded), and who devoted his considerable legal talents to the judicial support of ultra-conservative capitalism throughout a Court career destined to last for thirty-four years. It might have seemed that these five, at least, would vote to uphold the constitutionality of the close to half a billion dollars' worth of paper money issued, out of financial necessity, by the Lincoln-led U.S. government during its fight to preserve the Union—particularly since the railroads, by a strange quirk, were then on the side of the poor, the debtors, the easy-money class, because they were operating largely on bond-borrowed funds. But Chase, for all his close past connection with the issuance of the greenbacks, was more ambitious than consistent, and Field was more creditor-conscious than railroad-minded.

In the first of the Legal Tender cases, the Court, in conference, split four to four; but feeble seventy-six-year-old Justice Grier—the Northerner who had gone along with the pro-slavery Southerners in the Dred Scott decision after President-elect Buchanan so suggested—vacillated so vaguely in his views that his colleagues took the unprecedented step of unanimously asking him to resign from the Court. (By a sort of poetic justice, Field, who delivered the message to Grier, was himself the recipient of an identical request twenty-eight years later—at which date he was not too senile to mutter, when reminded of the Grier incident and his own part in it: "Yes—and a dirtier piece of work I never did in all my life.") Dirty work or no, Grier did resign, whereupon, early in 1870, the Court ruled, four to three, that the Legal Tender Acts were unconstitutional—with Chase, the Acts' chief sponsor, maintaining for the majority that Congress had no power to issue paper money and Miller, in blistering dissent, upholding the Acts as a "necessary and proper" (the Constitution's phrase) adjunct of Congress's unquestioned power to carry on a war. Had this decision stood until time encrusted it with sacredness—as has many a Court decision by a mere one-man majority—Congress's control of U.S. currency would still be limited, short of constitutional amendment, to the clumsy business of coining metallic money. But Congress, backed by its new ally in the White House, Ulysses S. Grant, was bound that the Court's hobbling decision should not stand long.

A month after Grant took office, and while the first of the Legal Tender cases was still on its way up to the Court, Congress, perhaps foreseeing trouble, had increased the number of Justices to nine (at which figure, despite Franklin Roosevelt's bid to raise the Justicial ante, it has remained ever since). Almost simultaneously with the announcement of the 4–3 decision, Grant named to the Court two more railroad lawyers—William Strong of Pennsylvania (Philadelphia and Reading R.R.) and Joseph P. Bradley of New Jersey (United Railway Companies of N.J.). Within a week after the quick confirmation of Strong and Bradley, the Administration started steps to bring the Legal Tender Acts before the Court—now a

slightly different Court—again. And the very next year—
with Strong and Bradley joining the former dissenters, and
Chief Justice Chase leading the former majority in futile
protest—the Supreme Court of the United States officially
and solemnly announced that the Constitution gives Congress the power to issue paper money, a power that Congress of course still exercises to this day. As when Justice
Roberts, in the New Deal era of the following century,
switched his views about the validity of minimum-wage
laws between one year and the next and, in so doing,
completely reversed the supreme law of the land as laid
down by the Court, so in 1871, the turnabout on the Legal
Tender Acts gave pause even to the most naïve of believers in the myth that Supreme Court Justices read the
law *out of* the Constitution instead of reading it *in*.

Made to look a little ridiculous by their own official flip-
flop (plus a push from Congress and the President) so soon
after Congress had made them look silly over Reconstruction, the Justices turned their primary attention, for more
than a score of years, away from the federal government
and toward the states. Now was the time when business
lawyers began to urge on the Court a free-wheeling version of the Fourteenth Amendment as a handy device to
keep unruly state legislatures in line. And as early as 1873,
the Court first listened, and almost succumbed, to this
functionally straightforward if legally tortuous argument.
The Louisiana legislature, probably bribed, had awarded
to one company a complete twenty-five-year monopoly of
all the slaughterhouse business in New Orleans—a move
made supposedly, and in part actually, as a health measure.
Competing slaughterhouse operators, faced with financial

ruin, hired former Supreme Court Justice Campbell to plead that they had been "deprived of property without due process of law" (and other things). Although the Court rejected this plea and resuscitated Taney's old concept of "state police power" to uphold Louisiana, it did so by a slim 5–4 margin. An entering wedge had been made and the wedge was wide.

But trenchant Justice Miller, speaking for the Court majority, produced perhaps the finest and certainly the most important opinion of his admirable twenty-eight-year career on the high bench. Like John Marshall, Miller had enjoyed very little formal legal training; indeed, he had been for years a practicing physician before he turned to the law. Like Marshall too, he had the practical capacity to cut through jungles of verbal legalism and hit a case or an issue in the jugular. Unlike Marshall, he did not consider the defense of private property rights as the prime duty of government or of the judiciary; one brief biographical sketch capsules him as "more concerned with the welfare of society as a whole than with the protection of vested property interests." Now, Miller, looking backward to the sources of the three post-Civil War Amendments, stated that "no one can fail to be impressed with the one pervading purpose found in them all, lying at the foundation of each, and without which none of them would have been even suggested; we mean the freedom of the slave race, the security and firm establishment of that freedom, and the protection of the newly-made freeman and citizen. . . ." Looking ahead, more prophetically than he knew, he warned that judicial acceptance of the newly proposed and far broader interpretation of the Fourteenth

Amendment "would constitute this Court a perpetual censor upon all legislation of the states. . . ." Despite Miller's historically accurate, humanitarian, and yet hard-
headed view of what the Amendment did and did not—or
should and should not—mean, four of Miller's fellows, including Chase, disagreed and dissented.

Within a matter of weeks after the slaughterhouse decision, death came to Chase, the most hapless Chief Justice
of them all—he who had been eclipsed on his own Court,
not only by Miller but by Davis and Field and Strong; he
he who had seen the one important majority ruling he ever
wrote, in the first Legal Tender case, overturned and con-
signed to operative oblivion the year after it was written;
he whose hunger for the higher office he coveted in vain
hamstrung and compromised his whole conduct of the high
office he held. Death may not have been unwelcome. But
the irony of events was to make Chase's minority slant in
the slaughterhouse matter the eventual law of the land,
while Justice Miller was to have his masterly majority
opinion, and all that it stood for, discarded by a differently
manned Court in the very year he died.

Even a Congress which, for the most part, coddled and
co-operated with President Grant could not quite stomach
the first two men he nominated to take the place of Chase;
each had little to account for his nomination save close
personal friendship with the President; one had recently
been publicly discredited as a Cabinet member and the
other was aged and also suspected to have been a Copperhead; both nominations, after widespread protest, were
withdrawn. Passing by a wealth of available legal talent,

including especially Justice Miller, who was generally rated, even by his ideological enemies, as the nation's finest judicial mind, Grant finally lit on a second-rate railroad lawyer from Ohio named Morrison R. Waite, conspicuous only for his inconspicuousness—and the Senate, with a collective sigh of relief that the choice had not been affirmatively worse, accepted him. It was under Waite's Chief Justiceship, if not precisely under his leadership, that the Court slid slowly away from Miller's humane and restricted reading of the Fourteenth Amendment and inched, under the insistent influence of railroad attorneys, both off and on the bench, toward a broader and more business-minded view. But before that view took precedence, there came, as a sort of death convulsion, a strong re-affirmation by the Court of the states' police power to regulate business, despite the due process clause, in a set of decisions known as the Granger cases.

The railroads, in their rampant push to the West, had been growing increasingly corrupt and contemptuous—buying and bribing state officials, charging shippers uneven and outrageous rates, counting for legal protection on the kind of constitutional doctrine laid down by John Marshall in the Dartmouth College case and others, whereby the property and the privileges granted by a state to a private concern were held sacred, as "obligation(s) of contracts," no matter by what malodorous means they were obtained. As the Supreme Court, following the Marshall precedents, began to uphold these claims to land and franchises, even though based on proven bribery (which the Court was to continue to do throughout the century), and as exploitation grew more arrogant and onerous, there had arisen in

the farm belt a political protest group, the forerunners of
the Populist Party. These Grangers had won control of the
governments of several midwestern states, and had passed
laws regulating railroad rates and reducing the charges of
grain warehouses and elevators as well. Immediately and
automatically, the owners of these businesses appealed to
the courts to save them from being deprived of their
property—meaning their considerable profits—without
due process of law. This time the Supreme Court failed
them—but not without planting the seeds of their future
success.

Speaking for an almost unanimous Court, with only
Field, that doughty defender of scot-free enterprise, dissenting, Chief Justice Waite announced that the businesses
in question were, by their essential nature, "clothed with a
public interest"—like ferries and stagecoaches and bakers
and millers under ancient English law—and that the prices
they charged could therefore be regulated as a proper
exercise of state police power. "For protection against
abuses by Legislatures, the people must resort to the
polls, not to the Courts." But by implication, might there
not be resort to the courts if a state tried to regulate a
business *not* "clothed with a public interest"? By implication, might not the due process clause then, and perhaps in
other instances, be used as a constitutional weapon to
strike down an offensive state law—since Waite had not,
as he might have, summarily dismissed the Granger cases
as based on a misconception of the meaning of the Fourteenth Amendment? Might not the hint of Waite be
coupled with the slant of Field—in contradistinction to
Miller's contemporaneously stated insistence that all "due

process of law" required was "a fair trial in a court of justice"—to veto whatever regulations of business the Court might choose to veto, especially if the Court's personnel should change?

Within five years of the 1877 Granger decisions, four Justices, all of them members of the majority that upheld the Granger laws, resigned or died. To replace them, Presidents Hayes, Garfield, and Arthur appointed three quite undistinguished but politically "right" legal personages named Woods (a carpetbag politician-turned-judge from Georgia), Matthews (an Ohio railroad lawyer whom the Senate finally confirmed by the margin of one vote on his second try), and Blatchford (a reactionary railroad-lawyer-turned-judge from New York)—plus one conventionally deserving legal choice, Chief Justice Horace Gray of the Massachusetts Supreme Court, as distinguished for his personal wealth as for his precedent-bound judicial orthodoxy and destined, in his twenty-year career on the federal bench, to write but one memorable opinion (which upheld, in the spirit of the eighteenth century's discredited Alien Act and the twentieth century's controversial McCarran Act, the unlimited right of the U.S. government to deport any aliens it pleased—and which even drew an acid dissent from so firm an anti-liberal as Justice Field).

Thus reconstituted, the Court soon gutted the Granger decisions by holding that a state could only regulate railroad rates for trips entirely within its own borders, since the Constitution's interstate commerce clause (not, here, the due process clause) gave control of all state-to-state transportation exclusively to Congress. (Of course, no such federal control was then being exercised; the Inter-

state Commerce Act had not yet been passed.) And an
astute cynic might well have commented that the Court's
switch on state regulation of railroad rates between 1877
and 1886 could be largely laid, no matter which constitutional clause was called in question, to the immediate
practical impact on the roads of each decision in its turn
and in its time. For in 1877, when the Justices sustained the
Grangers, rates had recently fallen so low, as an aftermath
of the panic of 1873, that the ruling did not, right then,
hurt the railroads at all; by 1886, rates were up again and
only the Granger laws were keeping them from going still
higher, so that the new ruling was a real financial boon.
Yet this explanation, however neat and plausible, inaccurately implies that the Court is a sort of continuing
unity, an integrated single force, instead of an ever changing group of men. They were a different group of men in
1886 than they were in 1877. And, although the interstate
commerce clause was their *technical* device for protecting
the railroads from regulation in 1886, the soon-to-come
perversion of the due process clause too to judicial defense
of *laissez faire*, in prosperity or depression, was telegraphed
by the politico-legal temper of the Court's new and business-minded members.

Meanwhile, the Justices had been busily perverting the
plain intent of the Fourteenth Amendment—and the
Fifteenth too—in another and even more indefensible
fashion. Through the 1860's and 1870's, Congress had
passed a series of laws designed to put teeth in the otherwise empty words of the post-War Amendments, by im-
posing criminal penalties on anybody who deprived the
Negroes of any personal or political rights, including "the

equal protection of the laws," which the Amendments were supposed to guarantee. Then, through the 1870's and 1880's, the Court imperiously and impatiently swept aside almost all of these so-called Civil Rights Acts, either by flatly branding them unconstitutional—no matter that the Constitution had been amended precisely to achieve what these laws were aimed to achieve—or by using legalistic chop-logic to "interpret" them out of effective existence. A federal statute that made it a crime for any state official to stop citizens from voting was vetoed by the Court as too far-reaching, and hence an improper invasion of states' rights—since the Fifteenth Amendment only forbids the states to stop people from voting "on account of race, color, or previous condition of servitude." (Actually, the statute did use the phrase, "on account of race and color," so the Court, by a weird contortion of words, had to hold that the statute meant more than it said in order to hold that, by meaning that much, by going that far, it was unconstitutional.) In another Negro voting case, the Court refused to let some Louisiana state officials be punished under federal law for their violent maltreatment of Negro would-be voters—simply because of a tiny technical slip in the wording of the indictment. Said the Court, quite straight-faced: "We may suspect that race was the cause of the hostility, but it is not so averred." On a broader and equally callous scale, the Justices gave a green light for the future to the brutality and terrorism of the Ku Klux Klan, by overthrowing a federal statute deliberately meant to curb the Klan—on the ground that the protections and guarantees of the Fourteenth Amendment could be enforced (if at all) only against official state acts, not against the acts of private persons. Amidst this judicial vandalism, one crumb was tossed to the Negroes in the form of a ruling that they could not be kept off juries just because they were Negroes—a ruling so obviously abstract and futile, in the light of Southern practices, that no effort was made by the Court to give it real effect for over fifty years.

Most important of all this group of cases, in its long-term effect on the Negroes' way of life in the South, was the decision that ditched, as unconstitutional, a congressional law that made it a crime for anyone to deny a Negro the same treatment accorded a white man in hotel or inn, restaurant or theater, or any public vehicle of transportation, whether horsecar, coach, ferry, or railroad—again on the ground that the Fourteenth Amendment had no force whatever to control the acts of non-official citizens. In eloquent, plain-spoken protest against the bland legalisms of his brethren, the Court's lone dissenter said: "I cannot resist the conclusion that the substance and spirit of the recent Amendments of the Constitution have been sacrificed by a subtle and ingenious verbal criticism. . . . Constitutional provisions adopted in the interest of liberty . . . have been so construed as to defeat the ends the people desired to accomplish, which they attempted to accomplish, and which they supposed they had accomplished by changes in their fundamental law." Broadening his protest to take in the whole fabric of judicial review, he went on: "The judiciary may not, with safety to our institutions, enter the domain of legislative discretion. . . . That would be sheer usurpation . . . which, if often repeated, and permanently acquiesced in, would work a radical change in our system of government."

The author of these wise but unhappily wasted words
was a former slave-owner from Kentucky and grandfather
of the present Justice who bears his name, John Marshall
Harlan. Appointed by President Hayes—strictly out of
political gratitude for his having swung the key Kentucky
delegation from Blaine to Hayes at the 1876 Republican
convention—Harlan had little in his past career to com-
mend him, then aged forty-four, for so high a post. Like
Marshall's and Miller's, his legal education had been
meager; an unsuccessful office-seeker, he had run twice for
the governorship of his state, and lost twice; his switch of
allegiance from Democrats to Republicans, not long before,
seemed to indicate an unstable political character. Yet what
looked like instability was soon revealed to be a rugged
independence of thought as Harlan proceeded to carve his
name large on the small roster of really great Justices. For
thirty-four years and under three Court Chiefs, consistent
in his earth-rooted liberalism if not always in the airier
niceties of legal logic, he waged a sniper's war that rolled
up more than three hundred dissents against the monolithic
drive of most of his colleagues to capture the Constitution
for unbridled conservatism, for a political philosophy
based—in the words of that illustrious contemporary attorney, Joseph H. Choate—on a belief that "the preservation of the rights of private property is the very keystone
of the arch upon which all civilized government rests."

No dissenter from this philosophy, but rather one who
rode it throughout his pre-Court and Court careers, was
the second Chief Justice under whom Harlan served. At
Waite's death in 1888, President Cleveland put in his
place another man practically unknown to the country at

large at his appointment and, despite his twenty-two years at the head of the nation's judiciary, practically unknown to history, even legal history, today. Melville W. Fuller, a Chicago corporation lawyer who had counted among his clients Marshall Field, Philip Armour, and the Chicago, Burlington, and Quincy Railroad, and who owed his elevation to the accidental fact that, despite having been born in Maine, he was a Democrat, made no substantial contribution, except his predictably pro-business votes, to the Court over which he presided, and wrote no memorable opinions save two—his slipshod emasculation, in the Knight case, of the Sherman Anti-Trust Act, and his clumsy killing of the income tax in the Pollock case.

Far more influential on the Fuller Court than its Chief was David Brewer of Kansas—nephew and idolator of Justice Field—who got his own Justiceship one year after Fuller, who in effect gave Field two votes on the Court while Field lived, and who faithfully followed his uncle's Choate-like philosophy after Field died. Like Rufus Peckham of New York—who was soon to join him on the Court and share with him its effective leadership, in Fuller's default—Brewer, as a lower court judge, had presumptuously refused to be guided in his own decisions by the Supreme Court's ruling in the Granger cases which upheld state regulation of railroads and other businesses. He had barely taken his seat on the high bench—and Justice Miller, long-time guardian of the principle of no judicial interference with state regulation of business, had just died— when the Supreme Court itself, quite differently manned than thirteen years earlier, gave the *coup de grace* to the Granger cases and opened the gate to unlimited judicial supervision of state laws under the aegis of the Fourteenth Amendment.

It is unimportant that this crucial case arose in Minnesota, where a railroad protested to the courts against having its rates regulated by a state commission set up by the state legislature. It is important only that a majority of the Justices ordered that any such regulation must always be subject to court review to make sure that the required rates were "reasonable," because any rates that a court might deem "unreasonable" would *therefore* be unconstitutional as well, in depriving the railroad—or any other regulated business—of its property without due process of law. As Justice Bradley, certainly no Granger, no Populist, no business-baiter, exclaimed in his dour dissent, "the decision of the court in this case . . . practically overrules [the Granger decisions]. The governing principle of those cases was that the regulation and settlement of the fares of railroads and other public accommodations is a legislative prerogative and not a judicial one. This is a principle which I regard as of great importance. . . . All human institutions are imperfect—courts as well as commissions and legislatures." But the bars were down now; in the next thirty years almost one-third of the cases heard by the Court, or roughly seven hundred cases, stemmed, at the Justices' open invitation, from claims that this state law or that ran counter to the due process clause of the forgotten Negroes' Fourteenth Amendment.

Having tasted power such as even Marshall never knew, having regained the institutional self-assurance that soured at the end of Taney's tenure and was badly battered right after the Civil War, the Justices were not to be denied. The biggest single year in all Court history, seen in the light of governmental dominance, of putting into practice the undemocratic theory that judges know best, was 1895. Three disparate but deeply intertwined decisions made their mark on the nation and the pattern of its laws; and one of them dealt directly with the most dynamic force—now for good, now for evil—of the latter part of the century: the railroads.

This was the Debs case, in which the railroads—now more plagued by their newly unionized employees, out for higher wages, than by their farmer-customers, out for lower rates—got a compliant federal district judge in Chicago to issue a shotgun injunction which, in effect, ordered the head of the Railway Union, former locomotive fireman Eugene V. Debs, to call off the Pullman strike or go to jail. It was not the injunction but federal troops, unnecessarily (there had been no violence) ordered in over Illinois Governor Altgeld's protest, that broke the strike; Debs, summarily sentenced to prison for contempt of court, appealed to the Supreme Court to release him; the Chicago judge had not granted him a jury trial, such as the Constitution seemed to require, and had acted without authorization from any law passed by Congress. Neither of these latter details bothered Justice Brewer, who, speaking for the Court in a manner to make his uncle proud, proclaimed for the federal judiciary the right to send men to jail, however arbitrarily, without benefit of jury, and the right to protect interstate commerce from interference, however peaceful, without benefit of legislation. The immediate results of the Debs decision were to turn the political wrath of organized labor plus its sympathizers against judges in general and the Supreme Court in particular, and to turn Eugene V. Debs into a militant Socialist —which, as is rarely realized, he had never been before. The chief long-term result was to make of federal labor injunctions, here given the highest possible benediction, the favorite and most widely abused weapon, for thirty-odd years (until the Norris-La Guardia Anti-Injunction Act put a stop to their abuse), of employers dealing with recalcitrant labor unions.

If the nation's economic health could be protected by court order from strikes by workingmen, even in the absence of statute, it could nevertheless not be protected by court order from business monopolies, even in the presence of a pointed statute. Such, at least, was the purport of another of the Justices' Big Three 1895 decisions—in the Knight case, where Chief Justice Fuller wrote one of his two notable, though less than admirable, Court opinions. The Sherman Anti-Trust Act, only five years old, carried the high hopes of the people and their Congress that it would serve as a legal sword to cut down or cut apart the more arrogantly anti-social of the growing group of industrial monopolies and trusts that were ingesting, octopus-like, a large chunk of the American economy. Involved in the Knight case, first real test of the new law, was the sugar trust; there was no doubt about the fact, which Fuller conceded, that by buying up the stock of four other companies "the American Sugar Refining Company acquired nearly complete control of the manufacture of refined sugar within the United States." However, Fuller continued—in a classic legalism that was to echo significantly through the Supreme Court reports for almost fifty years—there is a vital distinction between manufacture and "commerce"; Congress, under the Constitution, may only regulate commerce, not manufacture; hence the sugar trust, a manufacturing monopoly, may continue on its merry and profitable way, untouched and untouchable by the Sherman Act. As effectively as if the Act had been declared unconstitutional, which it was not, judicial operation had rendered it at least temporarily impotent.

Yet, of the 1895 trio of judiciary-triumphant decisions, the most audacious in its disregard of democratic government, and the most arbitrary for its lack of any basis in law, in logic, or in constitutional history, was the Pollock decision, which throttled the federal income tax until the slow process of constitutional amendment brought it back to life eighteen years later. To detail the devious processes of legalistic argumentation by which, first, a small segment of the tax was said to be banned by the Founding Fathers' edict that "direct taxes" (a phrase so ambiguous that the Fathers, in Convention assembled, could not themselves define it) had to be "apportioned"—and then the whole dog followed its tail backward into the ashcan of unconstitutionality—would be as tedious as it would be wide of the mark. This was not law, in any scholarly sense of the word, that five of the Justices laid down; their judgment was purely, or rather impurely, political. Lawyer Choate put the whole business in honest perspective when, pleading against the tax, he warned his audience of nine that the "Communist march" must be stopped and that it must be stopped "now or never." Chief Justice Fuller, in his opinion for the Court, took up the same tune, if pianissimo, in a sneering reference to "the speculative views of political economists or revenue reformers." And Justice Field, concurring a little louder, cautioned that "the present assault upon capital is but the beginning." Remarks like these from the bar and the bench, regardless of whether or not their ominousness was warranted, scarcely required or rested on legal wisdom—and gave the pseudo-legal show away.

Hence the four dissenting Justices, each one separately, sharply denounced their colleagues' economic overlordship for what it really was and called it utterly unjustified by law. One described the decision, accurately, as "a judicial amendment of the Constitution." Another protested that it "dislocates—principally for reasons of an economic nature —a sovereign power expressly granted to the general government." Said a third: "The decision involves nothing less than a surrender of the taxing power to the moneyed class. . . . Even the spectre of socialism is conjured up to frighten Congress from laying taxes upon the people in proportion to their ability to pay them." And the fourth— Howell Jackson of Tennessee, who had just recently come to the Court and who unfortunately died shortly after— expostulated: "This decision is, in my judgment, the most disastrous blow ever struck at the constitutional power of Congress." But none of these bootless rebukes allayed the jubilance of "the moneyed class" and their editorial spokesmen of the press. "The wave of the socialist revolution had gone far," exulted the New York *Sun*, "but it breaks at the foot of the ultimate bulwark set up for the protection of our liberties." And then, with a whiff of unwitting humor: "Five to four, the Court stands like a rock."

Within the couple of years after their 1895 triple victory, the Justices added a few further flourishes to their now blatant dominance of the nation's dual (state and federal) scheme of government. In a case severely limiting the effective power of the Interstate Commerce Commission, they embarked on a slow suffocation-by-"interpretation" of the Interstate Commerce Act—the law passed, under political pressure from farmers and small businessmen, to control on a national level the money-making shenanigans of the railroads, right after the Court had taken such control away from the states. This left the control nowhere—or rather, left it in the hands of the railroads themselves. In a case that finally engraved on the law of the land for decades to come the full perversion of the Fourteenth Amendment to business use, as urged by Justice Field in lone dissent from the Granger decisions twenty years before, the Justices jettisoned a Louisiana statute regulating insurance companies, and did it on the ground that the due process clause protected businessmen's "freedom of contract"—their right to make any deals they pleased—from meddlesome state interference. (Despite a slight backtracking by the Justices the next year—when they let Utah limit miners' working hours to eight a day as a health measure, with that dauntless duo, Brewer and Peckham, dissenting—"freedom of contract" soon became, in a profusion of decisions, the one kind of "liberty" most jealously guarded by the Court under the Constitution.)

The Justices also turned their attention once more to the neglected Negroes, who were now protesting, under the Fourteenth Amendment's guarantee of "equal protection" for everybody, against the Jim Crow laws of the South.

There was no doubt that these laws were official state actions, not the actions of private persons. But in the case of Plessy *v.* Ferguson, the Justices dreamed up and declared their famous, or infamous, "separate but equal" doctrine in defense of segregation. That the South, as was plainly to be expected, latched onto the "separate" and laughed off the "equal" did not bother the Court into discarding its impractical principle until almost sixty years after. One small bright spot in the late 1890's—and one of the three meaningful times in its history when the Court has defied Congress in behalf of civil liberties—came when the Justices overruled a federal statute in order to grant the protections of part of the Bill of Rights, such as trial by jury, to aliens, who thus fared better judicially in this period than did Negroes or union members, albeit these latter groups were citizens.

The century was now drawing toward its close. For the Supreme Court, it had been a century of fabulous fluctuations in the Court's fortunes, its power, its prestige. Judicial supremacy, hard-won and hard-held under Marshall, had been used, then abused and lost under Taney. No man, no two or three or four men, had won it back, but rather a jumble of ever changing, often clashing Justices—some weak, some strong, some stupid, some wise—with never a captain capable of ordering his crew. As the years after the Civil War had been for the nation years of awkward, adolescent growth and of adventurous, uninhibited expansion, territorial and industrial, so too they had been anti-government, don't-hold-us-down years. And it was this anti-government, free-of-all-fetters political feeling (it was scarcely a philosophy) that the Court first learned to ride and then to direct.

As the nation slid into the twentieth century, its eyes were shifted for a time away from internal affairs and toward the Spanish-American War, the most blatant U.S. experiment in imperialism. During this interval, few cases of any import came before the Court (save a couple dealing —and dealing imperiously—with the legal and political status of newly won Puerto Rico and the Philippines). Lolling easily in the governmental driver's seat, ready to call and take the turns as need should arise, the Court idled along, waiting.

Then, shortly after the turn of the century, an event took place that was destined to shake the Court out of its comparative complacence and give it, whether it heeded or not, a vocal conscience more eloquent than any it had known before. Theodore Roosevelt named to the bench, to replace pedestrian Justice Gray, a wise and witty sixty-one-year-old Boston Brahmin who then headed the highest court of Massachusetts and was soon to become, in the popular mind, the perennial prototype of the genus Justice—Oliver Wendell Holmes. Holmes in no sense, except intellectually, ever effectively led the Court he graced; if he had, he could scarce have been dubbed "the great dissenter." Yet everything significant the Court did while Holmes was on it is better illumined and understood—as a dark object is reflected, even though backward, in a bright mirror—if seen in the light of the Holmes dissents over almost three decades.

CHAPTER 6

Associate Justice Holmes, Dissenting

ONLY A HANDFUL OF MEN in all U.S. history have made with their minds so manifest a mark on their own age and on ages still to come as did Justice Holmes. Benjamin Franklin probably, Thomas Jefferson surely, John Marshall possibly, and after him Abraham Lincoln—and the list is closed. Serving always as an Associate Justice, under four Court Chiefs—Fuller, White, Taft, and Hughes—he was commonly called, with a sort of astute inaccuracy, Chief Justice Holmes. But not till fastidiously fictionalized, after his death, as the Yankee from Olympus (that retreat of the gods, remote, as Holmes never was, from the earthy affairs of men) did he become, in memoriam and for popular consumption, a heavenly hero. In life, there was little heavenly about the irreverent agnostic, the twinkling skeptic, the down-to-the-ground judicial realist, of whom legal historian Walton Hamilton was later to say: "It has taken a decade to elevate Mr. Justice Holmes from deity to mortality." There was little heavenly, that is, save the almighty power of his mind to cut through legal humbug (his favorite sneer-word) to clean common sense—and the almost godlike tolerance of other men's ideas, however idiotic they might seem to him, that became the byword of his dissenting blasts at his more benighted brethren and gave to the Court and the nation a fresh, new breath of freedom and a deeper faith in democracy, aflaunt and unafraid.

To label Holmes a "liberal," as he is universally labeled, is not to say that he was liberal in the current leftward-leaning connotation of the world. A stanch and solid Back Bay Republican from the time he fought for the Union and was wounded in the Civil War until, in the last five Presidential elections of his ninety-four-year life, he favored Hughes (over Wilson), Harding, Coolidge, Hoover, and Hoover again (over Franklin Roosevelt)—Holmes, in his personal politics, was a conservative. Almost by instinct (reinforced by environment) he tended to mistrust Democrats, and he brushed aside socialist talk and writing as "drool." Yet his passionate respect for the right of others to think differently than he did—that respect on which all of democracy is ultimately based—led him always to question even his fondest preferences and made him, in the truest sense, an *intellectual* liberal. His homage to human dignity (which he so effortlessly personified) made him, in defense of men's minds and persons, a *libertarian* liberal.

The two together, especially in contrast to the autocracy-grown-arrogant of most of his fellow Justices, made Holmes—for all his own political conservatism—the greatest *judicial* liberal the court had known.

This judicial liberalism found its chief targets, during Holmes's long span on the Supreme Court, in three different kinds of judicial illiberalism; indeed, the Court's record as a political power, throughout the first third of this century, can be written largely in terms of these three kinds of cases, where a majority of the Justices—not always but far too often—threw their we-have-the-last-word weight squarely against the brand of liberalism that Holmes believed in. One kind of case—and one that took up so much of the Justices' time that the Court's work fell as far as three years behind—was, of course, the complaint, coming in a flood, that some state law, using a new wrinkle to regulate business or tax wealth, was forbidden by the Fourteenth Amendment. A second and similar kind was the claim that some new *federal* tax or regulation, some law passed by Congress, was unconstitutional; and here there were two separate legal hooks on which the claim could be hung—either the due process clause of the *Fifth* Amendment, recently perverted like its younger brother to the protection of capital instead of the protection of criminals, or else a states'-rights sort of argument that something Congress had done went beyond what Congress had power to do by way of regulating interstate commerce. The third kind of case dealt with civil liberties, such as freedom of speech or freedom of the press, when some law, whether state or federal, threatened to cut them down.

To his colleagues' solicitude for property rights (in the
first two kinds of case) and their indifference to more personal rights (in the third), Holmes, over the years, made
multiple and always eloquent answer. Even when couched
in legal terms to hit the precise point at issue, those answers weave tightly together into an all-of-a-piece philosophy of law. In the first kind of case, he once said, naturally in dissent: "There is nothing that I more deprecate
than the use of the Fourteenth Amendment beyond the
absolute compulsion of its words to prevent the making of
social experiments that an important part of the community desires, in the insulated chambers afforded by the
several States, even though the experiments may seem
futile or even noxious to me and to those whose judgment
I most respect."

Dissenting against the Court's veto of a Congressional
law (on minimum wages) in the second kind of case,
Holmes got more specific: "In the present instance the
only objection that can be urged is found within the vague
contours of the Fifth Amendment, prohibiting the depriving of any person of liberty or property without due process
of law. . . . The earlier decisions upon the same words
in the Fourteenth Amendment began within our memory
and went no farther than an unpretentious assertion of the
liberty to follow the ordinary callings. Later that innocuous
generality was expanded into the dogma, Liberty of Contract. Contract is not specially mentioned in the text that
we have to construe. It is merely an example of doing what
you want to do, embodied in the word liberty. But pretty
much all law consists in forbidding men to do some things
that they want to do, and contract is no more exempt from

law than other acts." (Holmes's last words here were more wishful than accurate since, by the decisions of his brethren, in this and other cases, contract *was*, in fact, "more exempt.")

And when the attack on a Congressional law (this one restricting child labor) was hung, not on the Fifth Amendment's due process clause, but on a claimed overextension of Congress's control of interstate commerce so as to butt into the field of states' rights, Holmes roared, again in dissent: "If an act is within the powers specifically conferred upon Congress, it seems to me that it is not made any less constitutional because of the indirect effects that it may have. . . . Congress is given power to regulate [interstate] commerce in unqualified terms. . . . This Act does not meddle with anything belonging to the States. They may regulate their internal affairs and their domestic commerce as they like. But when they seek to send their products across the state line, they are no longer within their rights. . . . It seems to me entirely constitutional for Congress to enforce its understanding [of 'the national welfare'] by all the means at its command."

In situations like these, where ambiguous constitutional language was being stretched by his fellow Justices into a legal excuse to lord it over legislatures, out of a coddling concern for unfettered freedom-of-enterprise, Holmes's liberalism led him to defend the legislative will —even though, as a legislator himself, he might have voted against the very law that, as a judge, he fought to have upheld. Not so in the third kind of case, where civil liberties were involved and constitutional language was usually less obscure—as in the First Amendment's flat: "Congress shall make no law . . . abridging the freedom of speech or of the press. . . ." Here, Holmes would not have hesitated, as did his colleagues, to wield judicial supremacy in behalf of the personal rights of the unpopular and the persecuted. Perhaps the most famous of all his singing sentences were among those penned in protest against that part of the first World War's Espionage Act which made almost any kind of critical or nonconformist political expression a federal crime:

"But when men have realized that time has upset many fighting faiths, they may come to believe even more than they believe the very foundations of their own conduct that the ultimate good desired is better reached by free trade in ideas—that the best test of truth is the power of the thought to get itself accepted in the competition of the market, and that truth is the only ground upon which their wishes safely can be carried out. That at any rate is the theory of our Constitution. It is an experiment, as all life is an experiment. Every year if not every day we have to wager our salvation upon some prophecy based upon imperfect knowledge." Yet the moral courage and the intellectual humility of Holmes, emblazoned brilliant in these words, were rarely sufficient—and were not enough in this instance—to win a majority of the Justices to his cause. Only after his death were some, not all, of his dissenting essays and epigrams gradually turned, by judicial acceptance, into constitutional doctrine. It was rather as a critic than an actor, as a prophet than a present leader, that he made an indelible mark on the political law of his own time.

For the political law of Holmes's time was, with a few brief lapses and interludes, merely a more concentrated continuation of the let-business-alone-and-let-it-run-the-country jurisprudence that had come to full flower late in the preceding century. Theodore Roosevelt with his trust-busting crusade against the "malefactors of great wealth," and Woodrow Wilson with his New Freedom reforms might occupy the White House in between McKinley and Taft and Harding and Coolidge; they might get their progressive programs enacted into law; they might even name a few Justices less property-minded and business-dedicated to the Supreme Court. But there were never enough such Justices on the Court at any one time to change significantly its spots or its decisions. As state and federal governments stepped up their legislative efforts to control snowballing wealth and financial power for the welfare of all their constituents, the Court stepped up its use of the stop-sign, "Unconstitutional"; more federal statutes were branded void during Holmes's Justiceship— most of the important ones over his dissent—than during the 112 preceding years of the Court's existence; state laws went down the judicial drain by the hundreds. And this quantitative quickening of pace in their urge to exercise their government supremacy revealed how far the Justices were lagging once more behind the political temper of most of the nation.

Holmes saw quite clearly how his intransigent associates were steering the country toward a sort of anarchy by judicial decree. Let a state try to curb the self-serving excesses of big-and-growing-bigger business in the interest of workers or customers—and hence at the ex-

pense of investors and entrepreneurs—and the Fourteenth
Amendment's due process clause would likely be flashed as
a red light to regulation, a green light to business. But
let the central government at Washington try the same
sort of curb on a nationwide scale, and the bulk of business,
judicially divorced from interstate commerce and hence
from all Congressional control, would suddenly become
the private and exclusive stamping-ground of *state* regulation, although such regulation was largely imaginary,
being forbidden by the Justices under the Fourteenth
Amendment. In this Court-created vacuum from almost all
government restriction, this open invitation to a money-
making mazurka, the kings and captains of industry and
finance moved with loose-limbed abandon all the way from
McKinley's "full dinner-pail" to Hoover's "two cars in
every garage." And should any skeptical spokesman for
those whose dinner-pails or garages somehow remained
empty raise his voice too high in protest, he might be
slapped in jail—for all his supposed civil liberties—with
the passive, or sometimes active, approval of the Justices.
Holmes, as politically conservative, as economically upper-
class, as any of his fellows, could coin out of his wisdom-
lighted-by-wit such *bon mots* as: "The Fourteenth Amendment does not enact Mr. Herbert Spencer's Social Statics."
He could make such subversive statements as: "I do not
think the United States would come to an end if we lost our
power to declare an Act of Congress void." Yet, a constant majority of his colleagues continued to vote him
down.

Those colleagues, when Holmes first came to the Court,
were feckless Chief Justice Fuller; hard-hitting John

Harlan, growing a little less liberal with age; Brewer and Peckham, the tough-minded twins of ultra-conservatism; verbose but able Edward D. White of Louisiana, former sugar-planter and U.S. Senator, who was later to be elevated to the Court Chiefship; and three onetime railroad lawyers (along with Fuller)—Henry Brown of Michigan, George Shiras of Pennsylvania, and Joseph McKenna of California—of whom Shiras remained undistinguished and still a railroad lawyer throughout his term on the bench, McKenna was to become a sporadic spokesman against vested property interests under Holmes's tutelage, and only Brown ever flashed with any judicial fire, as in his searing dissent against the income tax decision. When Holmes quit the bench in 1932, at the age of ninety-one, his teammates were Chief Justice Hughes and Hughes's fellow switch-hitter, Owen Roberts; the close-playing conservative infield of Van Devanter, McReynolds, Sutherland and Butler; and Holmes's two cronies in dissent, Brandeis and Stone. During his not quite thirty-year tenure, Holmes outlasted seven other Justices—including a Chief Justice, Taft—who were appointed after him. Thus twenty-three men shared at different times—on the bench, around the conference table, in chambers, or at home—the searching sweep and the clean thrust of his mind. Yet rarely did more than three of them at once, and usually only one or two, go along with Holmes on the big issues. For no more than any government group do most Justices bow to reason when politics points the other way.

The chronological story of the Court from 1902 to 1932 —while his colleagues were too regularly ignoring the sweet reason of Justice Holmes—can be quickly told. During the last eight years of Fuller's technical Chiefship, the Court remained a citadel of economic conservatism— so much so that one unusual liberal ruling, allowing a state to limit women's working time on factory jobs to ten hours a day despite the dear old due process clause, came as a shocking surprise. Then, after Fuller was succeeded in 1910 by White, the Louisianan with the "rodomontade writing style," and the first man ever promoted from Associate Justice to Chief, the Court relaxed for six or seven years its *laissez faire* rigidity (a paradox of phrase but not of fact) until America entered the first World War. That this comparatively liberal interlude almost precisely coincided with the first of Charles Evans Hughes's two terms of service on the high bench was not entirely coincidental; Hughes was then fresh from the New York governorship that he had won from William Randolph Hearst, largely as an electoral reward for his exposure of insurance frauds and rackets in his state; until he resigned his Justiceship in 1916 to seek—and almost win—the Presidency, the better balance of the Court was witnessed by the temporary wane in Holmes's significant dissents.

Back to reactionary regularity went the Court even before the war was over and the typical postwar period of do-nothing (except sit on civil liberties) normality had set in. At White's death in 1921, President Harding played it straight and safe by appointing William Howard Taft of Ohio and, more recently, Connecticut—who thus became unique in U.S. history as the only person who ever served the nation in its two top posts, President and Chief Justice.

Physically the biggest man who ever held either job, easy-going Taft could at least compete, on his dual record, for the smallest accomplishment in both. Presumably he preferred the Chief Justiceship; as President he had once burbled: "I love judges and I love courts. They are my ideals on earth of what we shall meet afterward in Heaven under a just God." But regardless of this beatific personal feeling on the part of its Chief, the Taft Court was so anachronistic in its attitude toward law and government that Holmes was again led to step up the tempo of his bubble-bursting dissents until Taft died in 1930. Then an older, less legally limber Hughes came back to the Court, this time as Chief Justice—after a long interval of lucrative corporation law practice and over the anti-confirmation protest of twenty-six Senators, led by Borah, La Follette, and Norris. Holmes gave vent to a couple of dissenting swan-songs (including his "hardly any limit but the sky" crack against judicial veto of state laws under the Fourteenth Amendment) and soon resigned.

The only Justices other than Taft and Hughes (on his first run) worth passing mention, who both came and went while Holmes was dignifying the Court he never headed, were four in number. William Rufus Day of Ohio, appointed right after Holmes, had been—in triply classic mold—a successful railroad lawyer, a personal friend of a President, and a lower court judge. The friendly President, McKinley, made Day his Secretary of State during the Spanish-American War, and it was Day who decently insisted that the Philippines be bought (for $20,000,000) instead of claimed by conquest; McKinley then put him on the federal bench and Theodore Roosevelt soon raised him to the highest Court; for twenty years as a Justice, Day unspectacularly displayed his business-grown-imperalist background, tempered, in occasional dissent, by personal decency. By contrast to Day and his *noblesse oblige mais reste noblesse* philosophy, there was Mahlon Pitney of New Jersey, who sat with Holmes for ten years and actually dissented, in his unpredictably discordant fashion, more often than Holmes. Earlier known as a stiffly logical anti-labor judge in his home state (the unions bitterly fought his confirmation), he carried to the Court a near-compulsion to have his old decisions in the field of labor law approved by his new and nationally powerful brethren. His success was such, despite a few deviational pro-labor votes (most of his dissents were on rather trivial matters), that he set, for years to come, a hold-them-down Court attitude toward unions—and so raised the issue whether past judicial experience is always an asset in a Justice if that Justice is mainly out to justify his own judicial past. There was also, during Holmes's long tenure, gentle Edward Sanford of Tennessee, so in tune with his genial Chief that Taft could practically cast two votes and that the two men died almost simultaneously. And there was John Clarke of Ohio, whose slight and more than slightly liberal Court service was self-terminated so that he could devote himself to what he deemed the more important cause of world peace—and who, fifteen years after his resignation, as the only ex-Justice then living, emerged briefly from obscurity to publicly support (to the hush-hushing horror of most of the press) Franklin Roosevelt's plan to "pack" the Supreme Court.

But the thirty-year story of the Court under Holmes's chidance can best be told neither in strict chronological sequence nor in the specific records of specific Justices (other than Holmes)—most of whom managed most of the time to read their business-minded bents into the Constitution whenever the chips were really down. The story can be more meaningfully told in terms of the three different kinds of cases where the Justices used constitutional words to have their own political way. And of the three kinds, first billing properly goes to the cases where the Court pushed judicial review to its farthest limit by killing—as always, more in sorrow than in anger—Acts of Congress.

Most momentous of these judge-made murders of national laws were five decisions, each of them centered on some effort by Congress to better the not too happy lot of workingmen—or of working women or children. A typical legal mouthful entitled the Federal Employers' Liability Act would have made a railroad pay for death or injury to a worker if caused by the railroad's carelessness. There was no socialistic innovation here, since many states had this sort of law on their books; but because the Act failed to specify that only *interstate* railroad workers were to be protected (Congress can only regulate interstate, not within-one-state, commerce) five Justices—with Holmes, of course, captaining the four dissenters—cut down the entire Act as an unconstitutional trespass by Congress on states' rights. That Congress soon passed another law, properly limited in its scope, which the Court upheld four years later, did not stop the railroads from saving millions of dollars in the meantime (that being the obvious purpose of their winning legal gamble)—nor did it do much good for the workers, or their families, who were wounded or killed in the interval between.

In the same year, 1908, when the Court overruled Congress on making the railroads pay for avoidable accidents to their employees, it also forbade Congress to help the railroad workers help themselves. Congress had made it a crime for a railroad to fire a worker for belonging to a union—or to hold a worker to a so-called "yellow-dog contract," in which the worker, anxious for a job, had promised not to join a union. Unconstitutional, said seven Justices—under *both* the interstate commerce clause (Congress was again treading on states'-rights toes) and the Fifth Amendment's due process clause (Congress was interfering with freedom of contract). Strangely, the Court's opinion was penned by that old human-welfare war-horse, Justice Harlan, then nearing the end of a life that began when Andrew Jackson was President, and perhaps unable to fit his old-fashioned agrarian brand of liberalism to the facts of a far more mechanized nation. But Harlan's only-eight-years-younger colleague, Holmes, wryly remonstrated in dissent that he thought labor unions for railway workers had as much to do with interstate commerce as did safety-couplers on trains (about which the Court had recently let Congress legislate). Said Holmes, with his devastating directness: "I quite agree that the question what and how much good labor unions do is one on which intelligent people may differ . . . but I could not pronounce it unwarranted if Congress should decide that to foster a strong union was for the best interest, not only of the men, but of the railroads and the country at large."

It was again in defense of that will-o'-the-wisp, freedom of contract, that the Court struck down, some years later, a Congressional statute setting minimum wages for women workers in the District of Columbia. This law had been supported, in Congress and before the Court, as protective not merely of female health but also of female morals. But five elderly Justices thought, with something less than gallantry, that "the ancient inequality of the sexes . . . has continued 'with diminishing intensity.' In view of the great—not to say revolutionary—changes which have taken place . . . in the contractual, political, and civil status of women, culminating in the Nineteenth Amendment, it is not unreasonable to say that these differences have now come almost, if not quite, to the vanishing point." Where a Frenchman might have remarked:— "*Vive les différences*," the Court's majority continued with unwonted worldliness: "The relation between earnings and morals is not capable of standardization. It cannot be shown that well paid women safeguard their morals more carefully than those who are poorly paid." To which Holmes, less concerned here with the unwisdom of women than with the constitutional unwisdom of his colleagues, tartly replied: "The end, to remove conditions leading to ill health, immorality and the deterioration of the race, no one would deny to be within the scope of constitutional legislation. . . . When so many intelligent persons, who have studied the matter more than any of us can, have thought that the means are effective and are worth the price, it seems to me impossible to deny that the belief *reasonably* may be held by *reasonable* men."

Considerably farther-reaching than its Court-killed attempts to protect railroad workers and Washington women were Congress's two tries at getting rid of child labor throughout the United States. On its first try, Congress simply and flatly forbade the shipment from one state to another of any goods made in a shop or factory where children worked; whereupon the Court—as so often, by a bare five-to-four vote—simply and flatly upheld the exploitation of youth for the sake of fatter profits, on the old excuse that Congress had no right, even under its control of interstate commerce, to interfere obliquely with the right of the states to control (or, more accurately, *not* control) the way goods were manufactured within their borders. A shocked Holmes expostulated in doubly grounded dissent: "But if there is any matter upon which civilized countries have agreed . . . it is the evil of premature and excessive child labor. I should have thought that if we were to introduce our own moral conceptions where in my opinion they do not belong, this was pre-eminently a case for upholding the exercise of all its powers by the United States. But I had thought that . . . this Court always had disavowed the right to intrude its judgment upon questions of policy or morals. It is not for this Court to pronounce when prohibition is necessary to regulation . . . as against the product of ruined lives."

Balked in its first effort to do away with child labor through its control of interstate commerce, Congress tried again—this time by using its power to tax. What it did was to impose on all goods made by the exploited youngsters a federal tax at so high a rate that it would no longer be profitable to employ children, even at the low wages they were usually paid. The gimmick of using the taxing power for something other than raising revenue had been resorted to by Congress before—as in clamping down on the dope racket with a stiff tax on narcotics, and in protecting easily gulled housewives (as well as dairy farmers) with a prohibitive tax on yellow oleomargarine. Moreover, the Court had given these tax tricks official benediction, though the Justices were thoroughly aware that Congress's intent had not been to pour money into the Treasury. Came the child-labor tax and the Court decided, all of a sudden, that taxes could be levied only for revenue, not for regulation in disguise—though a realist might reasonably charge the Justices with somewhat greater concern for the economic welfare of dairy farmers (who far outnumbered the oleomargarine men) than with the physical welfare of children. Not until a New Deal Court, almost twenty years later, upheld the New Deal's Fair Labor Standards Act did the all-powerful Justices permit the nation to move as a nation, toward eliminating the curse of child labor.

In other, less spectacular ways, the Court cut down Congress's taxing power where it was really being used for revenue—and always over Holmes's dissent. A series of 5–4 and 6–3 decisions shortened the reach of the federal estate and gift taxes, in cases where well-advised wealthy men had used lawyers' stratagems, fully foreseen and planned against by Congress, to hand on their fortunes tax-free. Another 5–4 decision—which still plagues the U.S. Treasury today and still determines the dividend policy of thousands of corporations—opened the door to immense, and now legal, avoidance of income taxes, when a company's profits are paid out to stockholders in new stock instead of in cash. (Grumbled Holmes: "I cannot doubt that most people not lawyers would suppose when they voted for [the Sixteenth Amendment] that they put a question like the present to rest.") And in practically all these tax-cutting cases, the Court's slim but stubborn majority could find no more substantial justification for saying "Thou shalt not" to Congress than the Fifth Amendment's now grotesquely bloated due process clause.

But the most flimsily founded of all the Court's anti-tax decisions—and also the one that most clearly revealed how human, and humanly greedy, Supreme Court Justices can be—was the ruling by seven members of the Court that Congress could not, under the Constitution, tax the salaries of federal judges, including of course their own. To reach this remarkable result (reversed by a less selfish set of Justices many years later) the Court had to hold that, by making a judge pay an income tax along with everyone else, Congress would be lowering the judge's salary—which the Constitution does forbid. Here Holmes, with Brandeis alone joining in his dissent, could see "no reason for exonerating him from the ordinary duties of a citizen, which he shares with all others. To require a man to pay the taxes that all other men have to pay cannot possibly be made an instrument to attack his independence as a judge. I see nothing in the purpose of this clause of the Constitution to indicate that the judges were to be a privileged class, free from bearing their share of the cost of the institutions upon which their well-being if not their life depends." And Holmes, as did Brandeis, voluntarily paid as long as he lived the income taxes that his colleagues had ruled he did not have to pay.

Not only by branding Congressional laws unconstitutional, but also by "interpreting" others into comparative innocuousness, did the Court, during Holmes's tenure, serve as bodyguard for wealth undisturbed and business unbridled. Thus the Sherman Anti-Trust Act, whose teeth had been mostly pulled in the previous century, was fitted, for show, with false teeth that turned out to have no bite. With great fanfare, the Justices stopped the merger of the Northern Pacific and Great Northern Railroads, and later broke up—in name though not in effective fact—the American Tobacco and Standard Oil monopolies. But by balking at the use of the Act's criminal penalties and by reading into the statute Justice White's pet "rule of reason"—whereby only such "restraints of trade" as the *Court* thought "unreasonable" were to be forbidden—the Justices actually invited the big industrial combinations to continue, just a touch more politely, on their lucrative way. Labor unions alone, when they tried to use group pressure on behalf of their members, were really restrained from "restraining trade," with the Court's hearty approval.

When Congress, in Woodrow Wilson's time, added the Clayton Act to the government's legal armory against business abuses—and set up the Federal Trade Commission to stop such shameless shenanigans as secret price-fixing by supposed competitors, price-cutting to drive small rivals bankrupt, and the deliberate misleading of the public with false branding or false advertising—the Justices gaily began to "interpret" the new Clayton Act down to the defanged feebleness of the old Sherman Act.

Said the Court in one important case, overturning an F.T.C. ruling and telling the Commission bluntly who was boss: "The words 'unfair methods of competition' are not defined by the statute, and their exact meaning is in dispute. It is for the courts, not the commission, ultimately to determine as a matter of law what they include. . . . The Act was certainly not intended to fetter free and fair competition as commonly understood and practiced by honorable opponents in trade." (In fact, the Act had been precisely "intended to fetter" many of the dog-eat-dog practices considered both "fair" and "honorable" by business in its free-for-all fight for profits.)

But when the Commission turned from trying to protect little dogs from big dogs, and tried instead to protect the sheep-like buying public from all the pack—as Congress also clearly intended—the Justices suddenly saw the Clayton Act as meant only to keep competing businesses from unduly hurting each other, no matter how the public might be fleeced. Thus, in the classic Raladam case, where the Federal Trade Commission had ordered a patent medicine concern to quit fooling the fat with faked-up claims in its get-thin-quick advertising, the Court threw out the Commission's order—and actually did it on the ground that *all* "obesity remedies" were plugged with phony advertising, and hence none of the firm's competitors could be unfairly hurt. (Presumably, the Act was "not intended to fetter free and fair competition" between *dis*honorable "opponents in trade," either.) Just as under the Sherman Act, the only real losers under the Clayton Act as the Court read it (except, of course, the whole consuming public) were the labor unions, who saw an entire section of the new law—put in for the sole purpose of protecting peaceful union activities from the over-eagerly antipathetic orders of federal judges—"interpreted" to nothingness, with Taft, in sorry-but-this-won't-hurt-too-much manner, performing in person the major judicial operation.

As with the new Federal Trade Commission, so with the old Interstate Commerce Commission, especially when regulation of railroad rates was in the wind; Holmes's colleagues, determined to have their own economic and political views prevail, insisted on overseeing and often overruling the judgments of the technical experts to whom Congress had entrusted jobs requiring specialized knowledge; marketing or mechanical engineering, statistics or cost-accounting, whatever the field, the Justices thought they knew most and best. From the fruit of this assumed omniscience, Holmes frequently dissented; but his heart was less with these "interpretation" questions, for all their sometimes great significance, than with the constitutional cases where power of Court met power of legislature head-on. No less than when judicial autocracy was aimed at Congress did Holmes's voice ring in resonant protest when the solemn acts of state legislatures were treated cavalierly by his Court. And here it had the chance to ring more often.

To list in full the scores of instances when Holmes, with the patient persistence of water dripping on rock, repeated and rephrased and repeated his steady dissent, against his colleagues' misuse of the Fourteenth Amendment to veto state laws that they happened to disapprove, would be to elaborate—as Holmes was forced to—the obvious. Those laws ranged from a Nebraska statute fixing a standard weight for loaves of bread (to protect both buyers and honest bakers) to a Kansas statute setting up an "Industrial Court" to deal peacefully with wage and price disputes in vital industries, from a New Jersey regulation of the scandalous fees charged by employment agencies to a Wisconsin tax to stop the wealthy from giving their fortunes away tax-free just before they died. And the regular ritual for overriding some legislature's will was the magisterial mouthing of those magic words: ". . . deprived of property—or of liberty of contract—without due process of law."

Not that every state tax or regulation brought before the Court was ushered to "unconstitutional" oblivion; the due process plea was not quite an automatic ticket to freedom from any tax and from all restraint. During the Court's comparatively tolerant interlude—which ran from around the end of Fuller's Chiefship up to the nation's entrance into World War I—two important Oregon statutes limiting hours of labor, first for women, then for men, were upheld, albeit over strenuous conservative dissent. In a later case, which significantly did not involve business interests, Holmes himself spoke for the Court in permitting a state to sterilize congenital idiots—and remarked with some relish: "Three generations of imbeciles are enough." But the bulk of the state laws that ran the Fourteenth Amendment's gauntlet dealt with trivial matters or else forbade such obviously evil business practices as cheating coal miners by underweighing the coal they mined in a day.

Moreover, it is worth recalling here that the Court's power in constitutional cases is basically only the power to say No; when the Court says Yes—in Fourteenth Amendment cases or elsewhere—that fact is noteworthy only because it *might* have said No; for, beyond this, its saying Yes amounts to no more than letting the affirmative branches of government govern. Hence the many instances when Holmes's colleagues did *not* strike down state laws deserve little mention—except as the Justices might have been expected to say No, or came close to saying it. They came close in a couple of cases challenging the due-process propriety of laws passed by two Western states, Washington and Arizona, which set up slightly *avant-garde* schemes to make employers help pay for injuries to their employees; both schemes were upheld by five to four.

And the Arizona case is also notable because one of the due-process dissenters here gave expression, far more frank than discreet, to the kind of sentiments that so often swung a Court majority to their support—and so often elicited dissent, in somewhat less emotional vein, from Holmes. Said Justice McReynolds: "In the last analysis it is for us to determine what is arbitrary or oppressive upon consideration of the natural and inherent principles of practical justice which lie at the base of our traditional jurisprudence and inspirit our Constitution. . . . Until now I had supposed that a man's liberty and property—with their essential incidents—were under the protection of our charter and not subordinate to whims or caprices or fanciful ideas of those who happen for the day to constitute the legislative majority. The contrary doctrine is revolutionary and leads straight toward destruction of our well-tried and successful system of government." It was about nothing more than a rather routine but better-than-most "employers' liability act"—be it remembered—that McReynolds waxed so emotional.

By contrast to this sort of near-psychopathic concern for profits at any cost, including the cost of human limbs or lives (McReynolds and the rest never thought or suggested that "legislative majorities," however transient, should shut up their lawmaking shops entirely), came the cool and conservative clarity of Holmes. And four of his dissents against the due process doings of the Peckham-Pitney-McReynolds clan cry for special mention, and for quotation beyond what has earlier been quoted. Each appeared in a key case of considerable moment.

Holmes had been on the Court less than three years when a New York statute, limiting bakers' work-days to ten hours, came up for review in the Lochner case as the first real test of maximum-hour laws. For the Court's majority, Peckham, straight-faced, defended the constitutional right of bakery *employees* to work as many hours as *they* might choose—and listed, among the imaginary horrors that might ensue from upholding the statute, some future law "prohibiting lawyers' . . . clerks . . . to labor for their employers more than eight hours a day." Retorted Holmes: "This case is decided upon an economic theory which a large part of the country does not entertain. . . . It is settled by various decisions of this court that state constitutions and state laws may regulate life in many ways. . . . Some of these laws embody convictions or prejudices which judges are likely to share. Some may

not. But a constitution . . . is made for people of funda-
mentally differing views, and the accident of our finding
certain opinions natural and familiar or novel and even
shocking ought not to conclude our judgment upon the
question whether statutes embodying them conflict with
the Constitution of the United States."

In another test case, ten years later, Holmes tore into
his colleagues' veto of a state law, which protected the
right of all workers to join unions in much the same manner
as had the previously Court-vetoed federal statute for
railroad workers: "In present conditions a workman may
not unnaturally believe that only by belonging to a union
can he secure a contract that shall be fair to him. . . . If
that belief, whether right or wrong, may be held by a
reasonable man, it seems to me that it may be enforced by
law in order to establish the equality of position . . . in
which liberty of contract begins. Whether in the long run
it is wise for the working men to enact legislation of this
sort is not my concern, but I am strongly of opinion that
there is nothing in the Constitution of the United States to
prevent it. . . ."

As unions flourished despite the Court's efforts to help
business hamper their growth, business began to appeal
to local judges to prohibit such union activities as strikes
and picketing. Local judges, largely business-minded, com-
plied by issuing those peremptory court orders, called injunctions, which in effect commanded, as some parents do
their children: "Whatever you're doing, don't"—and the
price of disobedience was jail. The unions, in turn, went to
state legislatures to get laws passed which curbed the anti-
labor use of injunctions; and business, in its turn, went of

course to the Supreme Court to get these laws declared unconstitutional. In the first and definitive case, Holmes cut, as customary, to the heart of the matter: "The dangers of a delusive exactness in the application of the Fourteenth Amendment have been adverted to before now. . . . By calling a business 'property' you make it seem like land and lead up to the conclusion that a statute cannot substantially cut down the advantages of ownership existing before the statute was passed. . . . But you cannot give [a business] definiteness of contour by calling it a thing. It is a course of conduct. . . ." And then: "Legislation may begin where an evil begins. If, as many intelligent people believe, there is more danger that the injunction will be abused in labor cases than elsewhere, I can feel no doubt of the power of the legislature to deny it. . . ." It goes without saying that Holmes was speaking in dissent.

Though the major Fourteenth Amendment dissents, like the most important protests against judicial veto of federal laws, came in cases dealing with workers' rights, Holmes could be just as trenchant when other types of state statutes were struck down. Toward the end of his career on the Court, his brethren, still worrying the word-stuff of "state police power" and of businesses marked by "public interest" or "public use," rejected a New York statute aimed at Broadway ticket-scalpers. It seemed to Holmes that "theatres are as much devoted to public use as anything well can be." And this despite his regret that: "We have not that respect for art that is one of the glories of France." Beyond this personal touch, however, Holmes keelhauled his colleagues for their niggling manner of decision, even regardless of result: "We fear to grant power and are unwilling to recognize it when it exists . . . and when legislatures are held to be authorized to do anything considerably affecting public welfare it is covered by apologetic phrases like the police power, or the statement that the business concerned has been dedicated to a public use. . . . I do not believe in such apologies. I think the proper course is to recognize that a state legislature can do whatever it sees fit to do unless it is restrained by some express prohibition in the Constitution of the United States or of the State, and that Courts should be careful not to extend such prohibitions beyond their obvious meaning by reading into them conceptions of public policy that the particular Court may happen to entertain."

So strong was Holmes's belief in leaving legislatures alone that he once took a stand in their defense which many people consider his most illiberal view and vote. The problem was a tough one, for it pitted state-freedom-to-legislate-without-judicial-veto against a civil liberty of a sort—and hence was not only a due-process question but also one of the third major kind of case that the Court dealt with while Holmes was a Justice. In the anti-German hysteria during and after the first World War (which spawned such absurdities as calling German measles "liberty measles"), a few Midwestern states—where many recently emigrated German families lived—had banned the teaching of German in their grade-schools. When the Court declared these Philistine statutes unconstitutional, as offending the Fourteenth Amendment, Holmes—who would have thundered, as lawmaker, against these inroads on common culture—registered troubled dissent. His dissent was doubtless the more troubled by reason of the fact that McReynolds, scarcely a champion of human rights, was this time the Court's chief spokesman.

But where more important infringements of more clear-cut civil liberties were attempted by governments—national, state, or local—Holmes was almost always found on the side of the angels. He dissented against the Court's refusal to save, by a habeas corpus writ, a radical Northern Jew who had obviously been framed for a murder rap and then convicted by an anti-Semitic lynch jury in the South. (Novels have since been written about the case of Leo Frank.) In defense of a free press, he dissented against the Court's pat-on-the-head for a lower federal judge, who had held a Toledo newspaper in contempt of court because it dared to criticize that judge's own decisions; here, Chief Justice White, with his usual grave longiloquence, saw the "safeguarding and fructification of free and constitutional institutions" as "the very basis and mainstay on which the freedom of the press rests" and so declined to grant the defendant newspaper "the right virtually to destroy such institutions"; to which Holmes replied: "A judge of the United States is expected to be a man of ordinary firmness of character. . . . I confess I cannot find . . . in the evidence in the case anything that would have affected a mind of reasonable fortitude."

Holmes also dissented when a bare majority of his brethren, in three of the silliest rulings the Court ever handed down, barred from U.S. citizenship a well-known woman pacifist (Rosika Schwimmer), a minister who had

been a chaplain in World War I, and a religiously conscientious woman who had served as a nurse in World
War I—because none of the three would take an unqualified
oath to bear arms in any future war. Said Holmes, in one
of these cases: "I would suggest that the Quakers have
done their share to make the country what it is, that many
citizens agree with the applicant's belief, and that I had
not supposed hitherto that we regretted our inability to
expel them because they believe more than some of us do
in the teachings of the Sermon on the Mount."

Again, Holmes dissented on a point even more important today than it was then—the question whether a man
can be convicted of federal crime on evidence obtained by
wire-tapping, despite the Constitution's guarantee of "the
right of the people to be secure in their persons, houses,
papers, and effects [*there were no such things as telephones
when those words were written*], against unreasonable
searches and seizures." In 1928, it was big-time boot-
leggers, not Communist stooges or sympathizers, that the
wire-tapping feds were after—and a five-man Court
majority gave the wire-tappers the nod, with Taft doing
the talking as he read into the Fourth Amendment an
eighteenth-century literalness. ("There was no searching.
There was no seizure. The evidence was secured by the
sense of hearing. . . .") Holmes felt otherwise: "It is
desirable that criminals should be detected, and to that
end all available evidence should be used. It also is
desirable that the Government should not itself foster and
pay for other crimes. . . . We have to choose, and for my
part I think it a less evil that some criminals should escape

than that the Government should play an ignoble part."
Wire-tapping, said Holmes, was "dirty business"—but
he said it in dissent.

Yet, most crucial of all the civil liberties, in Holmes's
time and long before and since, is freedom of speech—or,
more pointedly, the right of every man to speak his mind
on political matters without being punished by some
government that dislikes what he has to say. Along with
majority rule, and here restricting majority rule, the
government ban against *government* action to shut men's
mouths or minds is one of the cornerstones, the *sine qua
nons*, of the system of government commonly called
"democracy." Outside such totalitarian states as the
Fascist and Communist countries, freedom of speech today
is taken for granted—up to a point; no U.S. Republican
seriously tries to stop or censor Democratic criticism, nor
vice versa; only against the extremists, labeled "dangerous," "destructive," "subversive"—against the Jacobins of 1798 or the Copperheads of 1863 or the anarchists
of 1918 or the Communists of today—do American laws
get passed, on any level of government, that do, in fact,
limit freedom of speech. Yet it is precisely in protecting
the expression of all views, however extreme or unpopular
and no matter how much it may hurt to protect them, that
freedom of speech has a more than mushy meaning. This
nation would not have become a nation had laws against
"dangerous" or "subversive" talk been enforced by the
local henchmen of a British king.

Hence, the eighteenth-century revolutionaries who
wrote the Constitution flatly banned, without one iota of
qualification, any Congressional law "abridging freedom

of speech." But, strange as it may seem, there is not one word in the U.S. Constitution, as written then or as since amended, which says that state or local governments may not abridge freedom of speech. Between these two constitutional extremes, the Court has taken, all on its own, a middle way—allowing Congress, despite the ban, to restrict some freedom of speech, and often forbidding the states to restrict it, despite the absence of any ban. Both these anti-constitutional trends, these clear examples of lawmaking by judges, came to a head during Holmes's tenure—and in both of them Holmes himself played a major part.

Judicial protection of freedom of speech against state laws actually had its source in a decision dealing with freedom of the press (though the two freedoms are political Siamese twins) and *not* protecting it. A New York Communist named Gitlow had published a pamphlet, full of the customary canned exhortations that the "proletariat" throw off their "bonds"—and had been convicted, during the Red scare that followed World War I, of violating New York's "Criminal Anarchy Act." The Supreme Court upheld the conviction despite Holmes's daring riposte in dissent: "If in the long run the beliefs expressed in proletarian dictatorship are destined to be accepted by the dominant forces of the community, the only meaning of free speech is that they should be given their chance and have their way." But the majority Justices, while not here agreeing with Holmes's vote, did express general agreement with his constitutional view when they said: "We may and do assume that freedom of speech and of the press . . . are among the fundamental personal rights and 'liberties' protected by the due process clause of the Fourteenth Amendment from impairment by the States." Approve or disapprove, this judicial use of the due process clause to protect *human* rights (and it has since been so used many times) was just as unwarranted by the words of the Constitution as was its earlier and far more abundant use to protect *property* rights. To read "liberty of speech" into the Fourteenth Amendment's "liberty" is quite as far-fetched a play on words as to read in "liberty of contract." And it is a mark of Holmes's humanity that, even at the expense of constitutional consistency, he encouraged the one after long deploring the other.

It was not humanity, however, that caused Holmes to join—and even to lead—his fellow Justices in diluting the strong, straight stuff of the First Amendment, with its absolute ban on Congressional meddling with freedom of speech. Holmes's motive here was presumably a compromising realism, which the test of time has revealed as a touch misguided. Indeed, Holmes's famous formula—allowing free speech to be abridged in the face of a "clear and present danger"—was perhaps his greatest, and only major, judicial error. The pat phrase was first used in a case where an anti-war extremist, who had urged that young men dodge the draft, was jailed for thus committing a federal crime. Holmes went along with the whole Court in upholding the conviction, despite the First Amendment—and may well have done so in order to write the opinion himself and make its grounds as narrow as possible. What Holmes said was: "The question in every case is whether the words used are used in such circumstances and are of such a nature as to create a clear and present danger that they will bring about the substantive evils that Congress has a right to prevent. It is a question of proximity and degree." (It was no such question to the authors of the First Amendment.) "When a nation is at war," Holmes continued—ignoring an earlier Court's words in the Milligan case, after an earlier war where Holmes was fighting, not judging—"many things that might be said in times of peace are such a hindrance to its effort that their utterance will not be endured so long as men fight and that no court could regard them as protected by any constitutional right."

Little more than a year later, Holmes himself had cause to regret the "clear and present danger"excuse for letting Congress curb freedom of speech, which he had handed his colleagues on the platter of his eloquence. Five ignorant Russian-born pacifists had tossed, off a New York City roof, a few leaflets reprinting the hackneyed phrases of Communist propaganda; the war, at that time, was not quite over; all five, including a girl, were convicted under the federal Espionage Act; three got the maximum sentence. Said Holmes, in deeply disturbed dissent (which also included his "best test of truth" creed): "In this case sentences of twenty years imprisonment have been imposed for the publishing of two leaflets that I believe the defendants had as much right to publish as the Government has to publish the Constitution of the United States now vainly invoked by them. . . . I think that we should be eternally vigilant against attempts to check the expression of opinions that we loathe and believe to be fraught with death, unless they so imminently threaten immediate interference with the lawful and pressing purposes of the law that an immediate check is required to save the country." But the "unless" was too much and the warning came too late. Future Courts would continue to widen the clear-and-present-danger breach in the wall of the First Amendment—and to give their free-speech-sapping operations the protective cover of the words of Holmes.

For Holmes was a legend—and his words were like scripture—long before he died. When he quit the Court in 1932, the nation was at the economic ebb of boom-turned-to-bust-turned-to-depression—and for the bread-lines and the apple salesmen, Holmes's brethren, with their business-blinkered faith in enterprise kept free from government control, were not entirely unresponsible. They had heard Holmes and—except when he sometimes talked to their taste—had politely or rudely overridden him. But a rising generation of lawyers, judges, plain politicians, had heard Holmes too—and had listened. This new generation took over the executive and legislative branches of the national government when Franklin Roosevelt went to the White House, the year after Holmes resigned. It required several more years, and a constitutional crisis, before the ever-lagging Supreme Court adjusted its judicial sights to the realities around it and to the prophetic views of Holmes.

Twenty years before the New Deal came in, Holmes had written of the Court: "We are very quiet there, but it is the quiet of a storm center. . . ." It was still the quiet of a storm center in 1933. But the time when the storm was to move off-center and hit the Court in the fullness of its fury was not far away.

CHAPTER 7

The Court Collides with the New Deal and Wins the Battle by Defaulting the War

IF MARBURY v. MADISON was the most important decision in Supreme Court history and the Dred Scott case the most famous or infamous, if 1895 with its trio of triumphs over Congress was the Court's biggest year from the standpoint of blatant judicial supremacy, still the most important and famous and exciting short-span period in the annals of the high tribunal, to date, was the three-year stretch from early 1935 through 1937 when the Justices clashed, head-on and eyes wide open, with Franklin Roosevelt's New Deal. Strong Presidents—Jefferson,

Jackson, Lincoln—had fought the Court or been fought by
the Court long before FDR was born; Jefferson in a major
way and Jackson in a minor way had been licked by mighty
John Marshall; Lincoln had been forced to resort to war to
undo what Taney's Court had done in time of peace. But
it was a single and immediately insignificant decision that
marked Marshall's major victory over Jefferson; it was a
few rulings on the faraway periphery of federal politics
that let Jackson know the judiciary was boss; it was an
edict issued before he ever took over the reins of government that led to Lincoln's battle with the men in black
robes. Never before Franklin Roosevelt's time had the
Court taken almost the entire governmental program of a
contemporary President plus his (the pronoun is accurate)
Congress and vetoed it law by law—as the Justices did with
the first New Deal. Never before had a President taken up
the challenge of a judiciary determined to dominate the
other two branches of national government and countered
it by peaceful political means—as did FDR with his
"Court-packing" plan. Never before had the proper place
of the Court in the constitutional scheme been so hotly and
ubiquitously debated, from tabloid headlines to subway
strap-hangers, as it became, first in the election campaign
of 1936, later and even more intensely after the President
sprang his plan on a taken-by-surprise nation. And it is a
tribute to the toughness and resiliency of American democracy that, in different senses, both the Court and the
President won.

To catch in retrospect the full significance of the most
acute constitutional crisis in the life of the nation as a
nation—the crisis that led an airplane-age President to

accuse the Court of a "horse-and-buggy" view of the Constitution and led one Justice, speaking for four, to exclaim, extemporaneously yet *ex cathedra*, "The Constitution is gone"—it is necessary first to recapture a touch of the mood of immediate urgency, of desperation barely buoyed by hope, that pervaded the U.S. people between Roosevelt's election and the first frantic Hundred Days of his incumbency, when the most pressing measures of the New Deal were hurried into law. History has already begun to record Franklin Roosevelt as primarily a war President. Recollection of what he did on the home front during his almost nine non-war years in the White House has already begun to fade into an oversimplified black-or-white, for-or-agin formula—into the adulatory poor folk of Harold Rome's song, "Franklin D. Roosevelt Jones," against the bitterly angry rich folk of Peter Arno's cartoon, "Let's all go down to the Trans-Lux and hiss Roosevelt." Largely forgotten is the well-nigh unanimous national sense of supplication for relief by a strong savior that greeted and cheered FDR in the otherwise dark days of early 1933; largely forgotten too is the frightened confusion that gripped the nation—as it never did on that December Sunday when the Japanese attacked Pearl Harbor—during the months before Roosevelt took the oath of office.

Those were the months of mounting unemployment, made visible on every street corner, for all of Herbert Hoover's whistling-in-the-wind assurances that prosperity lay just around it; those were the months of bank failures and business collapses, of barbers and brokers alike losing their life savings invested in Wall Street on margin, of farmers losing their farms although farm mortgages were

selling at less than ten cents on the dollar; those were the
months when the American bubble-dream of every-man-a-
millionaire turned into nightmare, and even businessmen,
their infallibility lying in fragments at their feet, were
begging, like a dying man who turns to God, for the
government intervention in industry and finance which
they had hated and successfully resisted for over fifty years.
They got it, close to the instant FDR was inaugurated;
starting with the immediate executive declaration of a bank
holiday to stop runs on banks, emergency regulations and
far-reaching laws dealing with every phase of the U.S.
economy were rushed through the Administration hopper;
and from the National Industrial Recovery Act, or NIRA,
on down, the onetime wizards of free enterprise applauded
and co-operated with the profusion of new federal agencies
to regulate and plan and direct—which less than a year
later, with catastrophe averted, would be damned by the
same free enterprisers as "alphabet soup." Aloof and remote from all this hoopla and hurly-burly, the Justices of
the Supreme Court read their newspapers and waited.

They knew, did the Justices, that soon or late these new-
fangled government innovations, these NIRA's and AAA's
and TVA's, these products of the pooled brains of bright-
eyed young lawyers and economists and college professors,
would come before the Court for final judgment. They
knew that the spate of non-political unanimity in support
of the President, bred as it was of sudden deliverance from
confusion and fear, could scarcely be so unanimous or ever-
lasting that nobody would take to the law and toss the
Constitution at the New Deal. They knew the continuing
truth of what Tocqueville had said almost a century be-

fore: "Hardly any political question arises in the United States that is not resolved sooner or later into a judicial question." And the oncoming conflict between Supreme Court and New Deal makes little sense on any but a flat, two-dimensional legal level without some picture of each of these eight survivors and one successor of Justice Holmes, who came to be christened the Nine Old Men.

Reading roughly and perhaps a bit perversely from right to left, just as their decisions were to read, first billing naturally goes to Van Devanter, McReynolds, Sutherland, and Butler (though not necessarily in that order, which was the order of their appointment), whom New Dealers were soon to dub the Four Horsemen of Reaction, and who followed the narrow-gauge, anti-government *constitutional* slant of Thomas Jefferson, whose *political* purposes they would have loathed, instead of the broad-interpretation slant of Alexander Hamilton, whose politics they would have embraced. The paradox, be it remembered, is a paradox of words alone; the constitutional theories of all politicians, including Supreme Court Justices, are no more than high-faluting ways of arguing for the political ends they are really after; in Hamilton's and Jefferson's time, the new federal government—whose "powers" under the Constitution can be argued to be broad or narrow—was pretty largely run by the same kind of "economic royalist" against whom much of the Roosevelt New Deal was aimed. It was their basic and bone-deep Hamiltonian empathy with the well-to-do that dictated the Jeffersonian constitutional talk of the Court's Four Horsemen.

Willis Van Devanter of Wyoming, dean of the Nine Old Men in length of service, had been an astute attorney for the Union Pacific Railroad, a chairman of his Republican State Committee, an Assistant U.S. Attorney-General (where he handled matters involving the Union Pacific—and always gently) and a federal circuit judge (where he decided cases involving the Union Pacific—and in the railroad's favor) when Taft named him to the Court in 1910. For all his frontier roots, a rather reserved and timid aristocrat with the technical-fine-point mind of a lawyer's lawyer, his contribution to the Court's work was largely oral, for a rare neurosis made the physical act of writing so difficult for him that he managed to turn out only three or four opinions a year during his twenty-seven years as a Justice. But his vote could almost always be counted beforehand on the conservative or corporation side, especially when a railroad or other public utility was a litigant, and he even remained active, behind the scenes, in Wyoming Republican politics for many years after he joined the Court.

Unlike the urbane Van Devanter, James McReynolds —whom Woodrow Wilson had side-doored onto the Court after a cantankerous year as Attorney-General—was a rough-cut Democrat from a small Tennessee town. His career had alternated, almost schizophrenically, between a lucrative law practice, both in Tennessee and in lower Manhattan, and some stints of trust-busting for the federal government. Although as an anti-trust attorney he had once called the American Tobacco Company a gang of "commercial wolves and highwaymen" (an outburst laid by some to the personal abhorrence of tobacco which led him to forbid all smoking in his presence), the anti-government part of his personality took full control soon after he reached the Court; for some years a lazy judicial work-man whose opinions were largely copied from lawyers' briefs, he became the New Deal's most vocal and violent Court opponent, and it was he who expostulated from the bench, after an early pro-New Deal holding (in the "gold clause" case) that the Constitution was gone. A crusty lifelong bachelor, whose intense and narrow prejudices led him to snub first Brandeis, then Cardozo, because they were Jews, he carried his bluster and bluntness over from personal to official matters so that his impatience with the polite legalisms of his three comrades-in-ultra-conserva-tism unwittingly gave a substance and a reality to the Court majority's stubborn resistance to Rooseveltian re-forms.

Ablest and hardest-working of the Four Horsemen was George Sutherland of Utah, a master at the lawyerly use of precedent and logic to paint a smooth-surfaced veri-similitude of unanswerable argument in defense of deci-sions actually arrived at for less lofty and more mortal reasons. Like Van Devanter, Sutherland, though born in England, had grown up with his Western territory-turned-state and had mingled politics with corporation law to become one of the top bosses of the new state's Republican machine. Repudiated at the polls after two terms as U.S. Senator—in which post his party regularity plus his soft-spoken scholarly manner had immeasurably impressed his heartier colleague, Warren Harding—the trim-bearded ex-Senator moved from a major brain-trusting job in Harding's 1920 "front-porch campaign" to become "the Colonel House of the Harding Administration," and thence to a Supreme Court Justiceship, courtesy of Harding, in

1922. Any doubts about how he would some day react to the New Deal could have been set at rest by reference to a typically mild-tempered sentence from one of his Senate speeches: "It is not strange that, in the universal fever of haste, government itself should be swept by this mad spirit of impatience which has given rise to this . . . demand that we shall abandon the methodical habits of the past and go careering after novel and untried things."

Fourth of the Horsemen, and least intellectually gifted of the Nine Old Men, was Pierce Butler of Minnesota, the farm boy become millionaire by his monolithic legal services to the Great Northern, Northern Pacific, and Chicago, Burlington & Quincy Railroads—whom Harding appointed as a second-rate successor, of sorts, to far abler Justice White, when he was pressed to put another Catholic on the Court after he had named Protestant Taft to White's place. Like so many risers from rags to riches, big, bull-headed Butler had an almost religious devotion to the status quo, and especially to the railroads; he was an expert at only one thing—the complicated accounting involved in figuring out railroad values and railroad rates—and his expertness was single-mindedly onesided. Confirmed by the Senate only after he had solemnly pledged that he would not sit in railroad rate cases, he got around his pledge by actually writing the Court's opinions in two major rate cases (dealing with water companies) which he knew would set a clear precedent for railroad cases to come; nor did he disqualify himself when railroad taxes, not rates, came before the Court—even though, in one big tax case, the railroad was his old client, the Great Northern (and Butler, of course, voted to cut the tax).

His attitude toward scholarship and civil liberties had been presaged when, as ruling regent of the University of Minnesota, he had engineered the firing of three professors because of their liberal views. The whole New Deal could not but prove anathema to his Philistine philosophy of politics and law.

These, then, were the four men, haphazardly appointed by three different Presidents for politically or personally opportune reasons, who were destined to dominate, anywhere from twelve to twenty-five years after their separate appointments, the government of the United States. These were the men, all products of earlier political ages, three of them over seventy years old (and the fourth, Butler, sixty-seven) when Franklin Roosevelt was inaugurated, who held the power to say No to the President, the Congress, and the overwhelming majority of the nation at a time of crucial crisis. To do so, they needed only one more judicial recruit to the cause of reaction-in-the-name-of-the-Constitution—and they found him, until he turned coat on them two long years after he joined them, in Owen Roberts of Pennsylvania.

Roberts is the perfect personification of the chanciness of government by judges. It was he who, during a Court career from 1930 to 1945, changed his mind and his major votes three separate times—from liberal to conservative to liberal to conservative—on the bed-rock issue of government power to regulate business; it was he who, by holding the decisive Court vote in the first three stages of his switch act, was for years the most powerful person in the United States; (and it was he who, with unintended irony, in the light of his own record, damned the law-

changing decisions of his New Deal brethren as comparable
to "a restricted railroad ticket good for this day and train
only," shortly before he resigned). More than this, it was
chance that made Roberts a Justice and gave him the
extraordinary power he held over 150 million fellow citizens. President Hoover had named federal Judge John
Parker to replace Justice Sanford; the Senate's liberals had
succeeded in defeating Parker's confirmation—the only
such Senate action this century—because of a Negro-
slurring speech he had once made and a routine labor injunction he had once issued; that they were misguided in
blocking Parker was subsequently proved by Parker's out-
standingly liberal judicial record for more than a quarter
of a century after. The same Senators had then nodded
Roberts onto the Court, looking mainly at his doggedly
able prosecution, for the government, of the Teapot Dome
oil scandal cases that had wrecked the reputation of Warren Harding. What they had overlooked about the ambitious plugger, who was right-wing-Republican Senator
George Wharton Pepper's protégé, was the rest of his
respectably eye-on-the-main-chance career as a conventional corporation lawyer with clients ranging from the
Pennsylvania Railroad to the Philadelphia affiliate of J. P.
Morgan & Co. Also overlooked was a speech of a few
years before in which Roberts had said: "The business man
in America today feels that he is doing business with a
minion of government looking over his shoulder with an
upraised arm and a threatening scowl. . . . Are we to go
into a state of socialism, or are you men, and men like
you, prepared to get out, take off your coats, and root for
good old-fashioned Anglo-Saxon individualism?"

Along with Roberts, whose basically pro-business bent of mind was cannily camouflaged by two tentative stretches of flirtation with his less old-fashioned-Anglo-Saxon-individualist fellows, the Chief of the Nine Old Men, Charles Evans Hughes, is regularly catalogued by legal historians as having shared the balance of power between the liberal and conservative wings of the Court that sat intact through the first four years of the New Deal. What the Court records prove is that Hughes held no such power at all. True, his votes did veer, as did Roberts's, from one side to the other; but never once in a major case did he cast the deciding vote; for never once in a major case was Hughes to the right of Roberts. Thus, with five brethren to right of him and three clearly to left, Hughes could only choose whether a conservative decision should be scored 5–4 or 6–3; he could never determine that a decision be liberal unless Roberts, the Court's swinging keystone, came along. Proof of this lies in the simple fact that Hughes dissented several times—and always on the liberal side— in the big cases that came up during that drastic age, whereas Roberts never dissented once. It was Roberts who, for practical purposes, steered the Court that Hughes headed, whenever the Justices called them close.

This so-near-yet-so-far futility in just failing to capture power was, of course, no new experience to Hughes. The slight, shy bookworm of a boy with a rigid Baptist background, who had lifted himself, by the strength of his mind, to the governorship of New York and thence through six stunningly liberal years at Holmes's side on the Supreme Court, had missed the Presidency of the U.S. in 1916 by the bare margin of 4,000 votes in one state, California. Obviously embittered, he had left public service to make a fortune in the practice of corporation law, then gone back to government as able Secretary of State under Harding and Coolidge, and again returned to the arguing of cases for a wealth of wealthy business clients, before the bench he had once sat on, at the remarkable rate of more than ten a year. Re-appointed to the Court as Chief Justice by Hoover in 1930, just twenty years after his appointment by Taft, he was now an austere, white-bearded figure, seeming taller than his medium height because of his stately carriage—and he was again somewhat embittered, this time by the slurs on his probable future judicial integrity cast by the twenty-six insurgent Senators who opposed his confirmation because of the character of his recent clients. In between his two Justiceships, Hughes had written a book on the Supreme Court, in which he had deplored his predecessors' lack of statesmanlike sagacity in the Dred Scott case, in the legal tender cases, and in the income tax decision of 1895; he was soon to be faced himself with an opportunity and an obligation of judicial statesmanship such as had never confronted the Court in all its long past history.

To join in judicial statesmanship at a time of national crisis, Hughes could scarcely look to any of the colleagues on his ideological right; the quixotically turn-back-the-clock quartet would give no inch in their creeds or convictions, come depression, panic, or possible constitutional revolution; vacillating Roberts might be persuaded or pressured if things got uncomfortably hot, but he lacked the fortitude to help lead. For assistance of this sort, for vision and wisdom, Hughes would have to look to his left, to the three great Justices who were carrying on, as immediate heirs, the Holmes tradition—Brandeis, Stone, and Cardozo.

Newcomer to the Court, though no newcomer to the job of judging, was Benjamin Cardozo, fresh from almost a score of years on New York's highest bench, the Court of Appeals, where, as Chief Judge, he had built that Court's prestige in legal circles well above the prestige of the Supreme Court of the United States under Taft. The saintly white-locked ascetic, whose private tutors (he was always bright beyond his years) had included Horatio Alger of rise-to-the-top-the-hard-way fame, had devoted his whole adult life trying to live down, for the Cardozo name, the political peccadilloes of his less idealistic father, a Tammany judge whose flagrant malfeasance in office had led him to resign rather than face impending impeachment. With a rare unanimity, practically the entire legal profession pushed Cardozo for the post left vacant when the legendary Holmes quit the Court in 1932; but President Hoover, unenchanted by the shy scholar's apolitical liberalism, dragged his feet on the excuse that there were already two New Yorkers on the Court—until one of those two (the other was Hughes) offered Hoover his resignation, if necessary to let Cardozo be named a Justice. The man who made the gallant offer was Harlan Stone.

Stone had been put on the Court by his fellow Amherst alumnus, Calvin Coolidge, in 1925, after serving one year as U.S. Attorney-General—during which year he had restored the Daugherty-depleted prestige of the Department of Justice, appointed J. Edgar Hoover as head of the FBI, and set in motion an anti-trust suit against the

Aluminum Company of America, to the considerable con-
sternation of Coolidge, who forthwith jumped his too
conscientious Attorney-General to a Justiceship. The
husky, heavy-set New Hampshire farm boy, whose penchant for slow-fused hell-raising had got him kicked out
of one college before he graduated from Amherst (Phi
Beta Kappa, president of his class, and, paradoxically, right
guard on a famous football team), had been causing con-
sternation in a conscientious way all his adult life. As a
Wall Street lawyer, a director of large corporations, an
intimate of Morgan partners, he had simultaneously been
a liberal law professor at Columbia, unreluctant to casti-
gate the financial skulduggery sometimes indulged in by
his clients and friends. A shambling, easy-going character
—nicknamed "Slug" and later "Doc"—he could still get
so indignant at the dictatorial tactics of Columbia's President Nicholas Murray Butler as to resign the law school's
deanship, only to be recalled by popular demand plus
presidential promises not to interfere. Once on the Court,
his open-minded honesty soon made him, despite his
dogged Yankee Republicanism, a disciple and co-dissenter
of fellow-Yankee Holmes and of a different breed of New
Englander, Louis Brandeis.

Brandeis was a New Englander only in the sense that
Stone was a New Yorker—that is, by choice, not by birth
—for Holmes's militant partner-in-protest through the
sixteen years they served on the Court together had been
Kentucky born. Attracted to the cultured intellectualism of
Boston during his Harvard Law School days, Brandeis had
settled there, made a fortune in the practice of corporation
law, and then—unlike his future colleagues who had

started the same way in Wyoming and Utah and Minnesota and Tennessee—had switched, as though suddenly pricked by a somewhat self-righteous conscience, to become a sort of counsel for the people, often without fee. Like Hughes in New York, he had fought the insurance overlords in Massachusetts—and had set up a model system of cheap state-run insurance which he ever after rated his greatest achievement; he had argued before the Supreme Court for such progressive state laws as Oregon's novel maximum-hour statutes, stressing economic facts instead of conventional legal abstractions in a manner that came to be commonly called by lawyers "the Brandeis brief." Named to the high Court by Wilson in 1916, his confirmation had been bitterly opposed by all the forces of legal conformity, from the unanimous past presidents of the American Bar Association to then-President Lowell of Harvard and future Chief Justice Taft—and the Senate debate had raged from January to June. As a Justice, the thin, stooped, deep-eyed aristocrat, though regularly teamed with Holmes in his votes, reached the same results by a quite different route; where Holmes was human and tolerant, Brandeis was austere and ruthless; where Holmes was the philosopher, Brandeis was the crusader. No less than McReynolds, on the far side of the fence, did Brandeis seek to write his own economic ideas into law. Chief of those ideas was a credo of economic democracy to supplement political democracy—a credo which would not tolerate the concentrated power of bigness (one of his books was titled "The Curse of Bigness"), whether it cropped up as big business, big labor unions, or big government; it can have been no surprise to those who

knew Brandeis any less vaguely than as "that other liberal
Justice" that he was to join with enthusiasm in the decision
that declared the New Deal's NIRA, with its overtones of
a corporate state, unconstitutional. But governmental experiment on a smaller scale fitted neatly into Brandeis's
somewhat nineteenth-century scheme of things; perhaps
his most famous opinion was his protest against the Court's
veto (under the Fourteenth Amendment's due process
clause, of course) of an Oklahoma law mildly regulating the
ice business. Said Brandeis: "It is one of the happy incidents of the federal system that a single courageous state
may, if its citizens choose, serve as a laboratory, and try
novel social and economic experiments without risk to the
rest of the country." Anti-bigness Brandeis might have
rated the same regulation less "happy" had it come from
the far-reaching federal government.

Yet the same opinion held words not limited to the
progressive pyrotechnics of the test-tube states: "To stay
experimentation in things social and economic is a grave
responsibility. Denial of the right to experiment may be
fraught with serious consequences to the Nation. . . .
This Court has the power to prevent an experiment. . . .
But in the exercise of this high power, we must ever be
on our guard, lest we erect our prejudices into legal principles. If we would guide by the light of reason, we must
let our minds be bold."

That these words were spoken in dissent and that they
were spoken in the very year when Franklin Roosevelt
was first elected President might have presaged to the
prophetic what the Nine Old Men—Van Devanter, Mc-
Reynolds, Sutherland, Butler, Roberts, Hughes, Cardozo,

Stone, and Brandeis—held in store, by their majority vote, for the conglomeration of new and experimental national laws that were to be known as the New Deal. Secure in their judicial supremacy, armed with their arsenal of constitutional word-weapons to achieve political ends, the Justices, *en masse*, made their customary courtesy call on the new President shortly after his inauguration. In the same month—March, 1933—the new President, polio braces and all, made a call that was considerably more than conventionally courteous at a little old house on I Street, where lived ninety-two-year-old retired Justice Holmes. This extraordinary gesture of homage hinted what was in the political wind.

The wind did not so much as touch the Supreme Court for well over a year; whether by design or happenstance, none of the test cases challenging the constitutionality of the congeries of laws that were lick-and-a-promised into shape to deal with the nation's economic crisis, in long-term or short-term ways, hit the high tribunal during its 1933–34 term. But a couple of key cases, involving state laws passed to relieve depression-bred hardships, did come before the Justices, whose duo of decisions were widely read as showing which way the *judicial* wind would soon be blowing on *national* legislation. That the predicters predicted in both directions was not so strange, considering what the Court did and said in the two cases.

A Minnesota statute, delaying the foreclosure of mortgages and obviously aimed to help the hard-pressed farmers hang onto their farms for the duration of the depression, was argued (by a modern version of a movie-

villain mortgagee) to be in violation of Founding Father
James Wilson's old constitutional ban against state laws
"impairing the obligation of contracts." Five to four, the
Court upheld the Minnesota law—with the four (who
scarcely need specification) having far the better of the
argument by logic and by legal precedent, if not by the
facts of life. Roberts, then in his early liberal phase, cast
the decisive vote but the Chief Justice wrote the majority
opinion. "Emergency," said Hughes, "does not create
power. Emergency does not increase granted power or
remove or diminish the restrictions imposed upon power
granted or reserved . . ."—and anti-New Dealers could
read this to their taste. "While emergency does not create
power," Hughes continued, "emergency may furnish the
occasion for the exercise of power . . ."—and pro-New
Dealers beamed. That the two statements in fact completely contradicted each other, as the dissenters bitterly
remarked, did not bother the predicters on either side; the
one certain thing, however, was that the law had been
upheld—barely.

By an identical 5–4 division, the Justices allowed New
York to help its dairy farmers by fixing minimum prices
for milk. This time it was the due process clause that was
hurled against the statute, and this time it was swing-man
Roberts who wrote the opinion, the most liberal of his
whole judicial career. Sounding almost like Holmes or
Brandeis, Roberts remarked: "The due process clause
makes no mention of sales or of prices any more than it
speaks of business or contracts or buildings or other incidents of property. The thought seems nevertheless to have
persisted that there is something peculiarly sacrosanct

about the price one may charge for what he makes or sells. . . . This view was negatived many years ago." At which point, Roberts cited as authority the old post-Civil-War Granger decisions, practically ignoring the multitude of contrary due-process rulings in between—and also misleading most of the country, including possibly his colleagues, as to what his stand would be in major cases soon to come.

They came in a rush, beginning in the winter of 1934–35. First of the New Deal's doings to be judged by the Justices was not in itself a matter of major import, but it carried the seed of a far more momentous decision, now only four months away; one small section of the "code" set up under the NIRA to police the oil industry—by letting the President stop state-to-state shipments of "hot," or illegally produced, oil—was thumbed to unconstitutional oblivion by the Court, with only Cardozo dissenting. It was the novel reason given for the decision that made astute lawyers prick up their ears; what the Court said was that Congress had improperly turned over part of its lawmaking power to the President, and so violated (though the Constitution nowhere forbids this in so many words) the ancient three-way separation of government powers. New Deal attorneys found hope in the fact that the ruling was so narrow, for the Court, had it wished, could have broadened its ukase to toss out the whole NIRA. Business attorneys—no longer so enamored of the NIRA, now that the nadir of business helplessness was almost two years in the past—wondered if this slap at the New Deal might not telegraph tougher punches in the near future.

In the very next month, the eagerly anti-Administration

wonderers were taken somewhat aback as the New Deal won—albeit by a cheerless five-to-four vote—its first major Court victory. This was in the "gold clause" case; the President and his Congress had followed the lead of England and France in taking the U.S. off the gold standard; hence the promise to pay old debts in gold (if the creditor asked for gold) which had commonly been written into private and public bonds (and commonly ignored) would be worthless—unless the Court should call the Administration scheme unconstitutional. The practical issue was simple; since depression had made gold more valuable, as measured in ordinary paper dollars, than it was when the bonds were issued, bond-holders hoped for the windfall that would come to them if their debtors had to pay them in gold, as promised. The legal issue was less simple; five Justices said that, for all bonds except U.S. government bonds, this action by the U.S. government was proper; the same five Justices then said that it was improper for the U.S. government to welch on its *own* promises, *but* that the machinery of the law provided no method by which the holders of U.S. bonds could collect on these broken promises to pay in gold. It was this last typically tortuous legal ruling that led McReynolds, heading his quartet in dissent, to exclaim extemporaneously from the bench: "The Constitution is gone." And it may well have been in order to hold Roberts's vote that Hughes, for the Court majority, gave the New Deal a verbal—but only verbal—spanking. If so, Hughes held Roberts for this case alone; by the next big decision, the Four Horsemen had won him away.

Where Roberts left the liberals and reverted to type as an old railroad lawyer, more comfortable among other old railroad lawyers than among bolder bedfellows, was in the rejection of the Railroad Retirement Act—to the dismay of the railroad workers, who thus lost their pensions, and to the pecuniary profit of the roads. As if to make a far-flung formal announcement of his reconversion to "old-fashioned Anglo-Saxon individualism," Roberts wrote the opinion that blasted the Act as beyond Congress's power to regulate interstate commerce and as a violation of the Fifth Amendment's due process clause too. The grave timbre of Hughes's potent dissent—in which Brandeis, Stone, and Cardozo joined—backed a tenor of warning to the country and the Court with a bass of mourning for a comrade apparently lost to the cause of judicial open-mindedness.

Yet when the most sweeping anti-New Deal decision of them all was handed down in the same month, May of 1935, it was Hughes who wrote the opinion that scuttled the NIRA, under which the nation's whole economy had been operating for almost two years—and wrote it for a surprisingly unanimous nine. The case that put an abrupt end to Administrator Hugh Johnson's government-guided co-operative empire—"codes of industry," Blue Eagle symbol, and all—was known officially as the Schechter case and popularly as the case of the sick chickens. Four broth-ers named Schechter who ran a small-time poultry business in Brooklyn had sold diseased fowl in brazen violation of the poultry code of the NRA (or National Recovery Ad-ministration, created by the National Industrial Recovery Act) and had been sentenced to brief terms in jail. Some-where along the ladder of appeal, the large and legendary Wall Street law firm of Cravath, de Gersdorff, Swaine, &

Wood had taken a sudden interest in the Schechters' plight
and had found the funds to carry their case to the Supreme
Court. Chief contention of the lawyers was that Congress
had no power, under the interstate commerce clause, to
regulate, even with industry co-operation, such little local
businesses as poultry markets—and this despite the widely
overlooked fact that, just four years before, the Court had
held that poultry markets were enmeshed enough in interstate commerce to bring them under the federal anti-trust
laws. Not only did the whole Court accept this argument,
brushing its own recent anti-trust decision aside; it went
infinitely farther and, taking its cue from the "hot oil"
case, branded the entire NIRA, even as applied to interstate businesses, an unconstitutional "delegation of legislative power to the executive." A few sick chickens had
murdered the mighty Blue Eagle.

That the Justices, almost simultaneously and again
unanimously, threw out—this time on a due-process excuse
—the New Deal's effort to lighten the load of farmers with
mortgaged farms (much as Minnesota had done, with five
Justices approving) came as utter anti-climax. It was the
Schechter decision that made headlines around the world.
On the stock market, prices shot skyward in a sheerly emotional reaction, quite out of character for financial folk, to
the prospect of government-free enterprise mercifully restored by the nine wise men of Washington. But conventionally sober second thought—of the myriad problems
suddenly dumped for solution in business's lap—sent the
soaring stock prices down the next day in a wave of heavy
selling. And an unsmiling President, at his weekly press
conference, spoke in solemnly ominous tones of the Court's

anachronistic attitude in trying to turn a mechanized and economically all-of-a-piece nation back to the "horse-and-buggy days" of here-a-little-there-a-little government. As for the Justices, they read their predominantly praise-laden press notices and went separately and serenely home to rest up over the summer for whatever further political problems, couched in constitutional clichés, might confront them the following fall.

This was the term of Court—from the fall of 1935 through the spring of 1936—that set off the fireworks. Most of the nation, while not joining in the jubilance of financial leaders (including publishers of large newspapers) over the NIRA decision, had been more surprised than dismayed; with the economy clearly on the upgrade, with employment rising and breadlines shrinking, Hugh Johnson and his Blue Eagle had become to many rather a minor nuisance than a boon; their demise had occasioned very little sorrow or anger throughout the country—just as the wind-sniffing Justices must have foreseen. But comparative popular indifference to the fate of the NIRA did not mean indifference to the New Deal as a whole; by the time of the 1936 nominating conventions, the Court had made itself a major issue for the coming Presidential campaign.

First and most manifoldly meaningful of the big decisions of that historic term of Court was the plowing under of the Agricultural Adjustment Act, or AAA. The Act was intended to raise the prices farmers got for their crops and other products by reducing the number of farm products for sale; to do this, farmers were, in effect, bribed by the government to produce less food, so that there would be no more of the surpluses that were keeping farm prices low; the money to pay these "subsidies" came from "processing taxes," not on the farmers but on those who handled the first step of turning farmstuff into food, as when wheat was milled into flour. It was, of course, a food processor, hit by the new tax, who challenged the constitutionality of the AAA. But it was no country lawyer—it was Justice Roberts's suave city-bred sponsor, George Wharton Pepper—who argued the case before the Supreme Court for a six-figure fee, and who wept like a Thespian trooper before the high bench as he perorated: "I pray almighty God that not in my time may the land of the regimented be accepted as a worthy substitute for the land of the free."

To the slight offense of those who were fastidious about the emulation of Caesar's wife by Supreme Court Justices, Pepper's protégé wrote the Court opinion that answered Pepper's—and the food processors'—prayer. The AAA was unconstitutional, said Roberts, in seven thousand words, because, despite Congress's uncontroverted power to raise taxes and spend money for the "general welfare," Congress could not use this taxing-and-spending power in ways that interfered with the states' right-of-regulation—and control of agriculture was the states', not the federal government's, domain. As if to try to ward off, beforehand, criticism of his quite unprecedented reading of the Constitution, based on a circular argument (for only those powers *not* granted to the federal government are "reserved to the States" and one of the powers *granted* is taxing-and-spending for the "general welfare"), Roberts wrote into his anti-New Deal tract one of the most ingenuous disclaimers of rule by judges ever penned: "When an act of Congress is appropriately challenged in the courts as not conforming to the constitutional mandate the judicial branch of the Government has only one duty—to lay the article of the Constitution which is invoked beside the statute which is challenged and to decide whether the latter squares with the former." By Roberts's metaphor, a draftsman with a T-square—or perhaps a chemist with his litmus paper or, at best, a philologist with a dictionary —would be adequately equipped to lay down constitutional law.

It was here that an outraged Stone—speaking for a three-man minority that embraced Brandeis and Cardozo —was moved to say, in one of the most magnificent opinions ever written: "Courts are not the only agency of government that must be assumed to have capacity to govern"—and "the only check upon our own exercise of power is our own sense of self-restraint." Stone also said, after wickedly ridiculing Roberts's parade of imaginary future horribles if the AAA were upheld: "The suggestion that it [*the governmental power of the purse*] must now be curtailed by judicial fiat because it may be abused by unwise use hardly rises to the dignity of argument. So may judicial power be abused. . . : Interpretation of our great charter of government which proceeds on any assumption that the responsibility for the preservation of our institutions is the exclusive concern of any one of the three branches of government, or that it alone can save them from destruction is far more likely, in the long run, 'to obliterate the constituent members' of 'an indestructible union of indestructible states' than the frank recognition that language, even of a constitution, may mean what it says. . . ." Not even Holmes ever flayed the-divine-right-of-judges-to-rule more tellingly or more truly.

And what of Hughes? The unhappy Chief Justice, completely aware that Stone's stark common-sense was infinitely righter and wiser than Roberts's nonsense, was torn between his twin duties as Justice and as Chief. As Justice, his intelligence-plus-integrity bade him join the dissenters; as Chief, his responsibility to the Court as an institution bade him beware what a 5–4 decision on so major a matter (the AAA had been second only to the NIRA in the Administration's alphabetical assortment) might do to the Court's prestige across the nation. There is no longer any doubt, despite the secrecy of Supreme Court conferences (the story has been told scores of times and never denied), that Hughes both talked and voted for the AAA's validity until, unable to win Roberts back to reason, he let himself be counted with the majority to make the score 6–3; his concession to personal conscience was in assigning the opinion to Roberts instead of writing it himself, as he had done in the unanimous NIRA case. Thus it was Roberts who bore the main brunt of Stone's cold-angry blast (indeed, Hughes practically never, during his eleven years as Chief, took on a majority opinion that would lay him open to the devastating dissents of his liberal colleagues) in the case that, more than any one other, sparked what Hughes had hoped to avoid—a direct attack on the Court by the President.

Not that the Court was yet through with the New Deal for the term. As if to apologize slightly for the AAA blow. the Justices upheld, on the narrowest and flimsiest ground possible, a part of the vast Tennessee Valley Authority, or

TVA, program—with only the immutable McReynolds dissenting. But this grudging concession by the Court was soon followed by another judicial veto of a vital New Deal statute—the Bituminous Coal Act (or "Guffey Coal Act") which regulated production, prices, and wages in that sick industry in such a manner that it was called "the little NIRA." Unlike the big NIRA, which was perforce loosely worded because it dealt with hundreds of industries, the Coal Act, dealing with one, was so specific that it could scarcely be thrown out of Court as an improper "delegation of legislative power"; unlike the little local poultry dealers of the Schechter case, the Carter Coal Co. (of the Coal Act case) was, like almost every coal company in the country, doing—and affecting—interstate business in an obvious and large-scale way; unlike the public apathy that had settled like a fog around the NIRA by the time of the Schechter decision, a continuing enthusiasm for the order-out-of-chaos results of the Coal Act persisted among most of the coal operators as well as the miners. None of these facts sufficed to save the law from a Court with the bit in its teeth.

Sutherland, for the other three Horsemen and Roberts, gave the rather personal slant of the anti-New Deal ruling away by the use of such adjectives as "obnoxious" and "intolerable," while resting the decision technically on the interstate commerce clause, with a due-process assist. It did not matter that the Court had catalogued the coal industry as deep enough in interstate commerce to let federal judges give orders, and jail sentences, to striking miners; it did not matter that every major coal-producing state filed a brief in favor of the Act, begging that the national government keep control rather than toss the ball back to them; with legal words winging and plain facts flouted, the majority Justices proclaimed that coal mining was a "local" business and hence federal regulation was an invasion of states' rights. Harried Chief Justice Hughes this time managed to split his vote between his colleagues to right and to left, going with the conservatives on wage control and with the liberals on price control (though the very next week, he completely capitulated to the liberals in a case that killed the New Deal's Municipal Bankruptcy Act by a clear-cut 5–4 vote). John L. Lewis, looking ahead undaunted, began to line up a contribution of almost half a million dollars from the United Mine Workers to Roosevelt's 1936 campaign.

It was at this point that the five dominant Justices, perhaps heady with power, made a grave strategic error. As matters stood, it was clear that one of the Republicans' rousing rallying-cries in the coming election would be Rooseveltian contempt for the Constitution, as conclusively proved by the Court's veto of most of the New Deal. To exploit this angle and to exalt the Court for saving the Republic, an organization of wealthy people and their lawyers, cleverly called the Liberty League, had sprouted fast and made many a headline. With nominating conventions only a few weeks away, one Justice was by no means unaware of popular interest in the Court and its members, nor unmindful of the fact that Hughes had been "drafted" from the Court to run for President twenty years before. This Justice, moreover, had for two years held the Court's close, tough decisions as much in the hollow of his raised or lowered hand as if he had sat on the Court alone. But it was not in a case involving the New Deal—except as the New Deal symbolized progressive help-the-people-who-need-help laws—that Roberts killed his chance for the nomination; it was in a challenge, under the Fourteenth Amendment's due process clause of course, of New York's minimum-wage statute for women.

Back in the 1920's, during prosperity, during Holmes's dissenting heyday, a Court ruling that no American government could require that workers, even women workers, be paid a living wage—since to do so would frustrate "freedom of contract"—would have caused little stir; those few lapses where the Justices had let legislatures limit business's right to bargain had dealt with prices or with hours of work, not with wages. But this was 1936; memories of poverty and hunger were still fresh in the minds of millions; more than one-third of the forty-eight states, plus twenty-one foreign countries, including England, had put laws like New York's on their books. As though thumbing their noses at a starving woman while self-righteously wrapping themselves in the flag, the Four Horsemen and Roberts held the law bad. Hughes, unable to stomach, even for his Court's prestige, such let-'em-eat-cake smugness, spoke in grim dissent of "the seriousness of the social problem." Said a Holmesian Stone in separate and stronger protest, with Brandeis and Cardozo agreeing: "The Fourteenth Amendment has no more embedded in the Constitution our preference for some particular set of economic beliefs than it had adopted, in the name of liberty, the system of theology which we may happen to approve." This pointed suggestion of something like religious fanaticism in the unbudgeable economic obstinacy of the majority was not unintentional.

Nor could the Court's final flourish after two years of knocking down laws like tenpins be laughed off as one last proof that the New Deal cared nothing about the Constitution. Here was no visionary product of professors and other brain-trusters who swarmed around that "traitor to his class" in the White House; here was a carefully drafted, badly needed law that had been backed by Republicans as well as Democrats in the nation's most heavily peopled state. Newspapers that had been chortling over the score —reported in sport-page fashion—of judicial "knock-outs" inflicted on the New Deal were plainly perturbed and troubled; the New York *Times*, no admirer of Administration experiments, called the decision "unfortunate in more than one respect." Among the "unfortunate" respects were the facts that the vetoed law had such wide approval, that the ruling was so close, and that the almost reverently respected Chief Justice rated the decision as radically wrong. Most significantly, if the majority Justices could perhaps misread the Constitution in a non-New Deal case, might they not have misread it in some of the New Deal cases too? The fervor of a save-the-Constitution crusade to stop Roosevelt's re-election simmered down; the Liberty League lost some of its luster; the Republican nomination went, not to Roberts, but to unjudging and almost unknown Alf Landon of Kansas.

Still, the Court and the Constitution by no means dropped out of the campaign. Senator Barkley, keynoting the convention that renominated FDR by acclamation, spoke of the New Deal as having been "cast aside by the rigors of technicality and the application of antiquated economic predilections"; of nine Justices who "could not agree on what the Constitution means"; of four dissenters "equally eminent, learned, and sincere, and equally alive to the compulsions of modern life," so that citizens were "relieved of any obligation to underwrite the infallibility of the five whose views prevail." On the other side, the anti-New Dealers, now a touch less aggressive and more apprehensive, made a slogan of Roosevelt's horse-and-buggy slur on the Justices and warned of sinister plans afoot to hobble the Court, to intrude on the vaunted independence of the judiciary, to debauch the Constitution, should Roosevelt win.

As always, a flock of factors—including especially the contrasting personalities of the two candidates—influenced the election; but the question of the Court's proper, or improper, place in the American scheme of government stayed a top-flight issue from start to finish. And when the voters gave their aggregate answer in November, Landon and the Liberty League lost every state save only Vermont and Maine. What effect this avalanche may have had in the marble temple, where the Court had convened for its new term a month before, must remain a matter of informed conjecture—at least until intimate memoirs are possibly published at a decent interval after the death of Roberts, last survivor of the Nine Old Men. What Franklin Roosevelt said, with bland and confident ambiguity, in his second inaugural on a rainy January day in 1937, was: "The Constitution of 1787 did not make our democracy impotent." Just what Franklin Roosevelt had in mind, not even his personal friends, much less his political enemies, knew.

As the government crisis approached its climax, a spate of literature about the Court and the Constitution kept increasing—not just in scholarly journals but in popular magazines and in books by professors and politicians, by lawyers and newspapermen, books that often hit the best-seller lists, so aware were literate citizens of the urgency and explosiveness of a problem long left to the learned discourse of academicians. As had happened sporadically throughout its history, though seldom since the nineteenth century, the Court was the target of all sorts of schemes, some new, some old, some mild, some tough, to break the impasse that had temporarily made "democracy impotent." Give Congress broad and specific power to pass laws promoting the "general welfare," regardless of old interstate-commerce or due-process limitations; let Congress overrule the Court's veto of federal statutes (as it can the President's veto) by a two-thirds, or perhaps three-fourths, majority; take away, partly or completely, the Court's *appellate* power (controlled by Congress) to rule on the rightness-or-wrongness of national legislation; require a 6–3, or maybe a 7–2, vote by the Justices to declare an Act of Congress void; on down to the pious plea: Educate the people to elect better Presidents who will appoint better Supreme Court Justices. But all the suggested schemes that held any real possibility of working needed an amendment to the Constitution—and that slow and, despite FDR's electoral avalanche, always uncertain procedure, however attractive for the long pull, seemed a less than practical answer to problems of the moment. By contrast, the big virtue of President Roosevelt's surprise package was the immediacy of its impact.

It was just two weeks and two days after he took the Presidential oath of office for the second time that FDR bombshelled the nation, including the bulk of his own most intimate advisors, with the proposal which the predominantly anti-Roosevelt press quickly branded, with semantic shrewdness, "the Court-packing plan"—and which might have been called, with equal accuracy and opposite overtones, "the Court-unpacking plan." Though obviously aimed at the intransigent Nine, or Five-out-of-Nine, the plan, on its literal terms, dealt with the entire federal judiciary. What the President asked was that, whenever a federal judge reached the age of seventy and failed to retire, another judge be appointed to supplement, not to replace, the old fellow—with the total number of new judges who could be so named not to exceed fifty, and with the Supreme Court held to a top membership of fifteen Justices. Since six sitting Justices, including all Four Horsemen, had reached the far side of seventy by 1937, enactment of the Court plan would have given Roosevelt the privilege and the pleasure of forthwith appointing six new Justices—enough to outvote with the liberal trio the Four Horsemen plus Roberts plus, if need be, Hughes. The beauty of the plan was its simplicity; the size of the Court had been varied several times before and the three post-Civil War shifts had been for strictly political purposes; nor was there any slightest doubt of the plan's constitutionality, since the Constitution left the size of the Court entirely up to Congress. Indeed the simplicity of the plan was part of its eventual undoing; it was so simple that it seemed to many diabolically clever—no amending of the Constitution, no curbing of the Court's power, merely (as FDR put it) the "infusion of new blood" into the otherwise untouched federal judiciary.

It has since become a commonplace to blame the bitter battle that led to the plan's ultimate defeat on the "deviousness" or "indirectness" with which it was presented —as simply a routine move to improve the whole federal court system. True, the President did stress in his message the need for more judges, to help the federal courts catch up with their calendars of pending cases and to cut down the frequent delays in handling litigation; and this argument, while quite warranted with respect to many lower federal courts, let Chief Justice Hughes enter the fray a little later by allowing publication of a letter in which he rather indignantly stated that the Supreme Court was "fully abreast of its work." But those who insist that the plan might have passed, had FDR come out flatly with his wish to get more liberal Court decisions by adding a few liberal Justices, overlook such remarks in his message as: "New facts become blurred through old glasses fitted, as it were, for the needs of another generation; older men, assuming that the scene is the same as it was in the past, cease to explore or inquire into the present or the future." Considering eighty-year-old Brandeis on the one hand and sixty-one-year-old Roberts on the other, Roosevelt erred in equating chronological age with conservatism. Yet it is scarcely accurate to say that he did not indicate his purpose to change, with the Court plan, the course of constitutional law.

What eventually defeated the plan, despite the so recently proved and overwhelming popularity of the Court-killed New Deal, was a host of little political factors—plus two big ones. One was the reverential awe-bred-of-ignorance, with which most Americans regarded the Court, however they might disapprove some of its decisions; this awe blinded both Republicans and Democrats to the blasphemous fact that the Court was a rather random collection of nine men exercising a political function atop one of the three branches of the federal government; and this awe was exploited to the hilt by more practical and purposeful folk whose motives were as mundane as the President's in that they wanted to keep the Court conservative as much as he wanted to make it liberal. Even granting a degree of obliqueness in FDR's tactical approach to the problem, there was no monopoly of masked motives on either side of the fight over the Court plan. The other big factor in the plan's defeat was the sudden and self-saving about-face by the Court itself in its constitutional decisions—an about-face which none could be so naïve as to call coincidental, and which made a cliché of "A switch in time saves nine."

Of these two major means of effective attack on the Court plan, the don't-touch-the-Court-it's-sacred stuff, while spread across the country by press, radio, and club-car conversation, was all focused on the Senate committee-room where heated hearings were under way. All the old saws about an inviolate, independent judiciary were dragged out and dusted off by the political descendants of those who had damned and ignored the Court after the Dred Scott case and had violated its independence to get the decision they wanted on Legal Tender. But strict party lines meant little as Democratic Senator Glass rushed to blast the plan on a national broadcast, Vice-President Garner took off for Texas "on vacation" until the shooting was over, and Democratic Senator Wheeler—La Follette's running-mate in 1924, whose long liberal record was unimpeachable—assumed, to the joy of Republican hearts, the leadership of the opposition. Many, like Wheeler, who attacked the plan did not defend the Court or its recent decisions; they thought the Court should be curbed but in a different, more dignified way, as by constitutional amendment; here was where the simple ease and essential directness of the President's proposal helped defeat it.

Yet, for all the forensics and falderol, political pressure would have pushed the plan through had not Hughes proved the most astute statesman of them all. Quite unnoticed—in January, 1937—was a Court decision upholding a minor New Deal tax, of a kind (it applied retroactively for a period before it was passed) that the Court had called unconstitutional a few years earlier; the Court plan had not yet been proposed. Noticed by the whole nation, however, and spread on every front page, the month *after* the plan was proposed, was a decision giving the Justices' bare 5–4 blessing to a Washington state minimum-wage law almost identical to the New York statute that the Court had scuttled, 5–4, the preceding June; and despite Hughes's gallant effort to save his re-won colleague's face by finding a technical difference, where none existed, between the two cases, it was plain to lawyers and laymen alike that Roberts had simply switched sides. But again unnoticed was the most intriguing, and revealing, fact of all; the Washington minimum-wage case, though the decision came down in March, had been argued in Court and decided in conference in January—*before* the President proposed his plan. Thus the circumstantial evidence is strong (Justices can, but very rarely do, change their votes after conference on a case is over) that Hughes had begun to counter the plan and save his nine-man Court a little ahead of when the plan was launched; for there can be no doubt that it was Hughes, as Chief, whose personal appeal, in the name of the Court's prestige, won Roberts away from the camp of the Four Horsemen. Whether there was a leak to Hughes from the Department of Justice where the plan was drafted, or whether, alerted by the election, he shrewdly foresaw what was coming, he got the jump, as few ever did, on Roosevelt.

Still, this one Court concession to the trend of the times, whatever it might portend, dealt only with a state statute, not a national New Deal law. The turning-point in the fight over the Court plan, and hence perhaps the biggest day in the Court's whole history, came a fortnight later, on April 12. In a series of five cases, headed by the Jones & Laughlin Steel Corp. case, the Court upheld the National Labor Relations Act—or "Wagner Act"—designed to protect labor unions and promote collective bargaining in industries throughout the nation. Factories and mills and mines and stores, whose activities had long been legally classified as "local," subject only to state regulation, and so immune, under the Constitution, from federal meddling, were suddenly found—in flat contradiction of the barely dry Schechter and Carter Coal Co. decisions— to "affect" interstate commerce "directly" enough to warrant Con-

gressional control under the commerce clause. In vain did
the Four Horsemen pull out all the free-enterprise stops
and invoke all the old precedents; Hughes, who read the
magisterial majority opinion himself, had held Roberts to
the twin causes of Court-saving and constitutional liberalism. Franklin Roosevelt's remark, when told of the
decision, was a smiling "It's been a pretty good day for
all of us"—but Wheeler and his Senate kill-the-Court-plan
cohorts were jubilant too. As one conservative Democratic
Senator put it, with I'm-off-the-hook relief: "Why run for
a train after you've caught it?"

Inevitably, all that followed was anti-climactic. Even the
Court's 5–4 decision, later in the term, sustaining the
Social Security Act—although its reasoning ran directly
counter to Roberts's unfortunate opinion in the AAA case
(and Roberts now was, naturally, with the majority)—occasioned no surprise. Like the child of the fairy tale, who
saw that the king's alleged fancy raiment was non-existent
and the king naked, the U.S. citizen was quite unfooled by
the fancy legal language in which the Justices dressed up
what they had done; with childlike clarity, the citizen saw
that the Court had nakedly succumbed to political pressure
—maybe wisely, maybe unwisely—and had beat a hasty
strategic retreat. The wisdom of the retreat was soon apparent. In June, the Senate Judiciary Committee, by an
appropriately Court-like margin of one vote, reported
against the President's plan as an "utterly dangerous abandonment of constitutional principle" which would "destroy
the independence of the judiciary" and which "violates
every sacred tradition of American democracy"—with
seven Democrats joining in this violent denunciation of

their party's chieftain. As the plan's supporters in the Senate went to work on a compromise proposal to let FDR add two, not six, new Justices, their leader, Senator Robinson—who had been Al Smith's running-mate in 1928 and whose loyalty had him marked for Roosevelt's first Court appointment—suddenly died. Back from his long Texas "vacation" rushed less loyal Vice-President Garner to help put the finishing touches to the burial of the whole scheme. The Court-plan battle was over.

But the war for a more up-to-date judicial reading of the loose-jointed (as was now plain to all) Constitution—the war that the President, while losing the battle, had begun to win—was to go gradually and steadily on. With emergency past, with the Court unviolated, might not Roberts, his job done, go home again to the conservatives; were the Court's decisions not still entirely dependent on its personnel? The first break in the five-year monopoly of the Court by the same Nine Old Men—and FDR's first chance to name a Justice (Taft had named six in four years, and Harding four in two)—came when seventy-eight-year-old Van Devanter, after the historic term was ended, took advantage of a new law that let Justices retire at full pay. This opened the way for Roosevelt to achieve as much in rebalancing the Court as enactment of the two-extra-Justices compromise would have done—for the subtraction of one conservative and the addition of one liberal is exactly equal, balance-wise, to the simple addition of two liberals. The President did not muff his opportunity.

Indeed, FDR took a double delight in dramatically appointing, during the summer, the militantly liberal Senator Hugo Black of Alabama. No possible appointment could

more have enraged the conservatives, in and out of the
Senate, who had done the Court plan to death; but the
silly rule of "Senatorial courtesy," whereby members of
the club never question very deeply the qualifications of a
fellow member named to a new post, made Black's confirmation—just as Roosevelt knew it would—almost automatic. Later in the summer, the President's master-move
almost backfired; a reporter on a reactionary Pittsburgh
newspaper found, in the easily available files of an Alabama paper, proof of what all Alabama had long known—
that Black, as a young Southern politician, had briefly been
a member of the Ku Klux Klan; the reporter's syndicated
stories, though wholly based on other men's work, won
him a Pulitzer prize and set the nation agog. But thoughtful
folk were well aware that the trumped-up furor over Black
in no sense stemmed from his old Klan membership (for
instance, McReynolds's openly Klannish race prejudice
had never stirred a whisper) but from a seething conservative sentiment of any-stick-to-beat-a-New-Deal-dog.
Black rode out the storm with the help of a radio talk, in
which he accurately assured the country that there was no
iota of intolerance in his record or in his bones, and his new
brethren greeted him to the Court in the fall.

Next of the Nine Old Men to go was Sutherland; at his
retirement, Roosevelt rewarded Stanley Reed of Kentucky
who, as Solicitor-General, had argued most of the big
New Deal cases before the Court with a patient passion
that had caused him once to faint in the course of argument.
Meanwhile, the slightly re-slanted nine were quietly re-
writing constitutional law; the Federal Power Commission, the New Deal's Labor Relations Board, and the New

Deal's finance-policing Securities and Exchange Commission were all upheld in anti-business actions that might have been slapped down two years before. A vital tax decision or two went for the government instead of against; soon to topple were some tax-law landmarks hoary with age—like the one that let federal judges out of paying an income tax and the series of cases, dating basically back to John Marshall's McCulloch *v.* Maryland, that exempted state employees from federal taxes and vice versa. Step by slow step, Roosevelt's war was being won.

Between 1938 and early 1939, the Court lost two of its all-time greats as Cardozo died and Brandeis resigned; to replace them, Roosevelt named two law school professors, selecting—with Ivy League impartiality—one from Harvard and one from Yale. The "scholar's seat" on the bench, previously warmed by Gray and Holmes and Cardozo, went to Felix Frankfurter, old friend and advisor of FDR, who had been sending his bright, young disciples to Washington to work in government (the Corcoran-and-Cohen team was among them) since long before the New Deal. To forty-year-old William O. Douglas, of the far West and, more recently, Connecticut—youngest appointee since Story, over a century before—went, appropriately enough, the seat of the financial expert and crusader; for Douglas had quit his academic job at Yale, first to help, then to head, the SEC, and had done it so well that Brandeis remarked to his less-than-half-as-old successor: "I wanted you to be here in my place."

When Butler died late in 1939, leaving McReynolds as the Four Horsemen's sole survivor on the Court, the politically sagacious President chose another Catholic—U.S.

Attorney-General Frank Murphy, who had formerly been a pro-labor mayor of Detroit and governor of Michigan. Thus, in a span of little more than two years, the inexorable processes of time had enabled Roosevelt to accomplish more, by way of reconstituting the Court's membership, than would have been achieved by his battered and beaten plan. With five Justices, a majority of the Court, now his hand-picked personal selections, and with old liberal war-horse Stone still going strong, it seemed as though the Court were set in a harmoniously leftward-looking pattern for years to come. But ever since the Civil War, the Court had tended to split, amoeba-like, along one or another political or constitutional line. Moreover, men who are granted great government power, to be wielded for the rest of their lives, with no real responsibility save to their own prejudice-propelled consciences, sometimes begin to mistake their separate selves—however liberal or conservative they may be—for God. And Supreme Court Justices are men.

CHAPTER 8

A Court Attuned to a Liberal Key Develops Its Own Discordance

THE TEN YEARS stretching from Butler's death and Murphy's appointment as the fifth Roosevelt Justice up to the summer of 1949—when those consecrated co-champions of civil liberties, Murphy and Wiley Rutledge, suddenly and almost simultaneously died (and their close associate, Douglas, was almost killed in a mountain accident)—were the years of the New Deal Court. Not merely that a majority of the Justices, throughout that decade, had been Roosevelt-chosen; that fact remained true of the Court for five subsequent years, until Justice

Jackson's death in 1954. Rather that the Court's political
and constitutional slant remained, for just that long—
and despite incessant and increasing internecine warfare
—a New Deal slant. New laws were upheld even at the
cost of overruling old decisions; old laws were given,
by new "interpretation," a wider sweep; protection of
personal freedoms, at least against the states, took precedence over protection of property rights; it was characteristic that, when Holmes's 1918 dissent against the
first child-labor decision became, in 1941, the new law of
the land, a unanimous Supreme Court so proclaimed. Indeed, inasmuch as FDR and the Congress began, in 1939,
to neglect and even negate the domestic New Deal as they
set their sights for war, it could be said that the Court—
in remaining the most liberal branch of the federal government—was once more, though on the opposite swing,
behind the political times.

Yet the outstanding fact about the New Deal Court was
not its over-all liberalism; it was what occurred within
the Court when liberalism, at long last and for the first
time in Court history, was promoted from a vehicle of
eloquent dissent to an instrument of actual judicial power
—when views that had been fine and brave and outvoted
five or fifty years before became taken-for-granted truths,
and the battle moved beyond them. Liberalism—or at
least, last year's liberalism—did not take to power
smoothly; where the Court, from the time of Taney on,
had split along fairly predictable political lines, it now
began to splinter; relieved of a common cause in resisting
reaction, the Roosevelt Justices were soon infighting
among themselves. Nor did they keep their quarrels within

the close confines of the conference room. As early as the 1940–41 term, scarcely a year after the New Dealers attained numerical court supremacy, close-reading lawyers could catch in occasional intramural dissents a note of annoyance and personal bitterness; not long after, Washington gossip columns began to "leak" word of a feud between Douglas and Frankfurter; by 1946, when Justice Jackson—from far-off Nuremberg where he was prosecuting Nazi war criminals—released to the press, despite President Truman's plea that he desist, an unprecedented attack on Black's character and integrity (which Black never dignified with an answer), the hostility of some of the Justices toward some of their colleagues was already common knowledge. If the New Deal Court had done nothing more—and it did a great deal more—it should have shown to even the most saint-seeking citizen that Supreme Court Justices are extremely human beings.

Still, the crossfire clash of personalities that once or twice went so far as to erupt into front-page headlines did not stem, at bottom, from simple man-to-man antipathies; it was not that Justice A could not stand Justice B's religion (shades of McReynolds) or mannerisms or morals—nor that Justice X was envious or contemptuous, on a purely personal level, of Justice Y. All the emotional aftermaths were marks of an originally and essentially intellectual disharmony; they came from the sudden catapulting of the liberals, long accustomed to the comparative irresponsibility of we're-so-few-we've-got-to-stick-together dissent, into the saddle of judicial leadership. The bickering and backbiting were symptoms; the basic fact was the splintering of the Justices in five or six or seven legal directions, once the liberals took control. And why did they splinter? The manifold answer can be rough-cut, for convenience, into two categories of explanation: They splintered because "liberalism" is so fuzzy-meaning a political concept, and "liberal" so inexact a political definition of a man, that neither prediction nor unanimity is possible when a group of liberals get together to decide a mass of many-faceted and mostly new political problems; in short, one reason why the liberal New Deal Court splintered was that different men thought differently on different *issues*. The other, and overlapping, reason for the splintering was more complex; it was the accept-or-fight-or-compromise reaction of each separate liberal Justice to the views of his fellow liberal Justices when *their* ideas of legal liberalism differed from *his*. In short, it was the different response of different *personalities* to intra-liberal differences on the issues. And both the *issues* and the *personalities* of the men who met—or failed to meet—those issues ranged (as those who would put "liberalism" or "Supreme Court" into a neatly patterned pigeonhole are so loath to recognize) over the whole of a colorful spectrum in which only black and white, the colorless colors, were missing.

In the time of Holmes and of the Four Horsemen, the political issues that hit the Court had seemed, if they had not always actually been, almost black-or-white simple—with a clear-cut conservative side, and with the liberals, although even then for dissimilar reasons (as was often true of Holmes and Brandeis) protesting, and thus being better classified as anti-conservative. Congress would pass a law to regulate business or tax wealth and the Court conservatives would talk states' rights or due process to veto it, over liberal dissent; a federal regulation or tax would come to the Court for "interpretation" and the majority Justices would read it—whether an anti-trust act or a new income tax wrinkle—with business-bound eyes, over liberal dissent; a state statute that regulated or taxed business or wealth would run afoul of the Fourteenth Amendment, courtesy of the Court, over liberal dissent; some federal or state or local law (or official) would trample on somebody's non-financial rights or freedoms, with judicial benediction, over liberal dissent. That was about all there was to it; to be liberal meant merely to disapprove, for whichever of dozens of reasons, the consistent conservatism, state and national, economic and civil-liberties-wise, of the Court's ruling clique.

After the New Deal Court took over, half of these major black-or-white areas of judicial disagreement disappeared. On the economic level, on the power of governments to regulate business, no further federal laws were vetoed outright on *any* constitutional pretext, and the Fourteenth Amendment's due process clause, that old sword of Damocles over the head of every new state control of finance or industry, passed into near desuetude. Yet a plethora of practical problems in government-by-judges continued to plague the Court. There was still the "interpretation" of federal laws, old and new, and there were still the delicate and democratically crucial questions of civil liberties, exacerbated first by hot, then by cold, war. Even in the economic field, where the Roosevelt Justices seemed, at surface glance, to have set government-regulation-of-business free, old political wine was often poured into new legal bottles; federal laws might not be flatly branded uncon-

stitutional but they could, on occasion, be so cautiously
Court-"interpreted" as to achieve almost the same conservative end; state statutes, rid of the threat of the
Fourteenth Amendment, might be, and often were, cut
down by another and newly-sharpened constitutional sword
—none other than the interstate commerce clause, once
used so recklessly against federal laws in alleged defense of
dormant and unexercised states' rights, now used with
equal abandon against state laws in alleged defense of
dormant and unexercised Congressional power. Indeed,
one or two of the Justices, apparently unaware that liberalism can never be static while the world moves, seemed
to feel they had done their liberal duty, and could call it a
day, once they had helped make majority doctrine of the
Holmes-Brandeis dissents that had thundered out the
judicial liberalism of a quarter of a century before.

It was over the complications and cross-currents of
newly raised or newly phrased issues of this kind that the
New Deal Court began to splinter. Might not a Justice be
an economic liberal and a civil-liberties conservative, or
vice versa?—the New Deal Court included both. Did
economic liberalism mean upholding all business-regulating and wealth-taxing, state or national, or did it mean
giving a clear priority to national laws and so rejecting
state laws that might, some time in the future, interfere?
—both views were represented on the New Deal Court.
Was economic liberalism always pro-labor and anti-
business when the two clashed, or was it always for the
underdog, the little fellow, as when a small company came
up against a big and powerful union?—there were New
Deal Justices on both sides. Where should an economic

liberal take his stand when a conservative Congress or Administration or a conservative state government passed a law or used a law to help the economic upperdogs at the expense of the economic underdogs (workers, farmers, consumers) and the underdogs came to a liberal Court for relief?—the New Deal Justices had half a dozen answers. Ought a liberal Justice defer to the legislative will, state or national, as readily on civil-liberties restrictions as on economic regulations?—both answers, plus a half-way-between answer, had adherents on the New Deal Court. Should civil-liberties liberalism give greater protection against national restrictions or against state restrictions, or equal protection against both?—each of the three views was held by at least one New Deal Justice. Did civil-liberties liberalism envisage a different degree of protection for one kind of civil liberty than for another, for freedom of speech than for fair treatment of suspected criminals?—some New Deal Justices thought Yes, some No. Should a liberal be a bit more tolerant of intrusions on civil liberties at home, during a real war against international illiberalism or a cold war against a powerful and illiberal enemy? —the New Deal Court was torn, and divided, both ways. Nor are questions like these a complex index—they are rather a set of illustrations—of the issues whose countless combinations-and-permutations of answers intellectually splintered the nine men whose job, as Justices, was to answer them. And strangely, the one complex of attitudes and answers that was paralleled by no member of the New Deal Court was that of its so-to-speak patron saint, Holmes, the civil-liberties liberal who, with rare exceptions, defended the legislative will on every level against

the economic conservatism of judges as zealously as he
defended civil liberties on every level against the legislative will—*and was himself an economic conservative.*

No less than the interlacing issues they faced, the separate and sometimes prima-donna-like personalities (Supreme Court Justices are human) of the members of the
New Deal Court helped splinter them six ways to Sunday.
There were two Justices, each of whom patently felt that
he and his views were entitled to special deference on a
Court at last controlled by liberals; one was Stone, sole
survivor of the Holmes-Brandeis-Stone team and, from
1941 on, the Court's senior member as well as its Chief;
the other was ex-professor Frankfurter, nationally known
as an expert in Supreme Court lore, to which he had dedicated most of an academic lifetime; when such comparative
upstarts as Black and Douglas declined to follow either of
their leads and began to push ahead of them along new
liberal trails, first Frankfurter, later Stone, seemed to sulk
into a sort of we-won't-play conservatism. There were two
Roosevelt Justices who lost, each for a different reason, the
first fine careless rapture of the New Deal crusade soon
after settling into the security of the Court; one was Reed
who, despite his intense and workmanlike advocacy of New
Deal laws when that was his job as Solicitor-General, had
always been more a Kentucky Democrat than an ardent
New Dealer; the other was Reed's successor as Solicitor-
General, Robert Jackson, whose chief intellectual attribute
was a forceful eloquence in support of whatever cause he
espoused (a not unlawyerly characteristic), and whose
command of language was increasingly dedicated on the
Court to a conservatism that better fitted both his per-

sonality and his economic status. Each of the rest of the Roosevelt Justices had his idiosyncrasies too—as do all men: Black, the self-made scholar from a dirt-poor part of the South, deeply offended at the uproar over his youthfully thoughtless joining of the Klan and at slurring references to him as a police-court judge (which he once briefly was), overdid his efforts to give an aura of legal respectability, through history and precedent, to his own constitutional views, which neither needed nor gained much from such excuse and semi-apology; by contrast, Douglas, temperamentally direct, forthright, and executive, was sometimes too impatient with the roundabout reasoning of the law to give his ideas their due in his opinions; Frank Murphy tended to think more with his heart than with his head, so that his unabashed humanitarianism (though Presidents are not belittled for their humanity) was often equated with legal incompetence; Wiley Rutledge, a scholar of a different ilk than the cocksure Frankfurter, regularly weakened his influence on the Court through a sense of super-fairness that made him worry interminably every angle and approach to a problem which might lead to a different conclusion than his. Small wonder that so kaleidoscopic a collection of men, each with his own Achilles' heel, splintered apart when confronted with politico-legal issues that were tough and many-sided and mostly new.

These were the eight Roosevelt Justices—with Stone, of the Nine Old Men, included because FDR raised him to the Chiefship, and with James Byrnes of South Carolina omitted because his one year on the bench, in between high administrative chores for the President, produced nothing worth noting. During the ten years of the Roosevelt Court, from 1939 to 1949, there were three different Chiefs (which fact also contributed to confusion)—since Hughes remained head man until he resigned in 1941, and Fred Vinson took charge, by Truman's appointment, at Stone's death in 1946. Along with Hughes and Stone, McReynolds for two years and Roberts for six lapped over from the old Court into the New Deal decade. Along with Vinson, Harold Burton of Ohio presaged the dawn of a different and duller span in the life of the Court when he replaced Roberts in what might well have been called "the Republican seat"—the only one to which Roosevelt never made an appointment. But the essence of the New Deal Court consisted of Stone, its five-year Chief, and those seven stars with their separate orbits—Black, Reed, Frankfurter, Douglas, Murphy, Jackson, and Rutledge. More pointedly than for any other period in its whole history, the Court's record, while these men wrote it, is quite incomprehensible except in the light of what they were like and how they got that way.

Hugo Black—first FDR appointee, more-or-less acknowledged (or else resented) intellectual leader of the New Deal Court, and dean of today's Court—was born in a crossroads cabin in the small-farm cotton country of Alabama, eighth child of a onetime volunteer in the Confederate Army, and, despite some slight formal schooling including less than two years of copy-book law, has been rigorously educating himself throughout most of the sixty-nine years since his birth. Like at least two great Justices of the past, John Marshall and Samuel Miller (and Black has already earned a place, in the minds of many, among the great Justices), Black turned his meagerness of conventional training into a see-things-straight boon rather than a confusion-ridden curse; unlike some of his recent predecessors who also rose from the bottom to the top under their own steam, Black continued to care about, and identify himself with, those less lucky or less gifted than he. As Alabama's ablest trial lawyer, he made a modest fortune selling his services, not to the big corporations, but for use against them; as a U.S. Senator, he was a New Dealer before there was a New Deal, and his tenacious yet trenchant investigations, notably of the shipping industry and of large-scale lobbying, led to new laws and also to a hatred and fear of Black on the part of the business world. By contrast, Black, a mellow and gentle-mannered man whose slight Southern drawl belies his tempered-steel mind, has the rare capacity of not transmitting his militant ideas and ideals into personal enmity toward those who disagree.

On the Court, his captaincy of the liberals was achieved from the start by the sheer power of his mind—to the sometimes quite unconcealed exasperation of Frankfurter and Jackson, who were less bold, and thought they were brighter, than he. His mental boldness was illustrated in an early dissent where he argued, brilliantly and alone, that, despite mountains of precedents running the other way, corporations should not be, and should never have been, judicially rated as "persons" entitled to the protections of the Fourteenth Amendment. It was shown again in a later dissent, which missed by only one vote carrying a Court majority with him, where he contended that the

Bill of Rights, with all its protections of civil liberties against *federal* encroachment, was meant to be carried over and used against *state* encroachment by the adoption of the Fourteenth Amendment. These two dissents also illustrate Black's general slant toward the whole Constitution: let judges use it to protect personal freedoms, not property rights, against the acts of lawmakers. Thus intellectual boldness supports human compassion in the judicial philosophy of the man who has been aptly dubbed "an evangelical progressive," and who once wrote, in overturning the murder conviction of four Negroes on torture-wrung confessions: "Under our constitutional system, courts stand against any winds that blow as havens of refuge for those who might otherwise suffer because they are helpless, weak, outnumbered. . . ." Black has also said—but this time in super-Holmesian dissent: "Freedom to speak and write about public questions is as important to the life of our government as is the heart to the human body. . . . If that heart be weakened, the result is debilitation; if it be stilled, the result is death." Except that Black is, as Holmes was not, an economic liberal, so that some of his votes come easier, Black approximates more than any other present Justice (though Douglas runs him a close second) a sort of Holmes-brought-up-to-date—and also most nearly approaches Holmes's stature.

Contrasting with Black, big, kindly, disconcerting Stanley Reed—least controversial, least intellectually gifted (save one-term Byrnes) and most conventionally law-minded of the Roosevelt Justices—never was poor and never had to be self-taught. From the rich tobacco land of Kentucky, where his father was a first-rate doctor and where Reed later owned a sizable farm himself, he was sent to Kentucky Wesleyan and Yale, to the University of Virginia and Columbia for law, and then abroad for a year at the Sorbonne in Paris. Characteristic of his middle-of-the-road political unmilitance (though he served briefly and capably in his state legislature) is the fact that the Hoover Administration, not the New Deal, first took Reed, who was naturally born a Democrat, from a successful law practice to a government post in Washington. As counsel for a couple of pre-Roosevelt alphabetical agencies, including the RFC, Reed did a workmanly lawyerlike job; staying on with the Democrats, he won the next-to-top spot in the Department of Justice (the Attorney-General heads the Department, while the Solicitor-General argues the big cases) just as the crucial two-years'-worth of tests of New Deal laws was about to hit the Supreme Court; his thanks for his work before the high bench was a seat behind it.

It has become common to assess Reed's record on the Court in terms of his allegedly inconsistent voting position and his consequent shifts between left, right, and center during his seventeen years as a Justice. Thus, it can be said that he started on the left, as a liberal dissenter with his first New Deal colleagues; that he moved to the center or swing-man position when the Roosevelt Justices achieved a bare Court majority; that at the height of the New Deal Court—roughly from Rutledge's appointment in 1943 to Stone's death in 1946—Reed was to right of center; and that he has since moved back through center to slightly left as death has reduced the Roosevelt Justices to four. All this is relatively, numerically, and superficially true. Yet, better than any other Justice, Reed illustrates why the New Deal Court splintered; for most of his votes have been neither inconsistent nor even unpredictable if read in terms of the different kinds of *issues* he has faced. From the beginning, he has been a strong federal-government man, upholding its laws and the orders of its administrative agencies, whether directed against wealth or against personal freedom of citizens; correlatively, he has been against state regulations and taxes where they might butt into national control. If he has sometimes seemed liberal on labor problems and conservative, or anti-tax, on taxes, it was partly because the labor cases dealt more often with pro-labor *federal* action and the new taxes came mostly from the *states*; beyond this, Reed retains proud memories of having sponsored two liberal labor laws in the Kentucky legislature, so that his anti-states'-rights slant is softer in this field; further, a well-to-do farming and professional background might tend a man to look more kindly on the restriction of industry, than on the collection of taxes, by government. In the civil liberties cases, where Reed, despite his personal good-will-toward-men, built up the most reactionary record of any Roosevelt Justice, he was simply deferring as usual to any federal government action, and also deferring here to state action where it did *not* interfere with the supremacy of the nation. Only in the Negro cases has Reed been regularly on the side of the angels (as in outlawing all-white primary elections in the South)—which might be due to the desire of a Southern gentleman not to seem guilty, as a judge, of racial prejudice. Finally, where Reed's votes fall outside this rather complicated yet consistent pattern, a look at the comparative technical competence of the lawyers who argued the cases might provide the answer—for Reed unduly but naturally appreciates precision of craftsmanship in the practice of the attorney's trade.

Viewed as the not abnormal product of the Justice's past life—born a well-to-do Southerner, reared in rich farm country, professional family, expensive but conventional education, respectable law practice, no real contact with industry or big-city finance, high federal administrative officer under both political parties, chief advocate and court defender of all the laws of the United States—viewed thus, Reed's judicial record loses most of its surface contradictions and begins to be consistent with the *man* who is Justice Reed. So too, the past lives of the next pair of Roosevelt appointees, named to the Court less than three months apart, help reveal why—despite the coincidence that both had been liberal law professors—Frankfurter and Douglas have differed so vastly and sometimes violently in their legal attitudes, their judicial temperaments, and the answers they give to the big issues of constitutional law.

Felix Frankfurter, technical successor to the magnificent Holmes and the great Cardozo, stands out as the New Deal Court's most controversial and unhappy figure, its most tragically wasted brilliant mind. Brought to New York at the age of twelve from Vienna, where he was born in middle-class comfort, he plunged precociously through public school, C.C.N.Y., and the Harvard Law School— which latter was to be forever after his intellectual home. Shunning private practice in Wall Street after a two-month try, he devoted his quick-witted capabilities to government service, with trust-busting stressed, until called back to Harvard in 1914 to teach. Except for a short stint in Washington during the first World War—worth noting only because he sat on the War Labor Policies Board beside an Assistant Secretary of the Navy named Franklin Roosevelt—Frankfurter spent the next quarter-century instructing, inspiring, befriending, and finding jobs for the cream of the crop who attended Harvard Law School. Fascinated by, and idolatrous of, that uniquely U.S. institution, the Supreme Court, intimate with both Holmes and Brandeis, whose law clerks he chose for years, he became a nationally acknowledged authority on the Court's works and ways; that he sometimes exalted form over substance ("Jurisdiction and Procedure of the Federal Courts" was his pet subject) seemed not out of line for an academician. His courageous and compendious defense of the murder-convicted anarchists, Sacco and Vanzetti, as victims of gross judicial injustice, made him a liberal hero, but did not prevent his being offered, a few years later, a seat on the stodgy Supreme Court of Massachusetts—which he declined. When the jaunty little scholar with the electric charm, the darting mind, and the hosts of high-and-low friends was named by one of those friends to a Justiceship, his appointment was applauded as a natural by both liberals and conservatives across the nation.

As a freshman Justice in the New Deal camp, Frankfurter helped turn old Holmes and Brandeis dissents into majority doctrine, while revealing in his one-man "separate opinions"—which were soon to flow in unprecedented flood—an insistence on doing and saying things his way. What happened next is best, if bluntly, described in the words of Professor Walton Hamilton, writing in 1947 of Frankfurter's first eight judicial years: "Mr. Justice Frankfurter has no feel for the dominant issues; he operates best when weaving crochet patches of legalism on the fingers of the case . . . it is a calamity that his skills happen to be petty skills." For not only did the ex-professor remain notoriously a professor, lecturing and heckling attorneys and Court colleagues alike; he also remained a rather narrow academician, engrossed in the trivia of formal legal propriety (he has been called "the Supreme Court's Emily Post") to the disregard of the tough stuff of judicial statesmanship. This reluctance to face the real issues (he once announced that he was "reserving judgment"—or refusing to vote at all—in a case on which he sat) may have had its source, long before the professorial years, in his earliest environment, for Continental education and scholarship are commonly more concerned with abstract ideas and patterns of logic than with down-to-the-dirty-earth problems of living people and working governments. Along with the sliding away from solid issues went an equally academic and Continental teacher-knows-best authoritarianism when Frankfurter was forced to face solid issues. Thus, an extraordinary outburst by mild-mannered Justice Black (in a patent-law case), written solely "in order that silence may not be understood as acquiescence in the views expressed in the dissenting opinion of Mr. Justice Frankfurter," exploded, with Holmesian indignation: "The dissent in question . . . mentions no statute at all. Instead the chief reliance appears to be upon . . . the writer's personal views on 'morals' and 'ethics.' . . . And for judges to rest their

interpretation of statutes on nothing but their own conceptions of 'morals' and 'ethics' is, to say the least,
dangerous business."

Despite this sort of "dangerous" authoritarianism,
Frankfurter kept proclaiming that he was strong for
"judicial self-denial"; hence he was usually against up-
setting state infringements on civil liberties (most blatantly in the flag-salute cases, where school-kids had
been locally ordered to violate, with a physical gesture,
their salute-only-God religious training—and where
Stone got a Court majority to back the children on the
second time around). Yet it was Frankfurter who spear-
headed the Court in using its judicial power, over multiple
dissent, to veto a series of state taxes that vaguely im-
pinged on business activities in interstate commerce.
Insistence on procedural propriety, self-assured authoritarianism, selective "judicial self-denial"—whatever the
excuse, Frankfurter was soon nestled, in most closely
contested cases, with the far-right wing of the New Deal
Court. Only where Holmes or Brandeis had voted liberally,
years before, on the identical issue, or where a liberal
answer fitted his private blueprint of how "the federal
system," as an abstract concept, ought to work—*and* where
strict adherence to impeccable legal etiquette left open no
side-door escape—might Frankfurter be found on the
liberal side. It was thus he, not Reed, who was the most
unpredictable of the Roosevelt Justices on major issues—
simply because those issues so often did not determine his
stand. And though the mediocre caliber of most recently-
appointed Justices has let Frankfurter lately shine brighter

by contrast, it was he—unable to wield among equals the preceptor-like personal influence he had long been accustomed to wield as a professor—who became, in the light of his great potential, the New Deal Court's outstanding disappointment.

Frankfurter's opposite on the Roosevelt Court, in so many different ways that their oppositeness soon flared into personal antagonism, was the other ex-professor of law who was named almost simultaneously, William O. Douglas. Where Frankfurter was the cautious and self-conscious scholar, Douglas was get-it-over-and-done-with decisive; (Douglas wrote two or three times as many opinions *for the Court*, per year, as did Frankfurter, whose anxiety to express his own views precisely led him, in one term, to talk for the Court in only seven cases while talking for himself, in dissent or "separate concurrence," on thirty-three occasions). Where Frankfurter was the circumspect backer-away from issues, Douglas, like Brandeis, his predecessor in crusade, wanted always to hit them head-on. Where Frankfurter was the whisperer, Douglas was the shouter. Where Frankfurter was ingratiating, Douglas was blunt. Where Frankfurter was the oldest man Roosevelt put on the Court, Douglas was by far the youngest in temperament as well as years. And perhaps most significantly of all (whether causally or only symbolically), whereas all the rest of their colleagues came from the comparatively small geographic area of the Eastern United States, between the Atlantic Ocean and the Mississippi River, Frankfurter's roots were thousands of miles to the East in a civilization long past its prime; Douglas, despite his Minnesota birth (he was still an infant when his family left the state), was a product of the Pacific Northwest, the last American frontier.

The forty pre-Court years of Douglas's life are straight in the Horatio Alger tradition—except that the riches he both sought and won carried no dollar mark in front of them. In the state of Washington, where the family happened to be when his itinerant-preacher father died, Douglas put himself through school and Whitman College with a ragtag succession of jobs ranging from newsboy to berry-picker to window-washer to sheepherder; (he also licked the after-effects of polio by mountain climbing, which strenuous pastime he has ever since indulged in all around the world). Riding east on a freight car, he arrived at Columbia Law School with less than a dollar to his name; earned while he learned with the help of a kindly dean named Harlan Stone; graduated number-two-man in a class that included, considerably farther down, one Thomas E. Dewey. Initiated into the intricacies of fancy corporate finance by a couple of years with a Wall Street law firm, the dour and rough-cut dynamo, who looks like a cross between a cowboy and a wary hayseed, took a law-teaching job at Columbia, quit it when President Butler flouted academic democracy in naming a new dean, was snapped up by Yale, and became a full professor just five years after he got his own LL.B. A less popular but far less orthodox teacher than was Frankfurter at Harvard, he worked with ideas more than with students and revolutionized the old-style approach to business law. When the New Deal's fledgling Securities and Exchange Commission asked him to investigate the mysteries and skullduggeries of "corporate reorganization," his report packed such a solid punch that Roosevelt made him a member of the SEC; the same sort of tough-minded expertness soon won him the SEC chairmanship. His executive skill, backed by knowledge and courage, as in bringing that holy-of-business-holies, the New York Stock Exchange, to heel, led many to rate him as the New Deal's finest administrator and to regret the submerging of this talent in the contemplative work of the Supreme Court—less than three years after the meteoric man-in-a-hurry hit Washington—even though the Court badly needed, at Brandeis's retirement, a member who knew all the ins and outs and underneaths of big-time business and finance.

From the start, Douglas teamed with the Court's other ex-poor-boy, Black, and for three terms the two never voted apart in a single case; some divergence began during the war and increased shortly after, but today, though differences still crop up, the phrase, "Black and Douglas dissenting," now that Murphy and Rutledge are gone, has become as common—and means the same thing—as "Holmes and Brandeis dissenting," thirty-odd years ago. Recognized, even by colleagues who disagreed with his conclusions, as the Court's wizard in matters financial, he was soon, except when outvoted, writing the bulk of the tough opinions in this field; for instance, in upholding the Interstate Commerce Commission in a major freight-rate case, he produced an essay to delight an economist, complete with seventeen tables and a graph. His Brandeis-like mistrust of bigness was best expressed in a pile-driving dissent against letting the U.S. Steel Corp. expand its huge empire into his beloved Far West: "Power that controls the economy should be in the hands of elected representatives of the people, not in the hands of an industrial oligarchy. Industrial power should be decentralized. It should be scattered into many hands so that the fortunes of the people will not be dependent on the whim or caprice, the political prejudices, the emotional instability of a few self-appointed men. The fact that they are not vicious men but respectable and social minded in irrelevant. That is the philosophy and command of the Sherman Act. It is founded on a theory of hostility to the concentration in private hands of power so great that only a government of the people should have it." "Government of the people" got his steady support, whether state or nation was doing the governing—except where civil liberties were stepped on, and sometimes even then. Through the New Deal Court days, Douglas ranked only fourth in defense of personal freedoms, behind Murphy, Rutledge, and Black; indeed, in the wartime cases—dealing with spying, with treason, and with the pushing around of Japanese-Americans on the Pacific coast—Douglas voted one hundred per cent with the government, regardless of claimed violations of the Bill of Rights. More recently, Douglas has become, both on the Court and off, the most vigorous and eloquent judicial champion of civil liberties. In cumulative dissents that vitalize cold facts with fire, he has damned all the "loyalty" programs and oaths and laws—like the Smith Act, under which the top native Communists have been jailed—as directed, in disregard of "the first article of our faith," against a tiny band of "miserable merchants of unwanted ideas. . . . Only those held by fear and panic could think otherwise." Blasting the New York "Feinberg

Law" that lets schoolteachers be fired "on a principle repugnant to our society—guilt by association," Douglas blended Brandeis and Holmes into his own mature credo: "We need be bold and adventuresome in our thinking to survive. . . . The Framers knew . . . the strength that comes when the mind is free. . . ."

As though time ran backward, the first four Roosevelt appointees—Black, Reed, Frankfurter, and Douglas—are today, and again in minority, the last four judicial survivors, each with more than sixteen years of service behind him. If joint survivorship, in the face of their five less luminous (Warren perhaps excepted) Truman-or-Eisenhower-appointed colleagues, has maybe brought them a little closer together, still Frankfurter misses the one intimate friend he found on the Court—his long-time ally in action, Robert Jackson; and Black and Douglas sorely miss their two stanch comrades against conservatism, mid-twentieth-century style—Wiley Rutledge and especially Frank Murphy.

Murphy—the New Deal Court's most underrated member, whose alleged lack of judicial skill or temperament led to such cracks, and not only by conservatives, as "Justice tempered with Murphy"—was a Michigan Irishman with a sense of mission, who might well have been a priest instead of a public servant. A onetime assistant U.S. district attorney, law teacher, local judge, mayor of Detroit, high commissioner of the Philippine Islands, he burst into national prominence when he refused, as newly elected governor of Michigan in 1937, to call out the state troopers to break up the sit-down strikes in the depression-hit automobile factories. Although his characteristically patient and unviolent handling of the explosive situation brought him thanks, not just from the unions, but from Ford and General Motors as well, he was defeated for re-election as an enemy of the rights of property. Roosevelt immediately named the non-drinking, non-smoking, bushy-browed bachelor, who looked a little like a saint with a red halo, to the U.S. Attorney-Generalship, where he spent a militantly liberal year—which included the setting up of a civil-rights section in the Department of Justice—before being elevated to the Court.

No Justice in all Court history—not Holmes, not Stone, not Black, not Douglas—was so consistent and passionate a judicial crusader for civil liberties for everyone, for Nazi spies and for Japanese generals, in peacetime and in wartime, as was Murphy. Not even his ardent Catholic faith kept him from defending the rights of the Catholic-hating sect called Jehovah's Witnesses ("To them . . . befalls the burden of testing our devotion to the ideals and constitutional guarantees of religious freedom")—nor from flaying official efforts to deport, as a former Communist, labor leader Harry Bridges ("The record in this case will stand forever as a monument to man's intolerance of man"). Despite his past as a federal law-enforcer, he insisted—as Reed so conspicuously did not—on giving criminals every constitutional break; dissenting in a search-and-seizure case, he pilloried his brethren for permitting a "shabby business: Lawlessness by officers of the law." His chief other legal-emotional slant was pro-labor—and his very first major opinion for the Court, upholding the right to picket peacefully as a form of freedom of speech, neatly combined the two. That Murphy was so predictable on civil liberties and labor, always finding some lawyer's-reason to reach the end he sought, was why lawyers belittled his ability as a judge; and yet John Marshall, for one, used exactly the same technique—though he used it to reach entirely different ends. "The law," Murphy said, "knows no finer hour than when it cuts through formal concepts . . . to protect unpopular citizens against discrimination and persecution." Marshall was never so forthright—nor so human.

As forthright as Murphy, but again not so human—in the sense of concern for others—was the New Deal Court's most obvious turncoat-to-conservatism and most gifted wielder of words, Robert Jackson. Maybe Jackson wrote so unlegally well—with the force of plain and pointed talk replacing lawyers' jargon—because he never went through law school nor won a law degree; indeed, though born on the proper side of the social and economic tracks, he never even went through college, and one ungraduating year of law study (shades of Marshall, Miller, and Black) was his only formal education after high school. Something of an adolescent prodigy, he learned law fast as an office apprentice and soon had a practice of his own in Jamestown, N.Y., sufficiently lucrative to let him be a gentleman farmer, with a stable of trotting horses, on the side. As that *rara avis*, a well-to-do upstate New York Democrat (his forte was lawyering for little companies against big ones), he did a chore or two for another gentleman farmer, Governor F. D. Roosevelt—and in 1934 a third New York gentleman farmer, Treasury Secretary Morgenthau, summoned Jackson to Washington "for six to eight months" to get the legal affairs of the Internal Revenue (or income-tax)

Bureau in shape. The solid and frog-mouthed man with the leisurely manner and mercurial mind never went back to Jamestown, except to vacation or visit. Jackson moved from tax work to anti-trust work (in both, he tackled and tamed the mighty Mellon financial interests), to the Solicitor-Generalship (he lost only one of twenty-four cases before the subdued Supreme Court in the 1938–39 term), to the Attorney-Generalship (with war in the wind), to a Justiceship shortly before war came. The most brilliant and vigorous verbal advocate the New Deal had known, he was counted on to continue his down-the-line New Dealing on the Court. Forgotten were three little facts: Jackson was ambitious—and a bit embittered that FDR had taken a third term when Jackson had high hopes and high chances to succeed him; Jackson was wealthy—the richest of the Roosevelt appointees; Jackson was independent, with far more than the turn-the-switch-either-way lawyerly independence of the counsel accustomed to fit his cause to his client—and the lifetime tenure of Justices invites the turning of legal and political switches.

For a term or two, Jackson used his freshness and pungency of phrase largely on the liberal side; he warned that, if California's keep-the-Okies-out law should be upheld (which it was not), "then our heritage . . . is only a promise to the ear to be broken to the hope, a teasing illusion like a munificent bequest in a pauper's will"; speaking for the Court, and for the schoolkids, in the second flag-salute case, he remarked that "compulsory unification of opinion achieves only the unanimity of the graveyard." But on economic issues, and soon on most civil liberties too, the gentleman of property early began to talk like a gentleman of property; as he edged right, to vote more and more often with his friend, Frankfurter, his virtue—as against the little scholar's pose of utter impartiality—was his plain-spoken approach to the job of judging. Dissenting against a liberal anti-trust decision, on policy grounds, he said: "To use my office at a time like this . . . to catapult Congress into . . . supervision of the nation's insurance business is more than I can reconcile with my view of the functions of this Court in our society." Dissenting against a liberal patent-law decision, he lampooned the majority view as based on "a legal concept which either is very profound or almost unintelligible, I cannot be quite sure which." Dissenting against a pro-labor decision, he protested: "This Court now . . . permits to employees the same arbitrary dominance, over the economic sphere which they control, that labor so long, so bitterly and so rightly asserted should belong to no man." And dissenting against a decision upholding religious freedom, his final metaphor must have made friend Frankfurter wince: "Religious symbolism is even used by some with the same mental reservations one has in teaching of Santa Claus or Uncle Sam or Easter bunnies or dispassionate judges." Jackson's frank disclaimer of judicial dispassion was made more pointed in his own case when, at President Truman's plea, he took a year off from the Court to prosecute war criminals in Germany—a diversion which bothered naïve believers in an independent and apolitical judiciary (as Justice Roberts's more judge-like investigation of Pearl Harbor, for President Roosevelt, had not) and also bothered Jackson's colleagues, mainly because a lot of 4-to-4 cases had to be held over for decision

until the following term. It was from his voluntary exile
that Jackson, uninformed or misinformed, bitter that he
did not get the hoped-for Chief Justiceship at Stone's
death, loosed his intemperate attack on Black, on whom he
blamed his disappointment; the attack put a finish to
Jackson's effective influence on his fellows. For the eight
years until he died, a frustrated man, in 1954, Jackson
followed an increasingly conservative line with only
occasional aberrations—though the quartet of Truman
appointees made him, like Frankfurter, look a little less
illiberal toward the end. But he never lost his mastery of
language; indeed, his Court career could well be capsuled
in the fact that an anti-labor, anti-civil-liberties "concurring opinion" which he wrote in 1950 was published—
and it read as though intended to be published—intact,
in the magazine section of the New York *Times*.

Where Jackson remained, as a judge, the aggressive
and hell-for-leather advocate, Wiley Rutledge—FDR's
last appointee and the only one with important past judicial
experience—precisely fitted the popular picture of a
Justice as a patient explore-every-angle-and-then-quietly-
make-up-your-mind sort of man. Roosevelt is said to have
named Rutledge partly because he "had geography"—in
that he could be designated "of Iowa," his last pre-D.C.
home, as Douglas had been designated "of Connecticut."
Rutledge did indeed have geography—in more than the
silly sense of scattering Justiceships East, South, West,
and North, according to George Washington's first-
Court precedent. Born in Kentucky—and, like Douglas, a
wandering minister's son—he had lived as a youth in
North Carolina and Tennessee, graduated from the

University of Wisconsin, taught high school in Indiana and New Mexico, taught law in Colorado and Missouri, and ended his peripatetic academic career as dean of the Iowa Law School. First plucked from his professorial swivel-chair to sit for four years on the federal court of appeals in Washington, the genial and slightly jowly scholar with the modest and slow-spoken mien was made a Justice to replace Byrnes (who had replaced McReynolds, and who now went back to more obvious politics, where he belonged).

Rutledge immediately joined the Black-Douglas-Murphy team and turned it, for six years and on most major matters, into a solid four-man core of living legal liberalism. Close to Murphy on civil liberties, more hesitant to go whole-hog on economic issues, as by blanket benediction of state taxes or of labor unions, he often gave to the Court's left wing, with his wordy, thinking-out-loud and respectful-of-precedent opinions, a more solid if stodgier support in lawyers' law than did the other three. If his touch was sometimes heavy, his rectitude was impeccable and could rise, on occasion, to heights of indignation. When the Court, with even Black and Douglas going along halfway, pretzel-twisted past law and plain common-sense in upholding—to most of the nation's emotional delight—an unprecedently tremendous fine for contempt of court, slapped on John L. Lewis and his striking United Mine Workers, Rutledge (and Murphy) refused to join in the lynching bee. In a magnificent dissent, running to forty-four pages and reminiscent in tone of Stone's dissent in the AAA case, Rutledge tore every majority argument to shreds, commented that one of several strange things the Court approved (the combining of a civil suit and a criminal suit in a single case) should be "shocking to every American lawyer and to most citizens," and hit a climax of superb and subtly double-edged disgust with: "No man or group is above the law. All are subject to its valid commands. So are the Government and the courts." Soon after, explaining his unpopular stand without apology, he said: "I could not see the law in any other guise than as I wrote. Accordingly there was nothing else for me to do than what I did." These words might well have served as Rutledge's epitaph.

Here then were the seven men, none a Chief Justice, whose separate, varied, and sometimes veering views of life-translated-into-law accounted, in main, for the Court's zig-zag-to-leftward course during its New Deal decade. For the two years from 1943 to 1945, when Stone and Roberts (until his retirement) made up the rest of the nine, the Court was—without even a close competitor—the most brilliant and able collection of Justices who ever graced the high bench together; the least of them would have stood out on many Courts of the past. Indeed, that very fact was one reason why they differed and fought and splintered. Another reason was the executive incapacity of Stone as Chief—for his tolerance of endless debate, New England town meeting style, in conference, made the early Roosevelt appointees, despite their respect for Stone as a Justice, look back longingly to the crisp but fair efficiency of headman Hughes. Still, the New Deal Court, for all its internal differences and its leaderlessness, laid down a lot of law, much of it new. And that part of its political, or government-guiding, array of decisions which has not already

gone with the conservative wind calls for summary even
in an effort to picture the Court's work with the focus set
for distance—as though what is still close were far away.

In the long perspective of time, probably no more than
a handful of the multitude of cases of great contemporary
importance decided during the New Deal decade will still
stand above the horizon as enduring landmarks of government law. Such a perhaps brash prediction stems from a
clutter of ill-assorted causes, chief among which is a hunch
that the Roosevelt Court's over-all slant and the more
compelling separate statements of its oh-so-individual
members are more likely than a ruling here and a ruling
there to affect the law's future course and to catch the attention of political and legal historians. The major break
with the past had been made by the Nine Old Men before
the appointment of a single Justice by FDR; what the New
Deal nine did, in main—and usually in otherwise unusual
unanimity—was to follow the lead that had been laid out
for them; it was of no special moment, except maybe sta-
tistically, that the Court, in a single year, 1941, overruled
no less than ten of their predecessors' decisions—decisions
ranging in age from five to thirty-three years back, and
ranging in importance from one that forbade a state to tax
a man on sales he made to the U.S. government, to the
one, made famous by Holmes's dissent, that vetoed the
outlawing of child labor. None of these overrulings
sparked more than casual comment, among laymen or even
lawyers—so accustomed was the country, in four short
years, to a radically new trend in constitutional law.
Moreover, many decisions that did hit the headlines,

because of their news value at the time, will soon fade to footnotes in Court annals; that the Justices upheld the National Labor Relations Board in letting the unions get away with a few selfish and generally resented tactics, under the terms of the Wagner Act, lost all long-term interest once those tactics were banned by Congress in the Taft-Hartley Act; whether granting children "released time" from public-school attendance for brief religious instruction menaces the "separation of church and state," or violates the constitutional guarantee of religious freedom (for whom?), is scarcely calculated to shake the law in proportion to the attention the public—and the Justices—paid it. Specific matters of immediate moment, or seeming moment—judicial or otherwise—rarely retain much significance unless they carry the seed, not merely the verbal symbol, of something larger and lasting.

Yet another reason why few of the New Deal Court's *decisions*—as opposed to some of the *opinions* of its brilliantly motley-minded members—are apt to achieve permanent stature is because, once the clean-up job on constitutional errors of past Courts was out of the way, those decisions lost the force of a united front. In "interpreting" federal statutes, in supervising federal agencies like the NLRB and the FTC and the FPC and the FCC and the old ICC, in reviewing state (and sometimes federal) taxes, and especially in dealing with claimed kicks-in-the-pants to civil liberties—by national, state, or local governments—not only did decisions go 5–4, or sometimes 4–4 or 4–3 (as one or both of the ex-Attorneys-General, Jackson and Murphy, disqualified themselves on cases started in the Department of Justice while they were there); decisions that went 5–4 or 6–3 or even 9–0, on many occasions, found the majority voting together for different reasons, so that no one could tell what the law was—or would be in the next case. And a decision made by five or six or eight or nine Justices, on two or three or four divergent grounds, is not the kind of decision that endures. In the John L. Lewis contempt-of-court case (where Rutledge superbly dissented), Vinson, who spoke "for the Court," based his ruling on two wholly separate grounds; Reed and Burton agreed with both; Frankfurter and Jackson agreed only with one; Black and Douglas agreed only with the other (and also, quite unrelatedly, protested against the penalty); Murphy dissented with Rutledge. What is the law and how likely is it to last?

One way to chronicle the New Deal Court's doings—and an easy and popular way with current commentators, lay or legal—is strictly chronological, so that "trends" to right or left can be stressed and spotted as the Court's personnel gradually shifted (for only the Black-Reed-Frankfurter-Douglas-Murphy five covered the whole ten years). Thus, it can be written that, during the 1940–41 session, which was Murphy's first *full* term, the nine (or enough of them) upheld the federal Wages and Hours Act; gave the federal government, for the first time, some control of state primaries where national officials, like Congressmen, are up for election; let the NLRB ban an employer from *not* hiring a job-seeker just because the man was a union member; broadened the control of Congress over "navigable" rivers in a way to give a legal boost to such public power programs as TVA; put labor unions almost all the way out of reach of the anti-trust acts; refused to let a judge, on his own and without a jury sitting, punish a newspaper editor for publishing criticism, however intemperate, of the judge's conduct of a case; gave its blessing to peaceful picketing, even by a union that had no members at work (or formerly at work) in the place being picketed—and made almost all these decisions by a divided Court. Or it can be written that, during the 1948–49 session, the last of the New Deal decade, the Court did almost nothing of note save uphold a Nebraska anti-union statute and a Missouri anti-union court order (labor by now, with the swing of the pendulum, had become, in many minds, too big and strong for its boots); restrict, though more in words than with any practical punch, over-eager "searches and seizures" by state policemen; and barely defend the right of even a filthy-mouthed native fascist to freedom of speech. Again, three of these four decisions were by a variously divided nine. Perhaps more meaningful and a little less boring than any such year-by-year catalogue of cases would be a quick over-all survey of the New Deal Court's work in different fields of government law, with special mention of some of the big decisions not already noted.

In the economic field, in the regulation and taxing of business, the old meat-axe of this-whole-law-is-unconstitutional rusted on the wall—except where a series of state taxes (as on state-to-state sales) and a few minor state regulations struck a slim majority of the Justices as interfering with national control of national commerce. Into judicial vogue came the stiletto of "interpretation," of deciding whether a legislature, almost always Congress, "intended" this particular use of a law when it acted—*or* when it did *not* act, to override, as it can, some old "inter-pretation" of that law by the Court. Thus, the bitterly argued case that made the insurance business subject to the anti-trust laws, by a 4–3 vote, revolved around what Congress meant or did not mean when it failed to specify insurance as coming under those laws—especially in the light of a seventy-five-year-old Court decision, here over-ruled, that held insurance was a *local* business and so subject to *state* control. Likewise, a strangely split trio of rulings, that left some corporation dividends, when paid in stock instead of cash, free of the income tax, centered on what Congress meant when it *did* amend (a further twist) the income tax law to deal with an old decision (Holmes and Brandeis dissenting) on just this point. Most of the Congressional acts the New Deal Court undertook to "interpret" concerned the anti-trust laws, the patent laws, and laws regulating the rates charged by railroads and other "public utilities," when some administrative agency (FTC, FPC, ICC) or the Department of Justice tried to give them a new or different reach. Sometimes the government won—notably in the insurance case, in a case blessing the more-often-damned Interstate Commerce Commission for lowering railroad freight-rates for South-ern and Western shippers while raising them for the here-tofore favored East, and in two cases letting the Federal Power Commission set gas company rates by a broader and far more consumer-conscious formula than an older Court had ordered, years and years before. Sometimes the government lost, as in most of the important patent and anti-trust cases, notably the one allowing U.S. Steel to expand its vast operations to the West Coast—which

Douglas's strong protest (for four dissenters) called "the most important anti-trust case . . . before the Court in years." Not one of these decisions was unanimous and most were not nearly so.

On civil liberties—on the protection of people's personal and political freedoms against some government's efforts to take them away—a tremendous fuss has been made of the New Deal Court's allegedly liberal record. It is true that that record is brighter than the record of any court in the past; it is true that in two overlapping ways—in speaking out against such barbaric police techniques as the third degree, especially as practiced by state and local officers, and in making a start toward granting Negroes the same living and voting and not-being-lynched-by-law rights as white people—the New Deal Court did make big strides toward giving life to the marble motto on the building where they work, "Equal Justice Under Law"; it is even true that, had there been one more Justice to regularly join the Black-Douglas-Murphy-Rutledge quartet, those strides might have been considerably longer. But the bulk of the New Deal Court's record, as a Court, on civil liberties consisted in deciding now this way, now that—with the Justices split in a dozen directions—a score of disparate little issues, some of them as petty as whether Jehovah's Witnesses (apparently the Court's pet religious sect, though none belonged to it) could peddle their literature on the streets without buying a cheap local permit. Chief basis of much of this backing and filling was the philosophic poser that not even Holmes had quite solved to his own satisfaction: If judges ought to respect the majority will when faced with *economic* laws (whether of nation, state, or village), if these laws were entitled to a "presumption of constitutionality," why were not laws that cut down or hemmed in civil liberties entitled to the same presumption? If the Court should not stop a state from regulating milk prices as the state saw fit, should it stop a state from letting its police officers tap telephone wires to get evidence of crime? It was Stone, not Holmes, who—in a famous footnote to an otherwise unimportant opinion (U.S. *v.* Carolene Products Co.)—first faced the issue squarely and maintained that, despite the loss of logical consistency, civil liberties deserved the greater judicial protection against lawmakers. But some of the Roosevelt Justices could not bring themselves to accept Stone's view; indeed Frankfurter once flatly, and at length, disowned it. Still another basic issue that bothered and divided the New Deal Court in civil liberties cases was how far the Fourteenth Amendment carried over, against state or local government action, the guarantees of the Bill of Rights against *federal* action. No Justice took the position—most sensible, if not necessarily most appealing, to any non-lawyer who reads the Amendment's words—that *none* of it was carried over; four Justices, headed by Black, argued and voted that the *whole* Bill of Rights was carried over; the rest thought some of it was and some was not—free speech, for instance, yes, but no-hint-of-self-incrimination in a criminal-case defendant's refusal to testify, no. Small wonder, then, that the New Deal Court's civil-liberties rulings were, for the most part, spotty and uncertain, and that a few of them have already been overturned.

As the slicing up of the Bill of Rights, where it hits the

states, suggests (with parts of it used, parts of it not used, by the Court majority's choice), there are many types of civil liberties and of civil-liberties cases. And the story of the New Deal nine's decisions in the field can best be told by dividing the cases, roughly and arbitrarily, into three different kinds: those stemming from the First Amendment's guarantees of freedom of religion, of speech, of press, and of the right of assembly; those dealing with the fair treatment of suspected criminals, before and during trial, to which most of the rest of the Bill of Rights is devoted; and those involving discrimination, political or personal, against minority groups (meaning, during this decade, for practical purposes, Negroes). Of the First Amendment's freedoms—which the whole Court thought carried over, though by no means in every instance, to the states—religious freedom got the greatest attention and protection; from the flag-salute cases to the released-school-time cases to the peddling-of-religious-propaganda cases to the question whether a state may pay to transport children to parochial schools by bus, the Court interminably worried comparative trivia in personalized opinions, and usually came out, by a close vote, on the side of free (unpaying and unpaid-for) religion. Far more important was the decision that upset, but only by 5–4, the rulings of the Nine Old Men that conscientious objectors against bearing arms could not become citizens—and there was something sadly symbolic in the fact that Stone, who had dissented with Holmes and Brandeis and Hughes in the old cases, here dissented in the opposite direction on the very day he died. Freedom of speech—which today practically embodies freedom of assembly—got some minor and divided support from the New Deal Court until the Communist cases and "loyalty" cases began to come in; neither then nor, especially, later were a majority of the Justices as alert to defend the right of radicals, including Communists, to speak their minds as the old Hughes Court had been, in a trio of anti-state-suppression-of-speech decisions during the 1930's. As for the freedom-of-press cases, they dealt chiefly with the right of news-papers to blast judges without being hauled into court for contempt; and with the protection of the courts from undue outside pressure weighing against press liberty, sometimes seen as license, the Justices—and the decisions—went both ways. The First Amendment got no great lift, no new breath of life, during the New Deal decade.

In the second big category of civil-liberties cases, where fair treatment and fair trial of suspected criminals was at stake, the New Deal Court's decisions defy all description. Not only did the Justices differ as to whether and which Bill-of-Rights guarantees here carried over to the states; not only were 5–4 decisions, on most points, the rule rather than the exception in cases going either way; not only did individual Justices switch back and forth on the same point (in one case, involving high-handed and highly questionable search procedures by the FBI, Black and Douglas voted to uphold the federal police while Frank-furter wrote a brilliant libertarian dissent, in which Jackson was one of three who joined); more than this, the very points at issue varied from protection against "unreason-able searches and seizures" (to get evidence of crime), to protection from third-degree confessions (here the Court was its best), to the right of indictment by a grand jury, to the right to be represented by counsel, to the right of a "speedy and public trial by an impartial jury," to the protections against self-incrimination and "double jeopardy" (for the same crime) and "cruel and unusual punishment" (shadows of the Georgia chain-gangs). It is enough to say that the Court's decisions ran about fifty-fifty where federal criminals and federal officials were concerned, and that civil liberties got less than an even break in the state-originated cases. This last fact led Black, in dissent against the 5–4 upholding of an Illinois burglary conviction, where the defendants had had no lawyers to represent them, to blister his colleagues' decision as "another example of the consequences which can be produced by substitution of this Court's day-to-day opinion of what kind of trial is fair and decent for the kind of trial which the Bill of Rights guarantees." Black's statement might stand as a summary of all the Justices' joint and separate treatment of this whole hodgepodge of issues—including on occasion his own.

It was in defense of the Negro race against discrimination that the New Deal Court struck its strongest blows for civil liberties—and may indeed have made its most enduring contributions to public law. Far fewer issues and far fewer cases came before the Justices in this field of personal freedoms (though many of the fair-trial decisions, as in banning use of the third degree to get confessions, were given double meaning and heavier Court support because the defendants were Negroes in the South). Yet what little, speaking quantitatively, the Court accomplished here was done with the force of unanimity or near-unanimity; most of it broke new ground; and its sheer momentum has already carried the post-New Deal Court farther and farther along this humanitarian line. What the Roosevelt Court did first was to toss out, as offending the Fifteenth Amendment (which forbids states to keep people from voting because of their race or color), the device then widely used in the South whereby states would turn over control of primary elections—the only elections that mattered—to the political parties, and the state Democratic Party would not let Negroes vote; in so doing, the new Justices overruled a less-than-ten-years-old *unanimous* decision by the Nine Old Men (who included Holmes, Brandeis, and Stone); further, when South Carolina tried to get around this by the gag of turning its Democratic Party into an un-state-authorized all-white "private club," the Court would not even listen to South Carolina's case after a lower federal court outlawed the gag. Next, the Justices, under the questionable cloak of the commerce clause, forbade Jim Crow arrangements on interstate buses, and upheld a state law forbidding similar segregation, even when applied to boats making excursion trips to Canada. Finally, "restrictive covenants"—whereby property-owners in "white sections" of Northern cities contracted never to sell or rent to people "not of the Caucasian race"—were dealt a long-range death-blow in a set of rulings which said that state courts could not enforce such contracts, even in private lawsuits, without violating the Fourteenth Amendment.

One supplementary and special group of civil-liberties issues arose directly from the war. Considerably more concerned for fairness than any of its predecessors who sat during previous wars, the New Deal Court overturned a

few treason and espionage convictions. But the most illiberal decision it ever handed down was in giving judicial
blessing, by a 6–3 vote, to the cruel, wholesale evacuation
from the West Coast, under Army orders, of all Japanese
and Japanese-Americans, regardless of their citizenship or
their later-proved loyalty and solely because of their race.
On the opposite or credit side of the Court's ledger—
though otherwise entirely unrelated—was a unique decision that branded a part of a federal law unconstitutional;
when Congress attached a rider to an appropriations bill,
specifically removing from the federal payroll three liberal
(though not Communist), high-placed employees, named
Lovett, Watson, and Dodd, the Justices struck down the
rider as a "bill of attainder"; this was the only time, in
the New Deal decade, that judicial supremacy was exercised to veto a Congressional act—and one of the three
times in the Court's history that it has been so used in
significant protection of civil liberties.

Civil liberties and economic, or bread-and-butter, matters meet and overlap in a third major area of government
law—that concerned with the rights of, or the restrictions
on, labor and labor unions. The overlapping is most apparent where the right to picket peacefully, obviously for
economic purposes, is judicially upheld as an exercise of
good old freedom of speech—as the New Deal Court, at
first, upheld it, only to repent and restrict its original
generosity in later cases. The overlapping was perhaps
most meaningful, during the New Deal decade, when the
unanimous Justices refused—though for different reasons
—to "interpret" the anti-union Taft-Hartley Act's ban on
the spending of union money for political purposes as for-

bidding political propaganda or palaver in union news-papers—a suggested curtailment of press freedom that might some day have led, had it been honored, to a government ban on political editorials in the supported-by-business-through-advertising New York *Times*. For all that the New Deal Court's labor decisions—from portal-to-portal pay to the legislative protection or, later, outlawing of the closed shop—were as publicized as they were numerous, they are perhaps the most ephemeral of all. What a majority of the Justices did (for unanimity was as rare in this field as in others) was, by and large, to follow the legislative lead—and thus the election returns —in consistently upholding statutes and administrative rulings made under them, on national and state levels, regardless of the about-face of both statutes and rulings from pro-union to anti-union during the decade. Although the aberrational and quite incomprehensible Lewis contempt case (where Rutledge's dissent is most likely to influence future Justices) and the first peaceful-picketing-is-free-speech decision (where Murphy's doubly self-expressive *coup* has already won consideration in literally hundreds of subsequent cases, largely in disagreement or qualification) can neither be completely ignored, little if anything that the New Deal Court did on the labor front—save bow, in general, to the shifting popular and legislative-or-administrative will—is likely to endure.

Yet it was a rather routine, and routinely divided, decision in the labor-law field that set off—or served as an excuse for—the most dramatic and symbolic single episode in the New Deal Court's ten-year tenure; this was, of course, Jackson's poisonous, public, long-distance attack on Black in the late spring of 1946. The excuse for the attack was that Black had sat and voted in a case where one litigant, the United Mine Workers, had been represented by a former law-partner of Black's, named Harris. Ignored in Jackson's intemperate and unprecedented yelp, and generally unknown even to lawyers, were several facts: Other Justices—Butler regularly, Roberts regularly, Stone once (though he preferred not to)—had sat in cases argued by former law-partners; Black's short partnership with Harris had ended nineteen years before, and the two men had scarcely seen each other since; Black's meticulous sense of propriety had led him to disqualify himself (disqualification, as even Jackson conceded, had always been left to the conscience of each individual Justice) in all cases involving the FCC, of which his brother-in-law was a member; the decision in the U.M.W. case would have gone the same way had Black declined to sit. But it was clearly not the case that caused the outburst; it was Jackson's deep disappointment that he had not been named Chief Justice when Stone died—plus stories that reached him abroad to the effect that Black was mainly responsible. Frustrated once, during his pre-Court New Deal days, in an abortive attempt to win the New York governorship, frustrated by Roosevelt's third term in his hope to become President, Jackson's last ambition was to head the Court—an honor allegedly promised him, long back, by FDR and left still unbestowed at FDR's death.

If Black blocked Jackson's elevation to the Chiefship (and there is some evidence that he indirectly helped do so), Frankfurter similarly stymied the naming of *his* arch-enemy, Douglas. President Truman compromised by appointing that long-time laborer in the Democratic vine-yard and top utility-man for the New Deal, Fred Vinson of Kentucky—with the hope that Vinson's conciliatory talents and slow patience might settle or smother the feuds within the Court. Vinson was Truman's second Justice, Harold Burton of Ohio having been named to the "Republican seat" a year earlier, at Roberts's why-bother-to-stay-on retirement. Three years later—when Murphy and Rutledge died, and Truman chose Tom Clark of Texas and Sherman Minton of Indiana—the New Deal Court, as a Court, with all its conflicts, its contradictions, its personal spats, and its splintered brilliance, passed into history. An era was ended.

CHAPTER 9

Yesterday's Court, the Court Today, and a Court That Could Be Tomorrow

FIVE YEARS AFTER the New Deal Court shut up shop in 1949, and adjourned for that sorry summer when Murphy and Rutledge died, the Justices were back in headlines and politics up to their robe-rimmed necks as they ordered the Southern states to let Negro children attend the same public schools as did white children. This is not to say they had not been front-page political news in the interim between; they had. In the May-or-June late spring of each of the four intervening terms, some matter of immediate moment—and of potential long-range reach—had been decided: In 1950, it was the 1954 ruling's feebler forerunner, which ordered the South to let Negroes into the classrooms of white universities and to let them eat in the same sections of the same dining-cars on railroads; in 1951, it was the blessing bestowed on Judge Harold Medina's prosecution (*sic*) of the eleven so-called "top native Communists," which blessing meant giving the Smith Act the judicial nod of constitutionality; in 1952, it was the refusal to bless President Truman's technical "seizure" of the steel plants to keep steel production going, despite a threatened strike, during the Korean War; in 1953, it was the back-and-forth legal and judicial moves —ending in an extraordinary special Court session after the Justices had adjourned—to decide whether the Rosenbergs should be executed as spies, which they were, within hours after the Court announced its final order.

Yet, if the Rosenberg business, because it was so dramatically personalized, made a bigger two-or-three-day public splash; if the you-mayn't-do-it-unless-Congress-lets-you spanking of Presidential steel-seizure had a more drastic short-term impact, in that it sparked the wartime strike that Truman had tried to avoid; if the Dennis decision that sent the unconcealed U.S. Communist leaders to jail—to be followed by lesser pip-squeaks of the party— was far more significant, seen in the light of U.S. constitutional history, since it all but obliterated the free-speech guarantee of the First Amendment by letting Congress ignore that guarantee at will—still, the anti-segregation-in-public-school decisions were clearly destined to affect more deeply, over a snowballing period of time, the day-to-day lives of the greatest number of citizens. A bit overenthusiastically described in parts of the press as the most important Supreme Court action since the diametrically opposed Dred Scott decision, this set of unanimous rulings led to silly talk of secession-again by a few Southern hotheads, and to plans for subtle disobedience of the Court's orders by millions in the South—including a former member of the Court, Governor Byrnes of South Carolina. Little mentioned or noticed was the fact that the post-New Deal Court was here moving, in a sense, on the momentum of the Roosevelt Justices in the one area where they had teamed *together* to blaze a new trail toward more liberal government law.

Little noticed, too, was the fact that all the Vinson-into-Warren (or Truman-into-Eisenhower) Court's big decisions, and a disproportionately large part of all its decisions, dealt with, stemmed from, or were mainly motivated by the cold war (or the Korean hot war) with Communist Russia. The relation of the steel-seizure case, of the Smith Act convictions of home-grown Communists, and of the Rosenberg spy rulings is apparent; nor is there any doubt that the pro-Negro pronouncements—as many Southerners have accurately, if angrily, charged—although following the New Deal Court's direction, were pushed to such unprecedented lengths to help counter Communist propaganda in Asia and Africa about American maltreatment of people whose skins are not white; and in free-speech cases, in "loyalty" cases, in cases on admitting or deporting aliens (or alien-born citizens), in Fifth Amendment self-incrimination cases, in such labor cases as that dealing with the non-Communist affidavit (for union officers) demanded by the Taft-Hartley Act—in all these and others, the dark shadow of the U.S.S.R. lay over the U.S.S.C. If there was ever any question that the Justices were primarily political figures, the past five or six years should have dispelled it; and never in the long history of this political group of men—not even when, acting separately on circuit, they were ruthlessly enforcing the Sedition Act at the end of the eighteenth century—did international politics, on a world scale, so overweigh and dominate their work and their decisions.

The tragedy—as history is sure, some day, to record it —is that the Supreme Court's majority, with the most magnificent opportunity ever granted so small a group to show the world the profound difference between the humanity of a democracy and the brutality of a dictatorship, so miserably failed; that the Court—except in the Negro cases—while purporting to fight a foreign tyranny, actually aped it. From the Dennis decision that makes a mockery of the First Amendment—in a way that would have shocked Holmes and Brandeis, and did shock Black and Douglas—on down to such seemingly little things as letting government servants be fired as "disloyal" on the random charges of unrevealed and so unanswerable informers, or letting an alien be torn from his U.S. wife and child, and deported, because he was once a Communist, though he quit them twenty-three years before (and eleven years before the law under which he was deported was passed)—the Truman-Vinson Court was more often the nation's shame than its pride at giving life to democracy's high ideals. Nor has the bare beginning of an Eisenhower-Warren Court significantly changed the picture yet, despite a few signs hinting to the hopeful that it may.

Although Vinson became Chief in name in 1946, the Court did not become his, in fact, until Clark and Minton joined him and Burton in 1949 to form a quartet of Truman-appointed Justices. In the three years between, two things about the Court's new captain had been made abundantly clear: One was that, despite his vast administrative skill as a compromiser of conflicting issues or men, and despite Truman's hope that this skill would suffice to suffocate or soften the Black-and-Douglas against Jackson-and-Frankfurter row, it did not suffice—because the real basis of that row was intellectual, not personal, and all four of the participants were Vinson's intellectual superiors. The other soon-apparent thing was that Vinson could not begin to fill the shoes of Stone, not even the slightly soured Stone of the last years, as a judicial liberal; perhaps by coincidence, perhaps not, Vinson's slant toward civil liberties was at least as ungenerous as that of his fellow-Kentuckian, Reed, and made the same exception for the rights of Negroes. Indeed, Vinson's views were so close to Reed's on most other matters, not just on civil liberties, that when Vinson at last became king of his Court, Reed, more often than not voting with the Truman-chosen four, became their chief spokesman as well as their ablest—though he had rated about at the bottom of the New Deal Justices.

For the four Truman Justices, judged by either ability or industry, in qualitative or quantitative estimate of their work, were the least happy choice of a Court quartet since President Harding picked Taft, Sutherland, Butler, and Sanford, about a quarter of a century before. Where the Hughes Court used to give complete treatment, meaning a hearing and a full-dress Court opinion, to about two hundred cases a year, the Vinson Court in only one of its four terms handled as many as a hundred—and its more industrious holdovers from the Hughes days chafed at their inactivity. Where the New Deal Court had pushed public law toward a greater respect for human dignity, the Fair Deal Court in a dozen ways pushed it back; prophetic and symbolic were the overrulings, less than a year after Murphy died, of a pair of paint-fresh Bill-of-Rights decisions he had penned. Fifty years hence, none of the Truman Justices, appraised by what they have shown up to now, will be any better remembered—or deserves to be better remembered—than the nameless Justices (save Johnson and Story) who sat with Marshall are remembered today. But since three of the Truman group are still on the Court, and the other ran it, his way, for the four unfortunate terms that preceded his death in 1953, a contemporary account demands that they be described as the men they were and are.

It would be neat, if less than profound, to lay Fred Vinson's judicial disregard of most personal freedoms to the fact that he was born, in a small Kentucky town, the son of the county jailer. Equally far-fetched would be the blaming of his bland and blighted hope to get the Court to work together, like a team, on the fact that he once played shortstop, in the semi-pro Blue Grass League, on a somewhat more coordinated nine. More likely, both attitudes stemmed from his more mature career. For over a score of pre-Court years, the mathematically-minded law-trained man with the ponderous split-personality face (one side looked like a strong statesman, the other like a weak, sly politician) worked for the federal government in all three of its branches in a shifting succession of top-flight jobs. As a Democratic Congressman, he was the Capitol's acknowledged-by-both-parties expert and chief spokesman on taxes; as a federal court of appeals judge (one rung below the Supreme Court), he was efficient enough to have Roosevelt choose him to head simultaneously an emergency court to hear OPA cases; drafted from his judgeship by FDR to be Economic Stabilizer, then Federal Loan Administrator, then "assistant President" as head of the Office of War Mobilization and Reconversion, Vinson next spent a year as Truman's Secretary of the Treasury before being named Chief Justice. It was the one-man power he held in his high administrative posts that perhaps led him to erroneously suppose that he could boss the Supreme Court in the same firm-if-gentle way. And if ever a Court member's past life clearly tended him toward upholding whatever the federal government did or wanted to do, it was Vinson's.

To Vinson—as to Reed alone of the Roosevelt Justices —Uncle Sam could almost do no wrong. Only against the states would Vinson use judicial power in important ways; of his six or eight major opinions for the Court, during seven years as Chief, the two indubitably liberal ones, on "restrictive covenants" in the North and on law-school segregation in the South, spanked the states for unconstitutional action against Negroes. When he voted against state taxes, his concern was for national control of commerce; when he cut down a couple of state limitations on labor's right to strike, it was not out of love for labor but because he thought they contradicted federal law. Let the

U.S. move against labor and Vinson would back any action to the hilt; it was he who spoke first and strongest in the splintered-four-ways decision that upheld the huge federal fine on Lewis and the miners; and it was he again who talked for the majority in letting Congress require non-Communist oaths from union officers. The outstanding instance of a pro-labor stand, however indirect, and perhaps his most forceful opinion, was his dissent—and Vinson dissented reluctantly and rarely—against the ruling that forbade pro-labor President Truman to seize the steel plants in the name of the federal government. When that government kicked civil liberties around, Vinson regularly wrote and voted in its behalf; "loyalty" programs or "loyalty" oaths, reviews of rough draft-boards or military courts, brutal treatment of aliens or of citizen-criminals—he could always be counted on the anti-libertarian side. Freedom of speech meant nothing to him, except as a pretty phrase; indeed, it was a state, not a federal, police action that let him write into the law of the land (with the backing of five of his fellows) the extraordinary rule that, when a political speaker is threatened with violence by some of his audience, the speaker, not the threateners, may be arrested. (Said Black, in dissent: "I will have no part or parcel in this holding which I view as a long step toward totalitarian authority.") But it was the Dennis decision, upholding the twentieth-century version of the Federalists' aged-in-disrepute Sedition Act—by letting native Communists be jailed simply for trying to spread their psychotic gospel—for which Vinson will be longest, and least admiringly, remembered. And it was fitting that the last official act of the thirteenth Chief Justice was to reconvene his Court and rush through a reversal of the stay of execution which Douglas had granted the spy-convicted Rosenbergs—in a manner that led even Frankfurter, no devotee of spies or of Douglas, to protest, but that let the Department of Justice do its electrocuting on schedule. For all his undoubted patriotism, chauvinist style, Vinson, less than any other man who ever headed the Court—less than Ellsworth, less than Waite, less than Taft—understood the real meaning of American democracy.

Chiming in with almost everything of any import that their Chief said or did were the three other Truman Justices—whose names have been linked and intoned by legal wags in imitation of Franklin Roosevelt's sneering campaign references to three right-wing Republicans, Martin-Barton-and-Fish. Certainly, Minton, Burton, and Clark, to date, have displayed nothing remotely resembling judicial statesmanship; and unless their new Chief, Warren, can (and wants to) win them away, as Black and Douglas could not, from their tame and timorous conception of their job—scared by legal precedents, scared by native Communists, scared to say No to the other branches of the federal government in the name of liberty—these three will continue to sog down the Court's work in a way that both the conservative Marshall and the liberal Holmes would have scorned. Rarely has there been such triple and simultaneous proof of the folly of letting even a pretty-good President carelessly pack the Court with his personal friends.

Harold Burton, the Court's senior non-New Deal member—who was once publicly designated as the least able Justice in a hundred years—is the product of a comfortable background, an upper-class education, a conventional career in corporation law, and a New England conscience (he was Massachusetts-born) that led him first to dabble, then to dive, into respectably conservative, and hence Republican, public service. Three terms as an upright mayor of Cleveland led to a U.S. Senatorship; a conscientious and not too partisan or reactionary Senate record led then-Senator Truman to ask for him as an opposition member of the famous "Truman Committee" to investigate defense contracts; the friendship that was cemented there—plus nationwide demands for a Republican replacement when the Court's lone Republican, Roberts, retired—led President Truman to pick the godly yet amiable white-thatched Ohioan, who looks like a small, neat version of a village storekeeper, as his first appointment to the high bench. At the start, Burton was clearly out of his depth on the Court; plodding along in pursuit of old cases to use as precedent like a lady shopper trying to match colors, exploring irrelevant trivia for page after dull page in near-parody of the job of judging, he managed, despite hard work, to turn out only five or six majority opinions a year (the figure was precisely six in one term when Black wrote twenty-nine and Douglas twenty-seven). But Burton has grown some in stature as the Court has shrunk; his nine or ten cases a term are today standard for a light and lazy docket; further, the New England conscience has pricked him, on occasion, into gingerly shucking off the anti-libertarian strait jacket which still binds the two other surviving Truman Justices. Indeed, the least-able-in-a-century label, once hung on Burton, would far better fit either Clark or Minton.

Tom Clark—who characteristically changed the Thomas to Tom, perhaps in fealty to his first sponsor, old-time U.S. Senator Tom Connally—has been a Texan Democrat all his life and a politician-prosecutor for most of it, his six years on the Court not excluded. From district attorney for Dallas County, when only five years out of law school, he moved in the mid-New Deal days to the Department of Justice, where he worked on anti-trust cases and later on war frauds, supervised without wincing the evacuation of Japanese from the West Coast, and was—by reliable report—about to be relieved of his assistant Attorney-Generalship by Roosevelt for comparative incompetence when FDR died. Instead of removing him, Truman—for whose political friends Clark had done a few Departmental favors—raised him to the Attorney-Generalship, where his running of the loyalty program took scant heed of civil liberties. That the smooth and smiling glad-hander, whose perpetual bowtie (worn today even under his robe) adds to the appearance of an over-aged college boy, would next be named to the Court was widely taken for granted; Vinson, who backed the appointment, was apocryphally said to have done so because he wanted someone on his Court who knew less law than he did; whether or not that was what Vinson wanted, it is what he—and the country—got. As a Justice, Clark has been uninteresting, unintelligent, and—in line with his own career and his late boss Vinson's lead—illiberal; left-wingers, aliens, suspected criminals, all who do not conform to the conformist picture of a one hundred per cent Amurrican, get from him short shrift. Given a chance to pen an exciting opinion when he joined a unanimous Court in long-delayed overruling of a

1915 decision that movies (then in their infancy) were not entitled to freedom of the press, he turned out a dull and muddy technical treatise. Or perhaps it was his law clerk who turned it out—for Clark's chief virtue is a rather appealing awareness of his own limitations as lawyer and as judge. More than any other present Justice, he votes with the pack and is rarely in dissent; more than any of his brethren, he depends on his young fresh-from-law-school assistants to outline and even write his opinions for him.

By contrast, Sherman Minton, fourth of the Truman appointees—whom freedom-defending Elmer Davis would doubtless like to disown as a fellow Hoosier—is conspicuously unaware of his judicial shortcomings. The very air of militant self-assurance that moved the lower-middle-class Midwesterner ahead, first in law, then in partisan Democratic politics, became a handicap and a vice once the goals to be reached were no longer chosen, the orders no longer given, by others. As New Deal whip during his one term in the U.S. Senate, the square-faced man with the quick anger, the quick tongue, and the build of a heavyweight boxer, forcefully backed—and followed —the whole Administration program. It was there, of course, and for that reason, that he became Harry Truman's friend. Licked for re-election in 1940, he served briefly as an administrative assistant to FDR before being hoisted to one of the federal courts of appeals where, for eight years—with nobody to give him the orders or tell him the answers (save the uncertain precedent of prior judges' opinions)—Minton turned out pedestrian, often off-the-point, but always flatly stated, law. None of this

stopped Truman—who knew him as a regular Democrat,
a personal friend, and a man with that overrated qualification for the highest Court, judicial experience—from naming Minton, over scores of other and abler federal judges,
to a Justiceship. With Minton still wanting and needing
to be led, and with Vinson—after three frustrating years as
Chief in name only—wanting to lead, it was inevitable that
the freshman Justice would immediately join the Court
captain's anti-libertarian camp. During his very first term,
he wrote one of the opinions (Reed wrote the other) that
discarded Murphy-penned Bill-of-Rights decisions only
two years old. Soon, as so often happens, the disciple's
ardor was greater than the master's; through the four
years they sat together, Minton's votes against civil
liberties exceeded by a few even Vinson's—and Reed's and
Clark's. Indeed, during Vinson's final term, when the
Court struck down one further device to deprive Negroes
of their voting rights (the Texas "Jaybirds," an all-white
club, held their private election *before* the state primary and
then joined together to vote officially for *their* winner),
Minton dissented alone. Highly out of line was Minton's
joining with Black and Douglas to protest the arrest of the
political speaker who was threatened by hostile members
of his audience. But it was characteristic that Minton wrote
the ruling which gave constitutional sanction to the dis-
graceful guilt-by-association doctrine, in the firing of New
York schoolteachers—and that he blithely blurted, in its
defense: "One's associates, past and present . . . may
properly be considered in determining fitness and loyalty.
. . . In the employment of officials and teachers of the
school system, the state may very properly inquire into

the company they keep. . . ." To which Black retorted: "Basically these laws rest on the belief that government should supervise and limit the flow of ideas into the minds of men. . . . Because of this policy, public officials . . : vested with powers to select the ideas people can think about . . . or choose the people or groups people can associate with . . . are not public servants; they are public masters." And Douglas recoiled from the whole idea as "repugnant," "alien to our system," and "a real threat to our way of life." But Black and Douglas were dissenting from what is now the law of the land, courtesy of the Vinson Court—with Minton here, as so often, its spokesman against freedom.

The mass attack on civil liberties by the 1949–53 Truman-Vinson Court—except that some semblance of legal decency for Negroes was carried a little way along from the start made by the New Deal Court, toward the big step since taken by the Warren Court—was one of two major contributions of those four years to Supreme Court history. The other—equally unadmirable if less portentous, though often employed to achieve the same end—was the new spendthrift use of "denial of certiorari," to refuse even to hear a lot of important cases and thus to cut the Justices' work-load down to a twentieth-century low. Just as Reed became the Truman quartet's elder statesman on anti-civil-liberties stuff, so Frankfurter, the stickler for propriety and reluctant facer of solid issues, became their leader and guide in the sparse use of their usable judicial power. Where Murphy and Rutledge had teamed with Black and Douglas to force Court consideration ("certiorari" is granted if four Justices vote for it) of many touchy problems, especially in the fair-trial field, the Court, at Frankfurter's open urging, now turned dozens of such cases down. More than that, Frankfurter went so far as to refuse to sit in several cases where, over his objection, Black and Douglas had managed to corral two more votes for a hearing; when this form of prima-donna pouting resulted only in his tossing away his chance to vote on the case itself, Frankfurter switched to a new tack; he began insisting, *after* a case was heard, that it be summarily dismissed because "certiorari" had been "improvidently granted"—a twist which it takes *five* Justices, not four, to prevent; this in turn provoked Douglas to protest, on the public records, against his colleague's persistence at having his own way. But Frankfurter usually did have his own way, thanks to the co-operation of the four Truman Justices—and the double result was to slice the number of cases the Court heard to less than half the number it used to hear ten years before, and to let the Justices duck making any decision at all on many a tough and vital constitutional problem, with Bill-of-Rights problems, of course, at the head of the ducked list.

Among the comparatively few public-law cases per year that Vinson's slowed-down nine did deign to handle, some —though a smaller proportion than ever in the past—dealt with economic matters, with the old question of regulation of business, or labor, by government. Topping these in contemporary and probable future importance was the steel-seizure decision, in which the legal issues were so tangled that each of the six majority Justices wrote his own separate opinion (though Black spoke "for the Court") and these, plus the three-man dissent, fill 133 pages of the official Court reports. The political problem was simpler: The steelworkers' demands for higher wages, refused by the steel companies, pointed toward a nationwide strike; the nation needed steel for the undeclared war in Korea; a pro-labor President, rather than use the Taft-Hartley Act of an anti-labor Congress to stop the strike, "seized" the steel plants in the name of the United States (which meant signing a legal paper and hoisting a few symbolic flags) without any clear authorization from Congress—just as Roosevelt had seized plants to stop strikes even before the U.S. entered World War II. With its three strongest let-the-federal-government-do-anything members, Vinson, Minton, and Reed, violently dissenting (and Clark joining the majority only on a comparative technicality), the Court forbade the President to poach on the preserves of Congress—and also precipitated the steel strike that Truman wanted, but in his own way, to avoid. Whether the ruling be rated good or bad, right or wrong, the outstanding fact—little noted at the time or since—was that the Court, while purporting to protect Congress under the old separation-of-powers theory, actually appropriated the top power and the last word, as usual, for itself. Few other economic decisions of the four Fair-Deal-Court years deserve so much as minor mention. State "fair trade laws," forbidding price-cutting on nationally sold products, were knocked out—to the delight of cut-rate drug stores, big low-price department stores like Macy's in New York, and consumers everywhere. The technical expertness of the Federal Communications Commission was honored by the Court in backing the Commission's choice between

two competing types of color television. A federal-minded
bench naturally upheld national claims over state claims to
tidelands oil (until overridden by a more oil-company-
minded Administration three years later). Tax laws, labor
laws, anti-trust laws, patent laws were applied and "interpreted" pretty much as during the preceding decade;
only in the civil liberties field was there significant progress—backward.

The most important and appalling of the Vinson Court's
assaults on human dignity and democratic decency, other
than those already touched on, concerned the treatment of
aliens in a manner to make the Statue of Liberty blush for
shame, and the treatment of citizens—especially those
subjected to "loyalty" checks or oaths by nation, state, or
city—in a manner to do a dictatorship proud. While President Truman was bravely branding the McCarran Act of
1952, before it was passed over his veto, as "worse than
the infamous Alien Act of 1798," his Justices were making
the new law almost superfluous by their blessing of official
outrages committed by his Department of Justice under
the not-quite-so-nauseous McCarran Act of 1940. Illus-
trative of the Vinson Court majority's sorry-but-what-can-
we-do attitude was the case of the twenty-three-years-ago
ex-Communist who was shipped back to Italy, his American family left behind—with Jackson seeming to say for
the Court that the issue was political and so none of the
Court's business, with Frankfurter explaining, in characteristic concurrence, that "the place to resist unwise or
cruel legislation touching aliens is the Congress, not this
Court," and with Black and Douglas of course dissenting.
But Jackson and Frankfurter joined Black and Douglas in

futile protest when the four Trumanites plus Reed let
Truman's Attorney-General arrest, on unproved "charges"
of Communism, and then hold indefinitely *without bail* a
whole batch of aliens—including a waiter, thirty-nine
years in this country, with sons in the U.S. Army, who
had donated blood seven times during World War II. And
the same five Justices outvoted the same four in apparently condemning to Ellis Island for life a man named
Mezei who had lived in the U.S. for twenty-five years, who
had gone to Rumania to see his dying mother, who had
been refused re-admission to the U.S. on his return, who
had been shipped back to Europe where no country on
either side of the Iron Curtain would have him (he applied
to more than twenty and the Western nations barred him
simply because the U.S. had barred him), who had therefore been forced to come back to the prison of Ellis Island
—and who never was granted a hearing nor given the
slightest notion what the "confidential" charges against
him were that kept him from going home to Buffalo. Said
Jackson, with the eloquence he could use so strongly on
either side: "This man, who seems to have led a life of
unrelieved insignificance, must have been astonished to
find himself suddenly putting the Government of the
United States in such fear that it was afraid to tell him
why it was afraid of him. . . . No one can make me believe we are that far gone." But five of his colleagues
clinched it that we were.

In some of those cases, too, where fear—which is the
only word for it—had spawned official infringements on
the rights of U.S. *citizens*, Frankfurter, sometimes Jackson,
and occasionally Burton (all three at the Court's far right

during most of the New Deal decade) looked liberal, by
contrast to the Vinson crew, as they now and then backed
Black's and Douglas's steady crusade. When the loose and
look-backward-Angelino "loyalty" oath that Los Angeles
demanded of all city employees was upheld, 5–4, with
Jackson casting the key vote, Frankfurter and Burton
agreed with the two stalwarts of dissent that the oath
requirement was an unconstitutional "bill of attainder"—
in that it punished people for their past doings, as Douglas
put it, "by legislative act, not by judicial process." When
the whole federal "loyalty" program, with its paid, secret
informers and its star-chamber methods, came up for review in the renowned Bailey case, it was Frankfurter and
jumping Jackson who teamed with Black and Douglas to
disown such totalitarian tactics. Part of the Bailey case's
renown stemmed from the fact that the Court, though it
heard the case at length, delivered no opinion—as it never
does when it splits 4–4; with Clark not sitting because, as
Attorney-General, he had played a major and partisan
part in the program, the official announcement merely said,
as is customary, that the lower court's decision (upholding
the program, 2–1) was "affirmed by an equally divided
Court"—and no names given. But the way the Court
divided was made clear, later in the same term, when one
small segment of the program—the listing of "subversive
organizations" by the Attorney-General without giving
them a hearing—was forbidden, by a 5–3 vote, with Burton
crossing to the liberal side on the narrow ground that this
particular procedure was a bit too arbitrary and high-
handed. Here, six of the eight Justices who sat wrote
separate opinions that revealed their views of the program

as a whole; Douglas, for one, openly discussed the Bailey case in damning the entire supposedly anti-subversion system as "subverion from within" and "abhorrent to fundamental justice"; the adamant-against-liberty trio of Vinson, Minton, and Reed were forced, for a change, into dissent. But the trio won Burton and Jackson back in the Dennis (jail-for-the-top-native-Communists) decision's aftermath, where Judge Medina had sentenced the Communists' *lawyers* to one-to-six months in prison for contempt of court, meaning contempt of him. This time, only Frankfurter stuck with Black and Douglas, and his long separate dissent with its forty-seven-page appendix is perhaps his finest judicial job; the bench and bar should have blushed with Medina to read in detail of "incontinent wrangles between court and counsel," as though in "an undisciplined debating society," which served to "weaken the restraints of respect" for a judge whose "self-concern pervades the record"; nor is it any derogation of his opinion here to point out that—as in the "loyalty" cases and as when he spoke up, way back, for Sacco and Vanzetti —it was procedural (or judicial) impropriety that stirred the scholar-Justice to liberal protest.

For Frankfurter—and Jackson and Burton—had been right up there with the pack in the Dennis decision itself, the biggest blot on the Vinson Court's blot-marked ledger. The importance of the Dennis case did not lie in the front-paged fact that a few leaders of Russia's feeble fifth column in the U.S. were jailed, to the undoubted delight of their propaganda-conscious party and their martyred selves; it lay in the fact that the Supreme Court of the United States, without renouncing its self-proclaimed power and duty to uphold the Constitution even against Acts of Congress, gave its ultimate benediction (as even the old Federalist Chase-Ellsworth Court had never done *in the name of the Supreme Court*) to a law that flatly violated the free-speech guarantee of the First Amendment. Dennis and the others were not convicted for, nor accused of, treason, spying, sabotage or any such *act* of any kind; they were put in prison for talking and writing—for "teaching and advocating" Communism. Although Vinson—for himself and Minton and Reed and Burton (with Clark again not sitting)—purported, by a strange sort of legal legerdemain, to be sticking to Holmes's old and unfortunate "clear and present danger" exception to the Amendment's clear command, he admitted that any danger to the nation *created by these defendants' known and nonsensical Communist activities* was not very clear and was certainly not present. This ignorant, or else intellectually dishonest, distortion of ideas by the wayward use of words was too much for Jackson or Frankfurter to stomach; yet each of these abler Justices, in his own characteristic fashion, went farther than Vinson had gone toward undermining the First Amendment. Jackson boldly urged judicial abandonment of the Amendment, "clear and present danger" rule and all, wherever a "conspiracy" was at large—despite the fact that the Amendment makes no mention of conspiracies and that Holmes originated his rule in a conspiracy case; Frankfurter, judicial-restrainedly timid and voluminously academic, deplored Congress's cavalier treatment of freedom of speech while simultaneously deploring his own obviously self-imposed inability to do anything about it. Equally characteristic of the men who wrote them were the

Black and Douglas separate dissents. Douglas hewed straight, in the Holmes-Brandeis tradition, to the clear-and-present-danger line: "Free speech—the glory of our system of government—should not be sacrificed on anything less than plain and objective proof of danger that . . . is imminent," not out of "prejudice nor hate nor senseless fear." Black, as bold as Jackson, but in the opposite direction, suggested scrapping the Holmes restriction "as to speech in the realm of public matters" and taking the First Amendment at its face; he also hoped, with a wistful note of near-despair which put the whole case in its proper light, that "in calmer times, when present pressures, passions and fears subside, this or some later Court will restore the First Amendment liberties to the high preferred place where they belong in a free society."

While Black's words might well stand as an epitaph for the Vinson Court, a couple of final and comparatively minor matters further italicize the tragic trend of that four-year span. One was the Court's backward stride in the fair-treatment-of-criminals field, where the New Deal nine had most steadfastly held the states to the Bill of Rights; during Vinson's final term, his Court did hear—as it rarely deigned to—a protest against barbaric police techniques; and with only Black, Douglas, and Frankfurter dissenting, it upheld the conviction of two New York thugs who had been kept incommunicado until confessions were literally wrung from them. But far more revealing of the whole temper of the four Fair Deal years was the hesitant, half-hearted way the Vinson-men handled the one issue that won them a semblance of liberal repute—the issue of segregation in the South. Back in 1896, when Fuller's Court gave segregation the judicial nod and invented the separate-but-equal excuse for it, the first Justice Harlan, in strong dissent, exclaimed: "Our Constitution is color-blind." Over half a century later, Negroes hoped that a Court majority might have caught up with Harlan; in the cases urging admission of Negroes to a white Texas law school, a white Oklahoma graduate course, and the white section of Southern dining-cars, the main plea was that the entire separate-but-equal doctrine be discarded; what the Vinson Court did was to sidestep the big point and order all the Negroes admitted on the old, narrow ground that the separate facilities offered them were *not* equal. But no such avenue of escape was handy when cases began to come up to the Court where the separate public grade-schools of the South—with the Negro schools sometimes newer and better equipped than the white schools—were attacked on the simple theory that "separate," *per se*, could never be "equal." Little appreciated is the fact that cases of this kind were duly before Vinson's Court for two full terms before he died; but by sending them back to lower courts for the flimsiest of reasons, by asking for later re-arguments after they were fully argued, by delays and postponements, Vinson managed to evade till his death the touchy political problem at their core. That Vinson himself was mainly responsible for ducking the high, hard one was made clear when the same eight Associate Justices faced it head-on during the first season of their new captain, Earl Warren of California.

If Vinson was a better and smarter real-life ballplayer than his successor—who never got beyond a symbolic center-field on a sandlot team—Warren already bids fair to eclipse the late semi-pro shortstop in the slightly more important job of Chief Justice of the United States. The handsome, blond hulk of a man, who looks like a kindly Viking (the family name was once a Norwegian "Varran"), grew up in the healthy and healthily unsegregated San Joaquin Valley of south central California. Son of a former railroad mechanic, Warren seems to have inherited the practical bent of mind that goes with use of the hands (a political opponent once said, intending it as an insult, that he "never had an abstract thought in his life"); Warren himself is ambidextrous; he writes right and throws left—which may again be symbolic. And he has the easy, outgoing manner with people, of whatever political persuasion, that marks the Westerner tinged with the politician. For Warren has been in politics—and, unlike any of his new brethren, in *state* politics—practically the whole of his adult life. Beginning a few years out of law school, he climbed a prosecuting ladder from deputy city attorney through several ranks in the county district attorney's office up to the state attorney-generalship; if the conviction of criminals seems a strange career for so inherently and almost indiscriminately friendly a man, he has said, despite his steamroller success as a prosecutor, that it used to make him sick to win a murder case. He was happier in the California governorship, to which he was elected for an unprecedented trio of consecutive terms with unprecedented bipartisan support. There, his budget-balancing Republicanism did not stop him from raising old-age pensions, nor from urging unsuccessfully a state plan for compulsory medical insurance; his prosecuting past did not stop him from taking a moderate stand against unbridled "loyalty" oaths for teachers; his scorn for race prejudice led him to name a Negro, for the first time in state history, to California's Superior Court, and also to write a gratuitous and indignant letter of sympathy to a Chinese family whom an all-white section of San Francisco had voted not to let live there. Though Warren's lone personal excursion into national politics was his run for the Vice-Presidency with Dewey in 1948, he was long a power in the party (and a recurrent dark-horse Presidential possibility) because he controlled the big California delegation. And it was partly as thanks for his state's support at the 1952 convention that Eisenhower named him Chief Justice; but the main reason for the President's choice was his view of Warren as a universally respected, reliable middle-of-the-roader—which is precisely what the ambidextrous ex-center-fielder had always been.

It is of course too early to make a substantial *judicial* assessment of the healthy sixty-four-year-old, who may have another ten, or even twenty, years to go. Yet his first term on the bench did begin to bear out Eisenhower's, and the nation's, confidence that Warren the judge, like Warren the governor, would be neither reactionary fish nor radical fowl. In the close civil-liberties cases, he occasionally forced Reed and Minton, instead of Black and Douglas, into dissent—as Vinson had rarely if ever done; indeed, where the Court split in this kind of case, Warren was on the Black-Douglas side almost half the time. In economic areas of dispute, a states'-rights tendency on the part of the new Chief began to crop up—as might have been expected; for whereas every one of the twelve Justices who immediately preceded him to the Court had been

picked from federal government posts (save only Frankfurter, who had once worked in Washington and whose
unofficial influence and activity in the New Deal had been
greater than those of most of its employees), Warren came
straight from a lifetime in state office. That he was thus
probably destined to be less federal-government-minded
than any of his colleagues was hinted, not only in his vote
to uphold the Eisenhower Congress's Submerged Lands
Act (giving tidelands oil back to the states), but more
pointedly in his dissent, with Black and Douglas, against
banning a *state* tax on sales to a company working for the
U.S. Navy—where the Court majority followed the old
dual-sovereignty line that Marshall started way back in
McCulloch *v.* Maryland. But Warren's pull toward real
and unseparate racial equality was considerably stronger
than his pro-state slant. And—despite the sport-paged
ruling that professional baseball was still as far out of
reach of the anti-trust acts as when Holmes had put it
there, long before the days of television (a ruling that was
anti-federal in both essence and origin)—the one major,
and clearly historic, move of the Warren Court in its first
term was its head-on handling of the Segregation Cases.

That the flat outlawing of separate public schools for
black and white children, as a violation of the Fourteenth
Amendment's "equal protection" clause, was done by a
unanimous Court and that the new Chief spoke for his
Court—without so much as a "separate concurrence" to
sap the strength of his words—are tributes to Warren's
executive skill and force. More impressive still was the
way he spoke; with no skirting around old cases or tight-
roping between them, with no pseudo-scholarly array of

legal or historical arguments, he simply said with refreshing straightforwardness that the separate-but-equal rule was out of date. Politely dismissing as "inconclusive" the exhaustive and, of course, conflicting efforts of both sides to "prove" what those who wrote and adopted the Fourteenth Amendment "intended," he added that, in any event, "we cannot turn the clock back to 1868." Hitting straight to the core of the issue, he said: "To separate them [*school children*] from others of similar age and qualifications solely because of their race generates a feeling of inferiority as to their status in the community that may affect their hearts and minds in a way unlikely ever to be undone. . . . We conclude that in the field of public education the doctrine of 'separate but equal' has no place."

Had this masterly performance, on every level, with its vast political repercussions, national and international, made up the Court's entire work for the term, the term would not have been wasted—and indeed, it very nearly did so; only sixty-five cases, the record low for over a century, got full treatment from the Justices. Presumably, a tremendous amount of backstage time was spent on the segregation matter; presumably also, it took some months for the man who had never been a judge, much less a Chief Justice, to adjust to the mechanics and the formalities of his brand-new job. If the Warren Court's slow gait continued into its second year, it was partly because the Justices were worrying throughout the term the complicated business, officially held over, of how and when to put their blanket anti-segregation order into effective operation, in different parts of the rumblingly rebellious South. But another reason for the snail's pace involved politics in an even more obvious way; for the Court kept putting off the hearing of many major and possibly 4–4 cases while a Senate Judiciary Committee run by maverick Senator Langer (who was demanding a top federal judgeship for some fellow-North-Dakotan), and then a new Committee run by Democrats, deliberately dawdled at confirming Eisenhower's choice for Jackson's seat—the second Justice John Marshall Harlan, this one from New York.

Prediction in print is a preoccupation for the foolhardy. And yet, if the prior lives of Justices help shape, and so help foretell, what their slants and bents on the Court will be, a rough guess—to be checked ten years hence—can be made about Harlan. Too conventional in background, too conformist in career, ever to match the fiery independent thinker and liberal dissenter who was his grandfather, Harlan may yet prove not so orthodox a Justice as many suppose; indeed, he is a new breed of cat on the Court. Though born in Chicago, he is a Princeton-to-Oxford-to-Wall-Street-law-practice product—the Court's first Ivy League "white-shoe boy," its first Rhodes Scholar, its first full-fledged Eastern Dewey Republican. That he has always been well-to-do and upper-crust does not necessarily betoken automatic conservatism; so was Holmes. Politically closer to Warren than to any other present Justice, despite major differences in their pre-Court work and lives, Harlan is also apt to be *judicially* closer, but without the Westerner's strength and simplicity. Like his Chief, he has never held federal office—except for a brief apprenticeship on a federal court of appeals—and his stints of public service (odd jobs of investigating or prosecuting) have been for the state; the national government will get from him no special preference. Again like Warren, his prosecuting was tempered with humanity, and the few criminal cases he heard as a court of appeals judge display concern for the fair treatment of defendants; he will be no Vinson at kicking the Bill of Rights around.

In all likelihood, the general slant of the new Justice will be just about the opposite of Reed's—except for a similarly super-lawyerlike over-attention to detail. On economic issues, where the country-bred boy tended anti-business, the big-city boy will tend pro-business; where the rural small-town lawyer tended pro-labor, the Wall Street financial lawyer will tend anti-labor; where the federal government servant tended strongly pro-national and somewhat anti-state on taxes and regulation, the private practitioner and occasional state servant will tend strongly anti-national and somewhat pro-state. It is on civil liberties that Harlan may turn the tables the other way; for where Reed, ex-Solicitor-General of the U.S., came close to thinking that government, especially the federal government, could not be wrong—no matter how it treated the Bill of Rights—Harlan may have that sense of *noblesse oblige* on such matters which so often goes with born-and-bred economic conservatism. True, Harlan, during the court-of-appeals prelude to his Justiceship, did deliver the decision that sent a dozen second-string Communist leaders to jail under the Smith Act; but it was not his job to question the Smith Act's constitutionality, so recently upheld by the Vinson Court in the Dennis case; and his patient, painstaking, sixty-page opinion reads almost as

though he were seeking some way to set the poor fools
free. It is far more meaningful that, in 1940, Harlan served
as special counsel to New York City's Board of Higher
Education in its futile effort, blocked by local judicial
Philistines, to bring to the City College faculty the
famous if unconforming philosopher, Bertrand Russell.
Just possibly, if hopefully, the appointment of Harlan may
give the Court one more and badly-needed vote for freedom of the mind.

There are other harbingers of hope. One is the sharp
drop in the proportionate number of Douglas's dissents
between Vinson's last term as Chief and Warren's first;
in 1952–53, Douglas set an all-time record by protesting
49 per cent, or just one less than half, of the Court's
decisions, the biggest batch of them in the civil-liberties
field—and by being concerned enough to write 33 dissenting opinions (while still carrying more than his share
of majority "opinions for the Court"); in 1953–54, the
proportion had gone down to 38 per cent—and he bothered to elaborate only 15 of his minority votes; Black's
dissents fell off too, but less sharply. Statistics also point
up another hopeful sign; Clark, so unsure of himself that
he always prefers to follow the pack and its current leader,
has dissented from less than 5 per cent of the Court's decisions, or a total of less than 25 times, since he came to
the bench six years ago; whenever Warren goes with Black
and Douglas, and takes Harlan or Frankfurter or maybe
Burton with him, Clark is sure to desert Reed and Minton,
and trot along. Moreover, the present Court's two most
determined defenders of the judicial bridge against any
influx of civil liberties may soon be cut to a single Horatius,

named Minton; for recurrent rumors of Reed's imminent retirement have recently grown louder. On a more tangible level, it is heartening that the Warren Court has "granted certiorari" in a new challenge (the Peters case) to the whole crux of the federal "loyalty" program, which was handled so inconclusively and unsatisfactorily by the Vinson Court in the Bailey case; what this implies—since Jackson was dead, and Clark probably disqualified himself again, and the Reed-Minton-Burton trio presumably stuck to their pro-"loyalty"-program stand of the Bailey case—is that Warren cast the fourth vote for "certiorari."

Indeed, the most hopeful and happy omen of them all is the apparent judicial character of the new Chief Justice. Unblinded by the tweedledum-tweedledee twaddle of much that passes for learned legal argument, unblinkered into the narrow vision so often so typical of those with past judicial experience, he seems essentially a direct, plainspoken politician who knows that his is primarily a political job. Of such, when they combine humanity with honesty, are judicial statesmen made. Not so wise as Holmes, not so intellectually daring as Black, not so dedicated as Brandeis or Douglas, not so independent as the nineteenth century's Johnson or Miller or Harlan, and clearly not so liberal as any of these, he comes closer to resembling a might-be twentieth-century Marshall. The same easy strength is there, and the same earthy approach to the esoterics of law. But where Marshall's achievement was to protect a weak nation, as a nation, from its people, Warren's opportunity is the precise opposite; it is to protect the people, as people, from their strong nation. Given the will and the good-will to do it, he can succeed.

O'Shaughnessy, the Irish poet, once sang: "For each age is a dream that is dying, or one that is coming to birth." Over eight score years and five, through age after different age, the men who are the Supreme Court of the United States have attended the birth and the death of different dreams. Today it would be a tragedy if the Black and Douglas dissents—which are rather affirmations of a faith—should prove a dirge for the bravest dream of all. For under the inspiration of those two great Justices and the aegis of a potentially great Chief Justice, the American dream of freedom may be reborn.

A

Adams, John, 10, *62, 66, 68, 69,* 71, 80, 91
Adams, John Quincy, *93,* 104, 110
Alger, Horatio, *225,* 274
Altgeld, John Peter, 171
Armour, Philip, *169*
Arno, Peter, *215*
Arthur, Chester A., *164*

B

Bailey case, *319, 331*
Barkley, Alben W., *242*
Barton, Bruce, *309*
Beard, Charles, *95,* 120, *150*
Beveridge, Albert J., *96*
Bingham, John, 149, *150*
Black, Hugo L., 16, *251–252,* 257, *262, 263, 264–266,* 271, *275, 276, 277, 278, 279, 282, 283, 287, 290, 291, 293, 294, 298, 304, 305, 308, 309, 310, 313, 314, 315,* 317, *319, 320, 322, 325, 326, 330, 331, 332*

Blaine, James G., *168*
Blair, John, *49, 61,* 137
Blatchford, Samuel, *164*
Borah, William E., *189*
Bradley, Joseph P., *158, 159, 170*
Brandeis, Louis D., 31, 187, *196, 219, 225, 226–229, 230, 233, 237, 241, 246, 253, 258, 260, 262, 270, 272, 273, 275, 277, 292, 295, 304, 322, 331*
Brewer, David J., *169,* 171, 187
Bridges, Harry, *278*
Brown, Henry, 187
Buchanan, James, *130,* **131, 132,** 157
Burr, Aaron, *92–93*
Burton, Harold H., *264,* 287, *299, 305, 309–310, 318, 319, 320, 321, 330, 331*
Butler, Nicholas Murray, *226,* 274
Butler, Pierce, 30, 187, *217, 220–221, 228, 253, 255, 298, 305*
Byrnes, James F., *263, 266, 283, 303*

C

Campbell, John A., 127, 128, 137, 160

Cardozo, Benjamin N., 31, 219, 225, 228, 231, 233, 237, 241, 253, 269

Catron, John, 127, 128, 132, 155

Charles River Bridge case, 122–123

Chase, Salmon P., 142, 143, 151, 156, 157, 159, 161

Chase, Samuel, 61, 62, 63, 64, 66, 67, 68, 69, 81, 83, 90–92, 93, 321

Choate, Joseph H., 168, 173

Clark, Tom C., 35, 299, 305, 309, 310, 311–312, 313, 316, 319, 321, 330, 331

Clarke, John, 190

Cleveland, Grover, 141, 168

Coal Act case, 239

Conkling, Roscoe, 149, 150

Connally, Tom, 311

Coolidge, Calvin, 9, 19, 180, 185, 224, 225

Cooper, Dr., 65

Curtis, Benjamin R., 128, 130, 145

Cushing, William, 48–49, 57, 61, 62, 68, 69, 83

D

Daniel, Peter V., 127, 128, 137

Dartmouth College case, 94–95, 122, 123, 162

Davis, David, 137, 154, 157, 161

Davis, Elmer, 312

Davis, Jefferson, 137

Day, William Rufus, 189–190

Debs, Eugene V., 145, 171–172

Dennis, Eugene, 320, 321, 329

Dewey, Thomas E., 274, 325, 328

Dodd, William E., Jr., 296

Douglas, William O., 16, 29, 145, 254, 255, 257, 262, 263, 264, 266, 269, 273–277, 278, 282, 283, 287, 290, 293, 298, 304, 305, 309, 310, 313, 314, 315, 317, 319, 320, 322, 325, 326, 330, 331, 332

Duval, Gabriel, 82

E

Eisenhower, Dwight D., 277, 303, 304, 325, 326, 328

Ellsworth, Oliver, 39, 61, 62, 68, 71, 80, 81, 309, 321

F

Field, Marshall, 169

Field, Stephen J., 157–158, 161, 163, 164, 169, 173, 175

Fish, Hamilton, 309

Frank, Leo, 206

Frankfurter, Felix, 9, 16–17, 253, 257, 262, 263, 264, 265, 269–273, 274, 277, 281, 282, 287, 291, 293, 298, 305, 309, 314, 315, 317, 318, 319, 320, 321, 322, 326, 330

Franklin, Benjamin, 39, 179

Fries, farmer, 49, 65–66

Fuller, Melville W., 142, 146, 169, 172, 173, 179, 186, 188, 200, 322

Fulton, Robert, 99

G

Garfield, James A., 164
Garner, John N., 248, 251
George, King, 38–39, 95
Gibbons v. Odgen, 94, 99–100
Gitlow, Benjamin, 209
Glass, Carter, 248
Granger cases, 163–165, 169, 170
Grant, Ulysses S., 142, 155, 158, 161, 162
Gray, Horace, 164, 177, 253
Grier, Robert C., 128, 132, 157–158

H

Hamilton, Alexander, 39, 217
Hamilton, Walton, 180, 271
Harding, Warren G., 8, 31, 180, 185, 188, 219, 220, 222, 224, 251, 305
Harlan, John M., 143, 168, 186–187, 192, 323, 331
Harlan, John Marshall, 168, 328–330
Harris, Crampton, 298
Hayes, Rutherford B., 164, 168
Henry, Patrick, 35, 46, 61
Hearst, William Randolph, 188
Hiss, Alger, 17
Holmes, Oliver W., 5, 9, 30, 74, 106, 143, 148, 177, 179–212, 217, 225, 226, 227, 229, 230, 238, 241, 253, 256, 258, 260, 262, 266, 269, 270, 271, 272, 275, 277, 278, 285, 290, 291, 292, 295, 304, 309, 321, 322, 326, 328, 331

Hoover, Herbert, 180, 186, 215, 222, 224, 225
Hoover, J. Edgar, 225
Hughes, Charles Evans, 7, 15, 31, 47, 84, 179, 180, 187, 188, 189, 223–224, 225, 227, 228, 230, 232, 233, 238, 240, 241, 245, 246, 248, 249, 250, 264, 284, 292, 293, 305

I

Iredell, James, 35, 49, 54, 62, 66, 67, 68

J

Jackson, Andrew, 10, 11, 78, 102, 104, 109, 110, 112, 116, 120, 121, 125, 126, 192, 214
Jackson, Howell E., 174
Jackson, Robert H., 9, 60, 257, 262, 264, 265, 277, 279–282, 286, 287, 293, 298, 305, 317, 318, 319, 320, 321, 322, 328, 331
Jay, John, 46, 47, 48, 54, 60, 71, 84
Jefferson, Thomas, 5, 45, 63, 65, 66, 68, 71, 75, 77, 78, 81, 82, 83, 85, 86, 87, 90, 92, 93, 106, 107, 112, 135, 179, 213, 214, 217
Johnson, Andrew, 142, 144, 155
Johnson, Hugh, 233, 235
Johnson, Thomas, 51
Johnson, William, 82, 83, 103, 105–106, 107, 306, 331
Jones & Laughlin Steel Corp. case, 249

L

La Follette, Robert M., 189, 248
Landon, Alfred M., 242, 243
Langer, William, 328
Lewis, John L., 240, 283, 287, 297, 308
Lincoln, Abraham, 75, 119, 134, 135, 136, 137, 138, 139, 141, 142, 151, 152, 156, 157, 179, 214
Livingston, Brockholst, 82
Lovett, Robert M., 296
Lowell, Abbott L., 227
Lyons, Matthew, 65

M

Madison, James, 65, 86–90, 94, 106, 107, 129, 213
Marbury, William, 86–90, 128, 129, 213
Marshall, John, 10, 19, 25, 34, 52, 71, 73–110, 111, 112, 113, 114, 115, 116, 117, 120, 121, 122, 123, 124, 125, 126, 130, 134–135, 139, 142, 143, 145–146, 160, 162, 168, 170, 176, 179, 214, 253, 264, 279, 306, 309, 326, 331
Martin, Joseph W., Jr., 309
Matthews, Stanley, 164
McCardle case, 155, 156
McCarthy, Joseph R., 91
McCulloch v. Maryland, 94, 96–99, 125, 128, 253, 326
McKenna, Joseph, 187
McKinley, William, 185, 186, 189
McLean, John, 128, 129, 130, 133, 137

McReynolds, James C., 9, 30, 187, 201–202, 206, 217, 218–219, 227, 228, 232, 239, 252, 253, 257, 264, 283
Medina, Harold, 302, 320
Mellon, Andrew W., 280
Mercer, John, 7
Merryman case, 136, 138, 154
Mezei case, 318
Miller, Samuel F., 137, 143, 146, 153, 157, 158, 160–161, 162, 163, 168, 169, 264, 279, 331
Milligan case, 154, 155, 156, 211
Minton, Sherman, 299, 305, 309, 310, 312–314, 316, 320, 321, 325, 330, 331
Monroe, James, 94
Moore, Alfred, 62
Morgenthau, Henry, Jr., 279
Murphy, Frank, 254, 255, 263, 264, 275, 276, 277–279, 283, 286, 287, 290, 297, 299, 301, 306, 313, 314

N

Nelson, Samuel, 128, 132
Nixon, Richard, 17
Norris, George, 189

P

Paine, Thomas, 63
Parker, John, 222
Paterson, William, 51, 62, 67, 68, 71, 83
Peckham, Rufus, 169, 187, 202
Pepper, George Wharton, 222, 236
Peters case, 331

Pitney, Mahlon, 190, 202
Plessy v. Ferguson, 176

R

Reed, Stanley F., 9, 252, 262, 264,
   266–269, 272, 277, 278, 287,
   305, 307, 313, 314, 316, 318,
   320, 321, 325, 329, 330, 331
Roberts, Owen J., 31, 159, 187,
   221–224, 228, 230, 231, 232,
   233, 236, 237, 238, 239, 241,
   242, 245, 246, 248, 249, 250,
   251, 264, 281, 284, 298, 299, 310
Robinson, Joseph T., 251
Rome, Harold, 215
Roosevelt, Franklin D., 9, 11, 19,
   20, 26, 35, 58, 74, 112, 142, 158,
   180, 190, 212, 213–217, 219,
   221, 228, 229, 240, 242, 243–
   256, 259, 262, 263, 264, 266,
   267, 269, 270, 272, 273, 275,
   277, 278, 279, 280, 281, 282,
   284, 285, 291, 295, 298, 303,
   307, 309, 311, 312, 316
Roosevelt, Theodore, 9, 177, 185,
   189
Rosenberg, Ethel, 302, 303, 309
Rosenberg, Julius, 302, 303, 309
Russell, Bertrand, 330
Rutledge, John, 47–48, 51, 60, 70
Rutledge, Wiley B., 255, 263, 264,
   267, 275, 276, 277, 282–284,
   287, 290, 297, 299, 301, 314

S

Sacco, Nicola, 270, 320
Sandford, John F. A., 129
Sanford, Edward, 190, 305

Schechter case, 233–234, 239, 249
Schwimmer, Rosika, 206
Scott, Dred, 110, 115, 118, 128–
   134, 142, 213, 224
Seward, William Henry, 132
Shiras, George, Jr., 187
Smith, Al, 251
Smith, J. Allen, 41
Spencer, Herbert, 186
Stanford, Leland, 157
Stanton, Edwin M., 155
Stone, Harlan F., 5–6, 9, 31, 139,
   187, 225–226, 229, 233, 237,
   238, 241, 254, 262, 263, 264,
   267, 274, 282, 284, 291, 292,
   295, 298, 305
Story, Joseph, 82, 102, 103, 106–
   107, 112, 113, 122, 123, 254, 306
Strong, William, 158, 159, 161
Stuart v. Laird, 89
Sturges v. Crowninshield, 104
Sutherland, George, 31, 187, 217,
   219–220, 228, 239, 252, 305
Swayne, Noah, 137, 157

T

Taft, William H., 36, 179, 185,
   187, 188, 189, 199, 207, 220,
   224, 225, 227, 251, 305, 309
Taney, Roger Brooke, 10, 11, 110,
   111–139, 142, 146, 151, 154,
   160, 170, 176, 214, 256
Tocqueville, Alexis de, 216
Trimble, Robert, 82
Truman, Harry S., 35, 138, 257,
   264, 277, 281, 282, 298, 299,
   302–318

U

U.S. *v.* Carolene Products Co., 291

V

Van Devanter, Willis, 30, 187, 217–218, 219, 228, 251

Vanzetti, Bartolomeo, 270, 320

Vinson, Fred M., 15, 24, 82, 264, 287, 299, 303, 304, 305, 306–309, 311, 313, 314, 315, 316, 317, 319, 320, 321, 322, 323, 325, 329, 330, 331

W

Waite, Morrison R., 142, 146, 162, 163, 168, 309

Warren, Charles, 113, 114

Warren, Earl, 277, 303, 304, 309, 314, 323–332

Washington, Bushrod, 62, 81, 83

Washington, George, 34, 35, 42, 45, 46, 47, 49, 50, 51, 55, 56, 57, 59, 60, 61, 75, 137, 282

Watson, Goodwin B., 296

Wayne, James M., 128, 130

Webster, Daniel, 94–95, 96, 102, 112, 113

Wheeler, Burton K., 248, 250

White, Edward D., 179, 187, 188, 197, 206, 220

Wilson, James, 39, 47, 48, 53, 61, 62, 101, 230

Wilson, Woodrow, 180, 185, 197, 218, 227

Woods, William B., 164

A B O U T   T H E   A U T H O R

FRED RODELL, Professor of Law at Yale University, was born in Philadelphia. He was graduated from Haverford College in 1926, took his LL.B. at Yale Law School in 1931 with a magna cum laude, and served as a legal advisor to Governor Pinchot of Pennsylvania. He has contributed to legal periodicals, but most of his articles have appeared in general magazines ranging from *Life* and *Look* to *Harper's* and *The New Republic*. He has been a contributing editor of *The Progressive*, and an editor of *Fortune*.

Mr. Rodell's three previous books were: *Fifty-five Men: the Story of the Constitution; Woe Unto You, Lawyers;* and *Democracy and the Third Term.* He lives in Bethany, Connecticut, with his wife and son.